Simple Gifts

To Bernadette our Treasured
friend — Sometimes the Simplest
of gifts are the most meaningful
and profound — Love, Commitment,
Loyalty, all unconditional —
May it be so for you and
those you love
Blessings *

10/17/2016
Luke 12:48b
Philippians 4:4~13
* See page 37

SIMPLE GIFTS

"Gifts Freely Given And Received, Priceless Gifts By Word And Deed"*

BY JOHN WOOLSLAIR SHEPPARD

"Much is required from those to whom much is given, and much more is required; and much more is required from those to whom much more is given." *JESUS, GOD The Gospel of Luke 12:48B (NLT)*

"I expect to pass this Way but once, any good therefore I can do, or any kindness I can show to any fellow creature, let me do it now; let me not defer or neglect it, for I shall not pass this way again." *Stephen Grellett. (Quaker Missionary)*

"The meaning of life it to find your gift, the purpose of life, is to give it away." *Pablo Picasso*

"We earn a living by what we get, we make a life by what we give." *Winston Churchill*

"The best sermons in life are lived, not preached." *Author Unknown*

*The title of the original painting of the Front Cover Art is by Ellen Sheppard, is "Simple Gifts Given and Received."

i

Scripture herein quoted except as otherwise noted, is taken from The New American Standard Bible. Copyright 1960, 1962, 1963, 1968, 1971, 1972, 1973, 1977, By The Lockman Foundation. Used by Permission (www.lockman.org)

ISBN-13: 9781537059327

ISBN-10: 1537059327

ACKNOWLEDGEMENTS

I wish to thank my best friend and wife, Ellen for her continued love, dedication, commitment and encouragement over these 62 and more years. The front cover artwork is an original painting by her.

The significance of the meaning of the original painting is, its title is "Simple Gifts Given and Received." Many people have seen the painting have commented that the man portrayed in the Art is so kindly looking, that his inner peace and the love for his dog shines through. Others have said that the man is a depiction of a kindly but well lived old man, some Santa Claus, and some even The Loving God. The painting is an expression of LOVE in its many forms. Scripture tells us GOD is LOVE and true LOVE is of GOD. The reader can attach whatever meaning she or he wishes, but we hope that it portrays LOVE in its best sense of freely giving Unconditional Love. I deem that we can learn much about Love through Man's love for his dog, and a Dog's unconditional commitment, love and loyalty to his or her owner. So touched by the communication of man and his dog one small section of this book, titled "A Dog's Tale" is included. We believe that the comments of people the world over and over history about "their" dog is instructive about the need of and meaning of unconditional love.

Thank you to all of my family, Andy and Carolyn, Sandy and Carl, and to all of my Grandchildren, Erik, Brett, Elyse, Carol, Lauren and JB. Special thanks to my granddaughter Lauren, who has helped me from time to time, assembling, and working through the maze, that I call the computer and electronics nightmare. And thank you to our very special friends, and all of the friends who have encouraged us in this effort.

Thank you too, to the staff at Create Space who have helped me to complete, assemble and this multifaceted project.

To all, they have given to me many kinds of gifts, and Simple Gifts with love.

DEDICATION

I dedicate this book to all of my family, Ellen, Andy, Sandy, and their spouses Carolyn and Carl, the memory of the lessons learned from our son Jay, my six grandchildren Erik, Brett, Elyse, Carl, Jr, Lauren and J. B. and to the increasing number of great grandchildren now at six, and to all of the many people who have befriended me and have been a part of my life, and including all of these 84 years, from whom I have learned so much and to all who have brought so much joy into my life.

Finally, I dedicate this book to The One Who Gives and Sustains All Life, Our Lord and My God. May each of us appreciate that life itself is a gift and each day of it a special gift which we can make a difference with others, often by the Simple Gift of care and love for each other, and even others we don't know.

TABLE OF CONTENTS

PREFACE

In the early 1960's when our children were very young, Ellen and I made one of our "big" early purchases a single speaker "Stereo" that played only Vinyl records. We purchased it as the Firestone Store in Main Street downtown, the cost eighty nine dollars. It was a splurge, but I felt it was important for Ellen, because we had three young children, and then of course we both loved music anyway.

My thought was that Ellen would have music in the home all day, and it might help and be beneficial for our young children. Our three were very close together, 18 and 13 months apart following the birth of our eldest son, Jay. Back then diapers and bottles were washed and sterilized so Ellen had little down time, day or night. She had the hard job in the family.

My hope was that with the music around all day long- with such classics as South Pacific, and other Rodgers and Hammerstein musicals, The Limelighters, Children's songs, would be uplifting for everyone. Among the recordings was one with the music of Aaron Copland. There were several of those works that especially touched both Ellen and I. It had on it, Fanfare for the Common Man, Appalachian Spring, Variations on a Shaker hymn, as well as selections from his Grand Canyon Suite. We listened to them often, yet knew nothing about it history, that is where the music came from. All we knew is that it moved both of us. Years later in the 1990's I heard the same theme music on a CBS TV series called "American Journal", yet still not knowing from whence it came.

In a book we had written in 2002 titled "Thy Word, A Light, Unto My Path" a verse taken from Psalms 119, verse 105. In that book we highlighted specific passages from the Bible that had made an impression on us. Interestingly, one of those passages was taken from a story of David in Old Testament Book of 2nd Samuel, about David and his Army dancing as they brought the Ark of the Covenant back into Jerusalem. David was dancing with joy, while wearing a religious robe. His dancing being spirited, while wearing the religious robe disgusted his wife, but David was joyous. As David's son, King Solomon said later in Ecclesiastes 3, "There is a Time to Dance." What better time than the recovery of the Ark of Covenant of the Lord, for his people.

In that book we titled the writing and the poem were titled "The Lord of the Dance,", but the poem was about our life dance through life, and the partners and tunes we will dance to. You can find the Scripture and poem on page 155, as well as the very simple words of the original Shaker hymn "Simple Gifts", and the words of the new hymn to that tune written in in 1963, by and Englishman named Sydney Carter. (His version is about Jesus and HIS Dance through life.)

And in 1996, Michael Flatley, used the tune once again in his celebrated dance Musical also titled "Lord of the Dance," which has been performed all over this country. That is where I next heard the "tune" again in seeing the performance of "The Lord of the Dance" here in Lee County. But not until about five years ago, did I hear the tune sung to the hymn that Sydney Carter wrote in 1963, when it was sung- to the same glorious tune, by our Church Choir, "The Lord of the Dance."

You may be as surprised, as I was to find that this beautiful almost majestic tune came from the hand, and the mind of a man, inspired by God who lived the simple life of the Shaker community.

In my research, I found that the music was a Shaker hymn written in 1848 by a Shaker Pastor, of the Shaker Community in Alfred Maine named Elder Joseph Brackett, Jr. Elder Brackett titled his hymn "Simple Gifts." And it is just that. Brackett's lyrics were written about the joy of living simply and following the way Jesus taught to live life.

The theme suggested that we live simply, live humbly, and to come down "off of our High or Human throne," to where God wants us to be. It concludes that we will live in the valley of love and delight.

The lyrics of the verse Brackett wrote, (and it has been suggested that it was written for a dance) were about as simple, yet as powerful as they could be. If you know the tune sing the lyrics to yourself, to the tune others have used so freely and for many different and wonderful purposes. Here they are:

> 'Tis a gift to be simple, 'Tis a gift to be free,
> 'Tis a gift to come down where we ought to be.
> And when we will find ourself in the place just right,
> 'Twill be in the valley of love and delight.
> Refrain:
> When true simplicity is gained,
> To bow and to bend, we shan't be ashamed.
> To turn, turn, turn, will be our delight,
> By turning, turning we come 'round right.

Research reflects that some of the later verses were added by others (apparently not by Elder Brackett) as follows:

> 'Tis a gift to be loved and to love in return
> 'Tis the gift to be taught and a richer gift to learn,
> And when we expect of others what we try to live each day,
> Then we'll all live together and we'll learn to say."
> Refrain
> 'Tis a gift to have friends and true friend to be
> 'Tis the gift to think of others, not only think of "me"
> And when we hear what others really think and feel.
> Refrain
> 'Tis the gift to be loving, 'tis the best gift of all,
> Like a quiet rain, it blesses where it fall,
> And with it we will truly believe,
> 'Tis better to give than it is to receive.
> Refrain.

You will note Brackett's "Simple Gifts" hymn, in its various versions in the Refrain has the words "Turn, Turn, Turn." Interestingly, the classic folk singer, in 1955, Pete Seeger wrote a song, using a different tune, based on Ecclesiastes 3: 3-8, variously titled as "To Everything There Is a Season," also called "Turn, Turn, Turn."

Interestingly, that was the same time when the United States conducted their last above ground hydrogen Bomb tests in the Pacific atoll island of Bikini. The blast destroyed every living thing and the atoll itself as well as a full armada of navy vessels as well as scores of goats and other test animals for many miles around. At that point even the military and the scientists concluded that they could not control, nor did they know the consequences for mankind, of further above ground testing. The above ground nuclear tests were stopped shorty after that.

Seeger wrote the song primarily as an anti-War song, yet didn't actually record it himself until 1962, in his album, "Bitter and Sweet." The lyrics follow the wording of the Scripture (Ecclesiastes 3:1-8) quite closely.

Verse 8 of the Scripture closes with the words "A time for War and a time for Peace." Seeger added the words "I swear it's not too late."

That song became a favorite of a number of Folk Rock performers, but the most noted and played was that by, the folk rock group "The Byrds." Their version came out in 1965. Not only was I a young, 33 at the time but very interested in Folk Rock music. I had also just begun any serious study of the Bible under the guidance of a wonderful teacher, named Lois Evans It was then I realized that the lyrics of that song nearly duplicated the King James Version of the Ecclesiastes verses. The song was even sung in Church meetings across the country. Several years later I attended a concert of "The Byrds" and heard that song again. Of course their song "Turn, Turn, Turn," was to different music, not that that Elder Brackett wrote.

Much later when I began to do research for this book beginning with the Shaker hymn "Simple Gifts", did I realize that the Shaker hymn's Refrain contained the words "Turn, Turn, Turn." Whether that old hymn had any connection with Pete Seeger's song, "To Everything There is a Season," I do not know. Nothing I found made any connection to "To Everything there is a Season" and the old hymn "Simple Gifts." Yet both are filled with the message that life is filled with everything, different things have different seasons in our lives.

And yet the end of the story of life in the verses of Ecclesiastes 3:1-8 nor the song, "To Every Thing There is a Season" is not the end of the story. For, if we skip ahead to Solomon's words in Chapter 3 to verses 11 & 12 hear Solomon's words of wisdom when he states clearly "HE has made everything beautiful in its time. Also he has put eternity into man's heart, yet he (man) will not (fully understand) what GOD has done from the beginning to the end."

Also, there are other verses to the Brackett music that have been written by others, and of course the totally different version by Sydney Carter as noted above. Yet the music to the hymn really came into its own on the American scene with Aaron Copland's work. It has been used as the theme music with variations on the work in various TV programs and Movies. It is one of those tunes that we've all heard but maybe did not know its origins.

The musical theme was arranged again by noted composer John Williams and was featured in the Inauguration Ceremony of Barrack Obama in 2009. This version was by a large orchestra and choir, and headed by such gifted and varied ethnic artists as Yo Yo Ma, Viola, Viola, Itzak Perlman, Violin, and Gabrielo Montera, piano.

What lies within the pages of this book then are a series of writings about living life in all of its "times an seasons."

An earlier book we wrote was titled "Little Things Can Mean a Lot, Pearls of Life of Great Worth." Its theme was about small things like the pearls, said or done can have great worth. That we cannot all do great things nor make great gifts, in the eyes of the world, but we can all do our own little things , and our little things said or done in love can change one life, and when passed on to others can change the world.

I hadn't thought about it until I began searching for a tile to this effort, but now that it is near completion, I can see that Simple Gifts are "simply," much more of things than Elder Brackett wrote and sang about in his hymn in 1848.

Likewise that the wise words of King Solomon in Ecclesiastes 3, did not end the story at verse 8, in other words in due time war may end and peace may prevail. Again, Solomon, in verse 11, adds to the story ""HE has made everything beautiful in its time, and HE has put eternity into Man's heart." May it be so for each of us!

SECTION I. SOME THINGS BORROWED, ALL THINGS TRUE, SOMETHINGS WRITTEN, JUST FOR YOU.

SOME THINGS BORRROWED, ALL THINGS TRUE, SOME THINGS WRITTEN JUST FOR YOU

Note: This section contains scores of quotes emanating from many different and divergent people, including the author, from many times of history. We hope that some will make such an impression on you that you might want to recall them. The author confesses to be a "book marker," (with pen and colored pencil) and for that reason never borrows books from others, lest they be returned to the owner in "marked down condition." That being said, please be at your leisure to mark the pages or make notes on the margin, for your benefit.

Items relating to giving

"Give people a fact or an idea, and you'll enlighten their mind. Give them a story and you'll touch their soul." *Hassidic Proverb.*

"For it is in giving that we receive." *St. Francis of Assisi.*

"At the end of your life you will never regret not having passed one more test, not having won one more verdict, not closing one more deal. You will regret the time not spent with your spouse, a friend, a child, or a parent." *Barbara Bush (Reflections: Life after the White House).*

"The rock that is an obstacle in the path of one person becomes a stepping stone in the path of another." *Unknown.*

"Never lose sight of the fact that the most important yardstick of your success in life, is how you treat other people." *Barbara Bush, (Reflections: Life after the White House).*

"We can't help everyone, but everyone can help someone." *Ronald Reagan.*

"What we do in this life echoes into eternity." *Maximus Decimus Meridius (The Gladiator Movie).*

"A person wrapped up in himself, makes a very small package." *Benjamin Franklin.*

"To keep a lamp burning, we must put oil into it." *Mother Teresa.*

"The true meaning of life is to plant trees under whose shade you do not expect to sit." *Nelson Henderson*

"We shall never know all the good that a simple smile can do." *Mother Teresa.*

"We ourselves feel that what we are doing is a drop in the ocean; but the ocean would be less without our drop." *Mother Teresa.*

"There are two ways of spreading the light: to be the candle or the mirror that reflects it." *Edith Wharton.*

"If you can't feed a hundred people, then just feed one." *Mother Teresa.*

"Help one another, there is no time like the present and no present like the time." *James Durst.*

"Plant Flowers in others gardens, and your life will become a bouquet." *Unknown.*

"Blessed are those who can give without remembering, and (receive) without forgetting." *Elizabeth Bibesco.*

"It's good to be blessed, it's better to be a blessing. *Unknown.*

"Success is not final, failure is not fatal, it is the courage to continue that counts." *Winston Churchill.*

"It is the heart that does the giving, if only the fingers will let go." *Unknown (Nigerian saying)*

"The best way to find yourself, is in the service of others." *Mahatma Gandhi.*

"If you want to touch the past, touch a rock, if you want to touch the present touch a flower, if you want to touch the future, touch a life." *Dillon Burroughs.*

"The heart of the human problem is the problem of the human heart." *Adrian Rogers.*

"He is rich or poor by what he is, not according to what he has." *Henry Ward Beecher.*

"Service is the rent we pay to be living. It is the very purpose of life, and not something you do in your spare time." *Marion Edelman.*

"The meaning of life is to find your gift, the purpose of life, is to give it away." *Pablo Picasso.*

"Only a life lived for others, is a life worthwhile." *Albert Einstein.*

"We earn a living by what we get, we make a life by what we give." *Winston Churchill.*

The best sermons in life are lived, not preached." Author Unknown.

"Giving frees us from the familiar territory of our needs- by opening our mind to the unexplained world occupied by the needs of others." *Barbara Bush (Reflections on Life after the White House).*

"Some people give time, some money, some their skills and connections, some literally give their life's blood, but everyone has something to give." *Barbara Bush (Reflections on Life after the White House).*

"Sooner or later, the only three things you can call your own, your mind, your body, and your spirit. So I want you to consider making your life, one long gift to others. *Stephen King.*

"Giving isn't just about the receiver, or the amount of the gift. It's also for the Giver, taking the focus of what we claim to own, but about putting it back where it belongs- on the lives we lead, the families we raise, the communities we nurture, and nurture us. A life of giving- not just money, but of time and spirit- repays." *Stephen King.*

"Life is no brief candle to me. It is sort of a splendid torch which I have got hold of for the moment, and I want to make it burn as brightly as I can before handing it on to future generations." *George Bernard Shaw.*

"It helps us to remember that we may go out being broke, but right now while we are here we're doing ok. Right now, we have the power to do good for others." So I ask you now to begin to give generously (and at your passing.) I think you will find… you gave and got more than you ever had and did more than you ever could have dreamed of." *Stephen King.*

"It is one of the most beautiful things in life… that no man can sincerely try to help another without helping himself." *Ralph Waldo Emerson.*

"I expect to pass this way but once, any good therefore I can do, or any kindness I can show to any fellow creature, let me do it now; let me not defer or neglect it, for I shall not pass this way again." *Stephen Grellett.*

"I am only one, but I am one. I cannot do everything, but I can do something. And I will not let what I cannot do interfere with what I can do." *Edward Everett Hale.*

"He who climbs highest is he who helps another up." *George Matthew Adams.*

"Too often, we underestimate the power of a touch, a smile, a kind word, a listening ear, and honest compliment, or the smallest act of caring, all of which have the potential to turn a life around." *Leo Buscalia.*

"I have never met and unhappy giver." *George Adams.*

"I can't sit back and fold my hands and think about the past, for there are thousands of yesterdays, but only one today and… maybe a tomorrow." *Red Skelton.*

"The one a day vitamin for the soul is helping another person." *Stephen Post, PhD.*

"You can give without loving, but you can never love without giving." *Robert Louis Stevenson.*

"It is not the things we get, but the hearts we touch, that will measure our success in life." *Unknown.*

"Sometimes you earn more by doing things that pay nothing." *Todd Ruthman.*

"It's not the dollars you make, it's the difference you make." *Benjamin Emanuel, Israeli Freedom. Fighter.*

"The best things in life aren't things." *Art Buchwald.*

"Great thoughts speak only to the thoughtful mind, great actions speak to all mankind." *Theodore Roosevelt.*

"What we do for ourselves, dies with us, what we do for others, carried on, is eternal." (Paraphrase) *Albert Pike.*

"Though no one can start life over from the beginning brand new, but everyone can re-start from the present, and make a brand new ending." (Paraphrase) *Carl Bard)*

Items from Scripture

"The world of the generous gets larger and larger; the world of the stingy gets small and smaller." *Proverbs 11:24-25 (The Message by Eugene Peterson).*

"Do not weary yourself to gain wealth, cease from your consideration of it. When you set your eyes on it, it is gone. For wealth certainly makes for itself wings, like an eagle that flies toward the heaven." *Proverbs 23:4-5*

"Mercy to the needy is a loan to God, and God pays back those loans in full." *Proverbs 19: 17 (The Message by Eugene Peterson).*

"Mark well that God doesn't miss a move you make; HE is aware of every step you Take." *Proverbs 5:21a (The Message, by Eugene Patterson).*

"Sitting across from the offering box, HE was observing how the crowd tossed money in for the collection. Many of the rich were making large contribution. One poor widow came up and put in two small coins- a measly two cents. Jesus called his disciples over and said, "The truth is that the poor widow gave more to the collection than all of the others put together. All the others gave what they'll never miss, she gave extravagantly, what she couldn't afford- she gave her all." *Mark 12: 41-44 (The Message by Eugene Peterson).*

"There is one who scatters , yet increases all the more, and there is one who withholds what is justly due, but results only in want. The generous man will be prosperous, and he who waters will himself be watered." *Proverbs 11-24-25 (The Message, by Eugene Peterson).*

"Like apples of gold in settings of silver is a word spoken in the right circumstances." *Proverbs 25:11.*

"Remember: a stingy planter gets a stingy crop. I want each of you to take plenty of time to think it over and make up your own mind what you will give. That will protect you against the sob stories and arm twisting. God loves it when the giver delights in the giving. And, God can pour on the blessings in astonishing ways so that you're ready for anything and everything, more than just ready to do what needs to be done. As one psalmist puts it: "He throws caution to the winds, giving to the needy in reckless abandon, right giving ways, never run out, never wear out." *2nd Corinthians 9:6-9. (The Message by Eugene Peterson)*

"Do not lay up for yourselves treasures on earth, where moth and rust destroy, and where the thieves break in and steal. But lay up for yourselves treasures in Heaven... for where your treasure lies, there will your heart lie also." *Matthew 6:19-21.*

"Now this I say, he who sows sparingly shall also reap sparingly; and he who sows bountifully, shall also reap bountifully. Let each one we do just as he has purposed in his heart; not grudgingly or under compulsion, for God loves a cheerful giver." *1st Corinthians 9: 6-7.*

"Do not be deceived, God is not mocked, for whatever a man sows so shall he reap... And let us not lose heart in doing good, for in due time, we shall reap, if we do not grow weary. So then, while we have the opportunity, let us do good to all men..." *Galatians 6: 9-10 (Selected NAS Version).*

"And from everyone who has been given much, much shall be required; and to whom much is entrusted, of him they will ask all the more." *Luke 12:48b (NAS Version).*

"Bring your full tithe (and offerings) to the Temple… Test Me on this and see if I don't open up Heaven itself to you and pour out blessings beyond your wildest dreams." *Malachi 3: selected verses. (The Message by Eugene Peterson).*

"How can I stand up before God (Who created and gives life), and show proper respect for God? Should I bring an armload of offerings, topped off with yearling calves? Would God be impressed with thousands of rams, with buckets and barrels of olive oil? Would he be moved if I sacrificed my first child, my precious baby, and cancel my sin? But, He's already made it plain how to live, what to do, what God is looking for in men and women. It's quite simple: Do what is fair and just to your neighbor, be compassionate and loyal in your love, and, don't take yourself too seriously-take God seriously." *Micah 6:6-8 (The Message by Eugene Peterson).*

Items by the Author

"You can't take it with you. Give of your time, your treasure, talent, and spirit. If you will take in your heart the joy of this sharing, you'll never miss what you've given away, and will see you've received much more in return."

"Turn your face to the light of the sun, and all of the shadows of the past are behind you."

"To blunt the sharpness of the emotional wound takes time, but what the wounded does with the time, and with whom, are much more important."

"It is important when one is grieved that he or she face the grief, and deal with it daily in whatever time it takes, and deal with and work through each of the stages of grief."

"Religion tells us that the grieving period is one year. It is not one year of time, it is not a specified time. It is whatever it time it takes for the grieving to work through his or her grief, and they need to take their time, both facing and dealing with the grief, the prayer, the labor, counselling, or effort it takes. Sometimes the healing scars of the loss may last a lifetime—it's just changed or different.

"Like the tip of the iceberg in sight above the water's surface, in life what we see with our eyes and hear with our ears, may be just a hint of what lies beneath the surface."

"Seize the moment, say or do a good thing, often it's the little things that can mean a lot."

"Yesterday is gone, never to return, we don't really know what tomorrow holds. All we have for sure is the present moment. Take care of today, what's on your plate today."

"While we don't always have a choice about the circumstances we find ourselves in in life, we do have a choice as to how we respond to every circumstance. Our attitude is the most important thing in determining each situation's final outcome."

"Every moment of every day is a gift, none to be wasted, all are special times, to be used wisely, enjoyed, and learned from, even the hard days."

"Life is not always fair, people are not always fair. Justice doesn't always meet our expectations. But trust that God has a plan for you, and for your good, and it will be revealed in due time. God doesn't always pay off on Saturday night."

"No one get a ticket to ride for a lifetime on the easy train. Difficulty is a part of life. Learn to dance in the rain."

"Today is today. Yesterday is gone, never to return. When tomorrow comes, today will be like yesterday, gone forever. In the place of each day gone by in our life, we have left something behind…let that something we leave behind each day, be something good."

"At times Life may not be the party we had planned, but we need to keep on dancing, until the music stops."

"Live each day with the wonder and enthusiasm as if it were the first day of your life, and the purpose and commitment as if it were the last day of your life."

"Sometimes doing our best to do good does not get it done, sometimes we have to do what is necessary to get good done, sometimes we have to do the best we can, and upon reflection, let it go."

"When hard times and events come, rejoice in what didn't happen, what you can learn by what has been lost, and treasure even more, that which hasn't been lost."

"In the road of life and faith, progress is taking the first step, even though you can't see past the bend in the road just ahead, and knowing that our path may need change from time to time.."

"To forgive is to let the offender and the hurt go free, for in that freeing act, the one who forgives is also set free of the lasting pain of hurt, anger and resentment."

"Even though a marriage may be conceived and made in heaven, there are on earth a lot of details to be lived out, adjustments to be made, things to be learned, love to be shared, patience with each other, and accepting of the other in love words and deed."

"Worry begins like a single droplet of water, a single negative thought. Unchecked, it can grow and become a flood or torrent of crippling anxiety within. Worry never passed a test, never paid a bill, or cured a disease, or hurt. It never finished a job, slew Goliath, or defeated Hercules. In all history, worry never won a battle, accomplished a single thing; but to make us less effective and to our doubts cling."

"Too often the bitterest tears of grief, when we have lost, are the words left unsaid and deeds left undone, after it's too late."

"In life, we should cross a bridge when we come to it, the bridges we cross before we get to them, are often the rivers that weren't there."

"The International Interstate Road to hell is paved with golden intentions, not met."

"Life is not about the number of years we live, but about what we do, we give and share of what we have to share, in the years that we have."

"There are great differences in sight and vision, talking and speaking, hearing and listening, even touching and feeling. In each case the first is a God given 'Sense", the second is how you develop and use those God given senses.

"There is something spiritual and sacredness in tears. There are not a mark of weakness, and unmanliness, but of power. They speak more eloquently that a thousand tongues. They can be healing and helpful in many aspects of life. They can send a message that no words can communicate. They are messengers of overwhelming pain and grief, of deep contrition and sorrow, for things said or done, or unsaid or undone. Yet they can also be evidence of indescribable joy" Tears can be the needed "pressure cooker release" of these deep emotions within us, release within positive endorphins, and grant relief for our body, mind and soul."

"With Inch by inch life's a cinch. And Foot by Foot may be sometimes best suited. But, Yard by yard is hard. We each have our daily doable limits. Know your limits of accuracy and good product."

"A wise wife is one who permits her husband to believe he is smart, the strong leader, and head of the family."

"Water, H_2O, its chemical elements, are critical to sustaining all human life. Likewise, Water is essential to cement create the lasting adhesive of concrete, binding the building blocks of construction. In the same manner, "Faith (in the future) and Trust (of the other)," are as the components of life giving "Water" which are critical to binding the structural building blocks of the of all lasting human relationships, whether it be two people married, a family, lasting friendships, an organization, a community, a nation, or the world."

"I have been a lawyer for more than 60 years of my life. My Father was a lawyer. He taught me when I was young that a lawyer and his client's confidences were no different than confession to a Priest, absolutely confidential, never to be revealed. He also taught me that in the advice that I gave to my clients be, to the best of my knowledge and belief, the truth as I knew it and saw it, and in the client's best interest, even if it was not what the client wanted to hear, and never because it might benefit me to conclude otherwise. He also wisely advised me, that I must conduct my personal life and my work life to be one that was not only one of not guilty of selfishness or indiscretion, but even beyond that, to avoid doing anything that might even have the appearance or hint of indiscretion. Further that the only thing that I could claim and own as having value was my integrity. I am thankful for that advice. I wonder if it might be good advice for all of us."

"Some people believe that all lawyers are dishonest. Other people believe that 99% of the lawyers give the rest of the lawyers a bad name. And, then are some people who believe that every lawyer other than their own lawyer, is dishonest. I was very fortunate in my professional life, to have many friends and clients who placed me in the latter category. I am blessed and thankful for that, as well as my Father's good advice."

"It is better to keep your mouth shut and seem a fool, than to open it and remove the doubt." (taught to me for oral recitation by my Father when I was 3 years old—except when I recited it the latter phrase was a bit off to "and remove it all of out.")

"My wife does not want to be liberated woman; she likes the fact that I honor and protect her, and place her first in all things, so long as I stay out of her kitchen. (Maybe that took some formulating on my part).

"You can't live someone else's life for them. Each must live out his own life. Don't blame yourself for things that you have no control over."

"A parent's love for their child should be unconditional. Though we may at times be very angry with them, frustrated with them, find their thoughts or actions as inexplicable, , not approve the choices they make, the things they may do or say, or not do and not say to us or others, while in discussion or observation, we never stop loving them, and wish the best for their future."

"With older children, we should give advice or offer opinions, when we are asked, and even then tell them frankly what we think, (without reminding them we are older, wiser, and more experienced than they), and then tell them to do what they damn please. If we are told our advice didn't work for them, remind them it was worth just what they paid for it."

"When I die, I'd like to go where my friends and family have gone, I hope that's in Heaven."

"I have learned with age not to be impressed with a person's position, rank, status, wealth, or Mensa intelligence. I am impressed by who and what the person is, what I see on the inside as well as the outside, positive words followed by positive action."

"Whenever we speak, or write a document by hand, on line, on face book or send it to the recipient, consider or read it carefully and repeatedly before sending. Once it has gone you can't take it back.
Once it is received by another, it is subject to many interpretations, depending on the hearer or reader, whether original or any recipient. The interpretation of the hearer or reader will be determined by their mood or stance, which may either not as you intended, affirm or offend. And always remember in today's world- once it's out there, it can come back to haunt the sender, hours, days or years later."

"I learned in Law School that in Property Law one could have both possession or "title" to property for a certain term (days, weeks, months or years).,or for an uncertain term (a Life estate), and even in "fee simple absolute forever. But in Life's School I've learned the real truth. In Life we can neither own nor possess ANYTHING whether real, tangible or intangible, such as a talent, a learned skill, a pot of gold, or buildings and property. All that we may think that we own is for an indeterminate time.

"Everything we have or do, for each of us it is only for a limited time, never the same, never equally, not always fair, but unique to each of us- determined by all the days of our life. All we have for sure, is the present moment of the present day. And, because of life's uncertainty, we need to use what we have, be it talent, time or treasure prudently, while we are in "Possession" of it. Use what we have and entrusted to us prudently, as good stewards, sharing those things abundantly with and for others for good. If we do this. If we do this, at the end, when our life is measured, we shall have truly lived The Good Life."

"Is what we say or do when no one is watching, the same as that which we say or do when the world is watching, or may discover later?"

"Storms in life in many forms and kinds will come to each of us, 'tis not a questions of weather or whether, but when. Will you let your personal storms be an incurable disease or a life destroyer, an issue to overcome, or just a little or temporary inconvenience, Much depends on the attitude and direction we assume choose to follow."

"When hard times and events come, rejoice in what didn't happen, what you still have, and what you can learn from what has changed or been lost, and what hasn't been changed or lost."

"Grief is, and can follow, any change or loss of anything or anyone in your life which you deem important. It can be a loss of a job, a loss of a spouse, parent, child, relative, friend, a relationship, a pet, the completion of a job, or the end of something. Depending on the change or loss and how it touches you personally, treat it with care and work through the process, rather than denying or burying it in busyness or distraction. Adjusting to the change or loss, may take time. The time it takes is your time, and not some else's time or an established or standard period. On the other hand, it takes work, labor and effort day by day, endeavoring to look forward and not back. It takes a realization that there is no rerun of time or of yesterday, it is past. It often involves negative emotions, including the "What if" and "If only" questions, anger, resentment, loneliness, doubt and regret for things said or done, or not said or done.

And particularly in the beginning of the change or loss sometimes it seems that the days are one step forward and steps back. Be patient with yourself, "Keep on keepin' on." Talk to someone, express your inner feelings, to a counsellor or a friend.
Hopefully you will find that in time that having worked through the change or loss, that there are positive lessons, and positive changes and gifts that come to you down the road in your journey."

"The span and time of our life is to God but a grain of sand, or the blink of an eye. But the story of love given and received, whether for a moment or a lifetime, is like God, it is eternal, for God is Love, and to Love unconditionally, is to be a part of God, and to make God a part of you."

"We bring nothing into this world, as we enter, and we shall take nothing with us when we leave, but our life lived for and with, as well as that which we gave will be our legacy."

"Most of us never know the day we will leave this world until it has arrived. Whatever we've thought or not thought, said or not said, done or not done while we are here, forms a part of the legacy we leave behind. But whatever we've possessed and given on or before that day does not go with us but stays behind. All that lasts of what you've said or done, as well as what we possess, our lasting imprint stays here, to benefit or burden those who receive what we have left behind, in thoughts, words, and actions. What will our legacy be?

"The greatest most valuable gift you can give or receive is love, which is priceless."

"Time and experience in life, give us, if not always the answers, but hopefully, wisdom, perspective and depth of understanding."

"Regret over missed or bungled opportunities teach us that there are no re-runs or replays of yesterday."

"Everything that occurs in life is not always fair and just, particularly when measured by our own standards."

"Life is sometimes like the "break" in a game of pool; if you get all of the balls rolling, there is a better chance of something dropping in the pocket."

"Love is saying you're sorry or regretful when you've had a disagreement with your loved ones, even if the issue was not fully resolved. Never let the sunset on our anger or go to bed angry. It will hurt both of you."

"When worry comes to knock at our door, say to it "No thanks, you've never solved one of my concerns, so I don't need your anymore."

"Don't worry about what happened yesterday, its done and over, don't worry about tomorrow, what you worry about tomorrow may never occur, or if it does, the realization may not even approach your anxious anticipation; just take care of today, it has a full plate."

"In life, always try to accentuate the positive, eliminate the negative, and don't mess with Mr. Indecision."

"The true value of a great tree is not known until it is felled. The true value of a person's life is often not appreciated until he or she is gone."

"The only person who has never made a mistake is a person who has never done anything."

"Never forget that it is not man or his accomplishments or a machine, but only God who gives and sustains life on earth."

"If you wear your heart on your sleeve, you are a candidate to be hurt, better to wear it inside, inside where God has placed it and in concert with your brain, it functions best."

"When we reach out to someone who is hurting, the right loving and caring word is always appropriate. But sometimes sitting silently, with just our very presence, may be the best gift we can give them."

"All we have for sure is the present moment of the present day; live each moment of each day with the enthusiasm as if it were your first day, and the commitment as if it were your last day."

"In business and in life others will usually forgive our imperfection and even mistakes, that are admitted, and if you are promptly responsive, and if they know that you care and have given it your best."

"A brilliant wife is one who plays to her husband's ego, letting him think he is the intelligent one and the head of the family. A little sugar goes a long way."

"In some situations in life, things that occur in our life or in the world for which there is no explanation or answer. So, after study and careful consideration, and without a rational explanation, let it go! We will have an explanation on the other side of the River. As we are told in Scripture, in some things "We don't yet see things clearly. We're squinting in a fog, peering through a mist. But it won't be long before the weather clears and the sun shines bright! We'll see it all then, see it all as clearly as God sees us, knowing Him directly just as He knows us now."

"The happiest people in life, those who have found joy, yet don't have the best of everything, but they make the best of what they have."

"Blessed is he who loves and shares unconditionally, with no expectation of reward in return, for he shall never be disappointed, and can rest on the effort of the gift he has made."

"People are like teabags, they and others don't know their real strength until they are in hot water."

"We cannot all do great things nor make great gifts as measured by the eyes of the world, but we can all do little things and our little things, said or done in love, can change one life, and when passed on can change the world."

"Do the best you are able to help another or a circumstance, but when it's done, note- do not labor over what might have been done. Then look for the opportunity to return and do something more."

"The most likely reason politicians work so hard, and raise so much money to be re-elected, is they are afraid to go back to working for a living, and especially making a living under the law's they've passed."

Political comments

"The more you observe politics, the more you've got to admit that each party is worse than the other." *Will Rogers.*

"Politics has become so expensive that it takes a lot of money even to be defeated." *Will Rogers.*

"I am not a member of any organized political party. I've been both a Democrat and a Republican, couldn't tell the difference." *Will Rogers.*

"You cannot legislate the poor into prosperity by legislating the wealthy out of prosperity. What one person receives without working for, another person must work for without receiving. The government cannot give to anybody anything that the government does not first take from somebody else. When half of the people get the idea that they do not have to work because the other half is going take care of them and when the other half gets the idea that it does no good to work because somebody else is going to get what they work for, that my dear friend, is the beginning of the end of any nation. You cannot multiply wealth by dividing it." *Adrian Rogers.*

"I cannot forecast to you the action of Russia. It is a riddle wrapped in a mystery, inside and enigma; but perhaps there is a key. That key is Russian national interest." *Winston Churchill (Radio Broadcast on October 1, 1939, 30 days after the beginning of WWII.)*

"A man who does not like dogs and want them about does not deserve to be in the white house." *Calvin Coolidge.*

"I love a dog. He does nothing for political reasons." *Will Rogers.*

"As we must account for every idle word, so must we account for every idle silence." *Benjamin Franklin.*

"To reach a port, we must sail, sail and not tie anchor,-sail and not drift." *Franklin Roosevelt.*

"The best argument against democracy is a five minute conversation with the average voter." *Winston Churchill.*

"What lies behind us and what lies before us are but tiny matters compared to what lies within us." *Ralph Waldo Emerson.*

"Civilizations do not give out, they give in. In a society where anything goes, eventually it will." *John Underwood.*

"The religion of Islam, above all others was founded upon the sword. Moreover, it provides incentives to slaughter, and in three continents has produced fighting breeds of men with a wild and merciless fanaticism." *Winston Churchill. (For more insights into his views, refer to his writings In "The River War," first Edition, (1899).*

Attitude, Love Joy and Living

"Vision is the art of seeing what is invisible to others." *Author Unknown.*

"You can't be a smart cookie if you have a crummy attitude." *John Maxwell.*

"Gratitude conserves the vital energies of a person more than any other attitude tested." *Hans Selye.*

"The heart of the human problem is the problem of the human heart." *Adrian Rogers.*

"Why wait? Life is not a dress rehearsal. Quit practicing what you are doing, and just do it." *Marilyn Grey.*

"There is only one happiness in this life, to love and be loved." *George Sand.*

"Uncontrolled anger is a strong wind that blows out the lamp of reason." *Benjamin Franklin.*

"When you fish for love, bait with your heart not your brain." *Mark Twain.*

"People don't care how much you know until they know how much you care." *Mike McKnight.*

"You are today where your thoughts have brought you; you will be tomorrow where your thoughts take you." *James Allen.*

"Change comes bearing gifts." *Price Pritchett.*

"Joy is not in things; it is in us." *Richard Wagner.*

Throw your heart over the fence and the rest will follow." *Norman Vincent Peale.*

"The best sermons in life are lived, not preached." *Unknown*

"The most important things in Life aren't things." *Anthony D'Angelo.*

"A gentle answer turns away wrath, but a harsh word stirs up anger. *Proverbs 15: 1.*

"Don't brashly announce what you are going to do tomorrow; you don't know the first thing about tomorrow, until it gets here." *Proverbs 27: 1 (The Message by Eugene Peterson.)*

"Know well the condition of your flocks, and pay attention to your herds; for riches are not forever, nor does a crown endure to all generations." *Proverbs 27: 23-24.*

"Do not wish to be anything but what you are, and try to be that perfectly." *St. Frances De Sales.*

"If we open a quarrel between past and present, we will find we have lost the future." *Winston Churchill.*

"Courage does not always roar. Sometimes it is a quiet voice at the end of the day, saying, "I will try again tomorrow." *Unknown*

"When you have a choice, and don't make it, that is in itself a choice." *William James.*

"Even if you're on the right track, you'll get run over, if you just sit there." *Mark Twain.*

"Wisdom is knowing the right path to take, integrity is taking it." *M. H. McKee.*

"When angry count to ten before you speak; if very angry count to one hundred." *Thomas Jefferson.*

"Who has not served cannot command." *John Florio.*

"Reputation is what other people think of us, character is what God knows of us, integrity is how only you and God know how you are really living your life." *Adrian Rogers.*

"A man's character may be learned from the adjectives which he habitually uses in conversation." *Mark Twain.*

"I am grateful for all of my problems. After each one was overcome, I became stronger and more able to meet those that were still to come. I grew in all of my difficulties." *J.C. Penney*

"Faith believes in spite of circumstances, and acts in spite of consequences." *Adrian Rogers.*

"Common sense is genius dressed up in work clothes." *Ralph Waldo Emerson.*

"Kindness is the language when the deaf can hear and the blind can see." *Mark Twain*

"Forgiveness is the fragrance that the violet sheds on the heel that has crushed it." *Mark Twain.*

"Courage is fear that has said its prayers." *Four year imprisoned Vietnam War Vet.*

"To be blind is a challenge, but worse is to having eyes and not see." *Helen Keller.*

"A bird doesn't sing because it has the answer, it sings because it has a song." *Maya Angelou.*

"What counts is not necessarily the size of the dog in the fight- it's the fight in the dog." *Dwight D. Eisenhower.*

"Worry is the interest paid by those who borrow trouble." *George Washington.*

"Anger is an acid that can do more harm to the vessel it's stored up in than to anything or anyone on which it is poured." *Mark Twain.*

"When you reach the end of your rope, tie a knot and hang on." *Thomas Jefferson.*

"Love is a fruit in season at all times, and within the reach of every hand." *Mother Teresa.*

"I have learned that people will forget what you said, people will forget what you did, but people will never forget how you made them feel." *Maya Angelou.*

"When one door of happiness closes, another opens; but often we look so long at the closed door, we do not see the one that has opened to us." *Helen Keller.*

"I've learned that you shouldn't go through life with a catcher's mitt on both hands; you need to be able to throw something back." *May Angelou*

"Be courteous to all, but intimate with few, and let those few be well tried before you give them your total confidence." *George Washington.*

"Friends are the family we choose for ourselves." *B.J. Gallagher.*

"Just because you get something doesn't mean you deserve it. And just because you deserve something doesn't mean you will get it." *Condoleezza Rice.*

"Happiness cannot come from without. It must come from within. It is not what we see or touch or that which others do for us which makes us happy; it is that which we think and feel and do for, first for the other fellow and then for ourselves." *Helen Keller*

"When it comes to life, the critical thing is whether you take things for granted or take them with gratitude." *G. K. Chesterton.*

"To feel gratitude and not express it, is like wrapping a present and not giving it." *William Arthur Ward.*

"Sow a thought and reap an action; sow an act and reap a habit; sow a habit and reap a character; sow a character and reap a destiny." *Ralph Waldo Emerson.*

"He that cannot forgive others breaks the bridge over which he himself, must pass." *Lord Herbert.*

"You win a few, you lose a few. Some get rained out. But you got to dress out for all of them." *Leroy "Satchel" Page.*
"If you have a tendency to brag, just remember it's not the whistle that pulls the train." *O. F. Nichols.*

"Life isn't about waiting for the storm to pass. It's about learning to dance in the rain."
Vivian Greene.

"We come into life naked and broke. When we go out, we may be neatly dressed well, but we are broke. Warren Buffett, broke! Tom Hanks, broke! Donald Trump, broke. Stephen King, broke, not a crying dime!" *Stephen King*

"To experience happiness we must train ourselves to live in this moment, to savor it for what it is not running ahead in anticipation of some future date, nor lagging behind in the paralysis of the past." *Luci Swindoll.*

"What lies behind us and before us are but tiny matters compared to what lies within us." *Ralph Waldo Emerson.*

"Gratitude changes the pangs of pain and memory, to tranquil joy." *Dietrich Bonhoeffer.*

"A friend is one who understands your past, believes in your future, and accepts you just the way you are." *Anonymous.*

There is often in people to whom "the worst" has happened, an almost transcendent freedom, for they have faced the worst, and survived." *Carol Peterson.*

Wise and Common Sense

"The secret of getting ahead is getting started." *Mark Twain.*

"We cannot change yesterday, it is gone. We can only make the most of today, and look with hope toward tomorrow." *Unknown.*

"If you tell the truth, then you don't have to try to remember what you earlier said." *Mark Twain.*

"A perfect marriage is just two imperfect people, who refuse to give up on each other." *Unknown.*

"No one can make you feel inferior without your consent." *Eleanor Roosevelt.*

"You may have to fight a battle more than once to win it." *Margaret Thatcher.*

"Stand by anybody who stands right, stand with him, while he is right, and part with him, if he goes wrong." *Abraham Lincoln.*

Success consists of going from failure to failure without loss of enthusiasm." *Winston Churchill.*

"Success is not final, failure is not fatal, it is the courage to continue that counts." *Winston Churchill.*

"A lie gets halfway around the world before the truth has a chance to put its pants on." *Winston Churchill.*

"Common sense is genius dressed up in work clothes." *Ralph Waldo Emerson.*

"It's not what you know or what you know. It's what you are that counts." *Zig Ziglar.*

"Children have never been very good at listening to their elders, but they've never failed to imitate them." *James Baldwin.*

"Real opportunities are seldom labeled as such, they are discovered or revealed to the opportunist." John A. Shedd

"God gave us two ears and one mouth, for good reason—that we might listen twice as much as we speak." *Unknown.*

"Success is not final, failure is not fatal: it is the courage to continue that counts." Winston Churchill. "The best things in life aren't things." *Art Buchwald.*

"You cannot discover new oceans unless you have the courage to lose sight of the shore." *Lord Chesterfield.*

Children's Question and Answers for God

"At that time, Jesus declared I praise You Father, Lord of Heaven and earth, because you have hidden these things from the wise and the learned, and have revealed them to little Children. Yes, Father for thus it was well pleasing in Thy sight." *Matthew 11:25-26*

Matthew 21: 16…"And he said to them, Yes, have you never read, "Out of the mouth of infants and nursing babes Thou hast prepared praise for Thy-Self?

"You have taught children and infants to tell of your strength, silencing your enemies and all who oppose You." *Psalms 8:2 (New Living Translation)*

NOTE: The following are a few of partial extracts from the wonderful book, "Children's Letter to God (The New Collection)" by Stuart H. Hample and Erik Marshall, Illustrated by Tom Bloom, published by Workman Publishing Company, New York, New York (First Printing 1991). We include several extracts that you might consider the above Words of Scripture and what Messrs. Hample and Marshall found through children's words.

We highly recommend the book for your consideration and reading, available through Bookstores and available through Amazon, and other online book shops. We think you will be touched by the many questions and observations of the children, all aged ten years or younger.

All of the one line "letters" in the book begin with the "Dear God" followed by a question or an observation, apparently written in their own ways of understanding and writing. Most have the salutation "love," and the handwriting of each is beautifully different and preserved.

DEAR GOD, (at the beginning of each letter, and finishes with their first name.)

"I read the bible. What does begat mean? Nobody will tell me."

"Are you really invisible or is that just a trick?"

"Is it true my father won't get in heaven if he uses his bowling words in the house?"

"Did you mean for the giraffe to look like that or was it an accident?"

"Do Animals use you or is there someone else for them?"

"I like the Lord's prayer best of all. Did you have to write it a lot or did you get it right the first time? I have to write everything I write over again."

"It's o. k. that you made different religions but don't you get mixed up sometimes?"

"Is Reverend Coe a friend of yours, or do you just know him through business?"

"Did you really mean to do unto others as they do unto you, because if you do, then I'm going to fix my brothers?"

"When you made the first man did he work as good as we do now?"

"My Grandpa says you were around when he was a little boy. How far back do You go?"

"I am an American, what are You?"

"Thank you for the baby brother but what I prayed for was a puppy."

"Please put another holiday between Christmas and Easter. There is nothing good in there now."

"If we come back as something-please, don't let me be Jennifer because I hate her."

"Maybe Cain and Abel would not kill so much if they had their own rooms. It works with my brother."

"I want to be just like my Daddy, when I get big, but not with so much hair all over."

"I think about you sometimes even when I'm not praying."

"I bet it is hard for you to love all of everybody in the whole world. There are only 4 people in our family and I can never do it."

"Of all the people who work for you I like Peter and John the best?"

"My brother told me about being born but it doesn't sound right."

"If you watch in Church Sunday I will show you my new shoes."

"I would like to live 900 years like the guy in the Bible."

"I don't ever feel alone since I found out about you."

"We read Thos. Edison made light. But in Sunday school they said you did it. So I bet he stoled it from you."

"I love you because you give us what we need to live, but I wish you would tell me why you made it so we have to die."

"It is great the way you always get the stars in the right places."

"I do not think anybody could be a better God. Well I just want you to know but I am not just saying that because you are God."

"I didn't think orange went with purple until I saw the sunset you made on Tue. That was cool."

"Dear God, I am doing the best I can."

SECTION II. BY THE NUMBERS (ASSORTED THINGS, ESSAYS, WRITINGS, AND ALL THINGS NUMBERED)

SEVEN PROVERBIAL PRINCIPLES OF WEALTH

Honor the Lord your God with all of your life, and all you do, And He shall in turn, pour out His blessings, and honor you. Consider Him in all that you own and all that you earn, and He'll open the Windows of Heaven to overflowing, and see what you learn. *(Proverbs 3:9-10; Malachi 3:10.)*

Be not concerned about hoarding, storing and stacking up your wealth, gold can have wings like eagles' and fly away, or as a lion consume you with his stealth. Focusing on riches, like our life, can be here today, and gone tomorrow, you'll find you've missed life's key things, and be left with only remorse and sorrow. *(Proverbs 23:4-5.)*

Even though what we possess, and claim as ours, is just on loan from God, Then, we are merely tenants of His gifts, as through our life we trod. May we then use wisely those things, riches and titles we claim as ours, we are entrusted with both great and small things, for at best, our living hours. *(1st Chronicles 29: 10-16.)*

Our money can never buy, at any price, Life's most precious treasures, Love, joy, family, friends, a purposeful life, are best by any measure. And to own a respected name, integrity, honesty, trust, are worth much more, than all the combined gold on earth, in Fort Knox, and north of Singapore. *(Proverbs 15:6; 17:15; 22:1; 28:6.)*

Yet, if you have received in your life the gift of prosperity, to he whom much is given, much more is expected, in responsibility. Be alert, for the love of money is the root of many evils that cause lives to sour, our life's central purpose to pile up wealth upon wealth, and power upon power. *(Proverbs 8:11; Luke 12:13-21; 1st Timothy 6:8-10.)*

So also, if God has blessed you with children and a spouse, He has entrusted them to you, to protect, to nurture beneath the roof of your house. For God has told us through the Apostle Paul, in words both loud and clear, "He who does not provide for his own household, has denied the faith, he holds so dear." *(1st Timothy 5:8)*

We have come into this world naked, leave with nothing, no more to achieve, so what we have while here, we must use wisely, a good and prudent legacy to leave. Giving a portion to God's Storehouse work, serving people, even the least of these, leaving a prudent inheritance, a good life and name, to our family as our true legacy. *(Psalms 39:5-6; Proverbs 13:22; Job 19:21; Malachi 3:10)*

ONE LITTLE THING

One little seed can grow a tree, One little Tree can begin a forest.
One little smile can make a good day,

One little affirming word can change the course of a life.

One little moment of one little day, may be the most important one thing in someone's life,
One little spark can start a glowing and warming fire.

One little idea can change the world, One little voice can begin a great cause.
One little hand offered can lift one up who is down,

One little release of angered bitterness can cure the angry cancer that is growing within. One little positive glance
can convey an affirming thought,
One little candle can bring darkness into light.

One little hand held squeeze can bring confidence, One little kiss can make it well.
One little laugh can change an attitude,

One little bit of love shared can become a lifetime of shared joy. One little embrace can give one immediate
comfort,

One little bit of faith can carry someone through the darkest night. One little touch can ignite a lifeless spirit,

One little forgiveness can bring lasting relief to the hurt, and the one who did hurt. One little act of kindness can
relieve a tortured soul,

One Little life of sharing, passed on can change the world. One Solitary Life can change mankind,

YOU CAN BE THAT ONE LITTLE THING.

THREE THINGS

1. Three things that can never come back:
    a. Time- there is no re-run of yesterday,
    b. Words written or spoken,
    c. An opportunity- that we let slip by us.

2. Three Things that can destroy the life of the one harboring it- or the That of the recipient:
    a. Anger that is not let go,
    b. Hurtful words spoken or written,
    c. A failure to forgive- not letting go of hurt.

3. Three things you should never lose:
    a. FAITH AND HOPE,
    b. LOVE,
    c. INTEGRITY.

4. Three Things in Life that are invaluable:
    a. Respect and acceptance of self and Love of others,
    b. Family and Friends,
    c. Sharing your time, your talent and your treasure.

5. Three Things to strive for Daily:
    a. Total Commitment,
    b. Truthfulness and Sincerity,
    c. Tenacity in our purpose.

6. Three Things that are uncertain in Life:
    a. What tomorrow holds,
    b. What we possess tangibly today,
    c. That we'll fully finish what was unfinished today.

TEN COMMANDMENTS OF MARRIAGE

1.   Thou shalt love thy spouse with all thy heart and all thy soul, warts and all, for better or for worse, but thou shalt also respect, preserve and defend thy spouse as the special and unique person that he is, even thyself. *(Ephesians 5:22-31)*

2.   Scripture instructs us that man shall leave his father and his mother and cleave unto his wife. Thou shalt put thy wife above all things and above all the world, including thyself, thy mother and father, and yes even thy children, for it is together as one you shall raise your children in the way they should go, for even when they are old they will not depart from it. *(Genesis 2:24; Proverbs 6:22)*

3.   Thou shalt communicate and share with thy spouse all the days of your life together, through all of the God given sense, of listening, speaking, touching, seeing with understanding; and thou shalt be slow to speak, quick to listen and slow to anger. Speak in thoughtful comforting words, and do not let the sunset on your anger. *(James 1:9)*

4.   Thou shalt not set thy goals on material things, neither money, nor status, nor power, nor control, nor position or office; but thou shalt set thy life's purpose on those intangible yet eternal things such as love, sharing, caring, and a purposeful life, for what profit a man, if he shall gain the entire world but has no eternal conviction or life purpose. *(Matthew 16:24-26)*

5.   Thou shalt forgive and forget with a full heart, and thy family shall call you blessed, and thou shalt love your spouse for what he, forgive for what he is not, and shall not seek to remake thy spouse in they own image. *(Matthew 5:7)*

6.   Thou shalt remember that thy body, which has been given to you, is the Temple of the Holy Spirit, and you shall therefore neither defile thy body nor mind with excessive, food drink, foreign substance, nor addiction of any kind, but thou shalt preserve thy body as an endowment given to you to the best of thy ability. *(1st Corinthians 6:19-20)*

7.   Consider the beauty of lilies of the field, and unduly worry about the future, for today has enough problems to occupy your hours, for thy worry adds nothing to the solution of your concerns, only lessens your effectiveness as a spouse, a parent, and as a person. *(Matthew 6:7, 34)*

8.   Cleanliness is next to Godliness, and thou shalt render all reasonable effort to maintain and orderly home a clean body and mind and a neat attire. *(John Wesley)*

9.   To thine own self, thy spouse, thy family, friends and others be truthful and true, for you shall be a blessing to your children, and shall come to know the Truth and the Truth shall set you free. *(Proverbs 20:7; John 8:32)*

10.   Together Love the Lord thy God with all thy Heart, mind and soul, love your spouse and your children with the same commitment and fervor, and love your neighbor as yourself, doing unto them as you would have them do unto you. *(Matthew 7:12; 22:37- 40)*

THE MEASURE OF A LIFE

Not how did he die, but how did he live? Not how did she gain, but how did she give?
Not who did he beat, but who did he help?

Not how pretty was she, but to whom she gave a cold water's cup?
Not what was his station in life, but did he have a giving heart?

Not her many given gifts, but how did she use them to fulfill her part?

Not how eloquently he spoke, but did he have an affirming word to share? To bring forth a smile, an "I can do it,"
or wipe away a tear?

Not how religious she was nor even her memorized verses and creeds
But how she befriended others, even strangers, supplied other's needs?

Not that he was a captain of industry, and "did it my way,"
But the positive impact of his life on others, as he lived day by day?

These just some of the measurements of one's life's worth,
Of each man and woman, boy or girl, not their wealth, their color, title, or birth.

It is that person who had true wealth he was loved had a good name, and a legacy,
What we've done for self, dies with us,
But what we have given and done for others in life and passed on to others lasts for eternity.

THINGS MONEY CAN'T BUY

Money can buy a bed and fancy numbered mattress;
But not restful sleep.

Money can buy books, a computer, a tablet, or an "I phone;"
But not knowledge, intelligence or wisdom.

Money can buy food;
But only people feed the hungry mouths.

Money can buy beautiful clothes, a face lift or outer body reconstruction;
But not inner beauty nor a loving heart.

Money can buy a house;
But not a Home.

Money can buy surgery or medicine;
But not insure total health.

Money can buy a name;
But not integrity.

Money can buy effective and laudatory advertisements;
But not honesty.

Money can buy office furniture, maybe even an office;
But not a good reputation.

Money can buy luxuries and amusement;
But not happiness.

Money can buy a laborer; But not a friend.

Money can buy a relaxing vacation;
But not inner peace.

Money may be able to prolong our continued existence;
But not a meaningful life, nor negate the certainty of death.

Money can buy your love expensive rings;
But not her love.

Money can buy your children expensive toys and cars;
But not their respect.

Money can buy a Church Pew;
But not a priceless ticket to heaven.

Money can buy a religious sacrifice;
But not forgiveness.

Money can buy a Bible or religious symbol;
But not a Savior.

Money, as all tangible things are entrusted to us but for a time;
To use wisely and for good, whether it be millions, a nickel or a dime.

I WISH YOU ENOUGH*
(A Blessing)

"HE gives HIS best to all, the Sun to warm and the Rain to nourish, the good and the evil alike" Matthew 5: 45. (Paraphrase)

I wish you enough gain to meet your needs, and ample to share those without enough, but only enough loss to appreciate all that you have now, and have not lost.

I wish you enough success to climb to the mountain top,
But only enough failure to know the road is rocky not easy, and not all reach the top.

I wish for you enough confidence to know that you are a unique and gifted person, but enough humility, to know these gifts must be nurtured and used for good.

I wish you enough strength for each of your days,
But only enough weakness to be patient with yourself and the weakness of others.

I wish you enough sun to keep your attitude bright, even when the day is gray,
But only enough rain that you appreciate the sun, and as do plants, by rain, grow stronger.

I wish you enough courage to bring whatever challenges you may face, under control, But only enough fear, that you realize that no one is an island, we can't do it alone.

I wish you enough happiness and joy to keep your spirit alive, hopeful, and everlasting, but only enough pain that you realize, often the smallest life joys are the most treasured.

I wish you enough love, that you know the life gift we have in love given and received, But only enough rejection, that you understand loneliness, and reject no one in need.

I wish you enough understanding that God is near us always, the choice to call is ours, but only enough self-doubt, that you make the choice to call for His help and vision.

I wish you enough of God's Eternal Peace, to carry you thru life's deepest waters, But only enough turmoil, that you appreciate the quiet eddies of life.

I wish you enough time to find true friends, and a long lifetime to love them,
And enough wisdom to see, that all things in God's time, have a season and reason.

I wish you enough Faith to know things unseen are alive and real, that God has a plan, and enough self-inquiry, to find the Truth that sets you free, to know you are in His plan.

I wish then, that you might know that whenever I say to you "Blessings", or "I Wish You Enough,"
That these are the things, I pray for you!

*This written for a dear friend during an extended last illness.

FIFTEEN LITTLE PASSING THOUGHTS ABOUT LOVE, LIFE AND FRIENDSHIP

1. Always put the needs of the ones you love before your own wants.

2. Just because two lovers don't argue, doesn't mean they don't love each other.

3. Just because two lovers don't argue, doesn't prove they do love each other.

4. If two spouses always agreed on everything, it would be a boring life.

5. We don't have to change our friends, if we understand that our friends do change.

6. True love will always have pain, because at some point it or life comes to an end.

7. It may take a lifetime to become the person you'd like to be.

8. As good as you think you may have become, you can always become a bit better.

9. When you think you are the best- don't bother to step around the corner.

10. You generally can keep on going longer than you think you can.

11. Never let your young children go to bed without telling them you love them, even when it's been a trying day.

12. Control your anger or it will control you.

13. Wisdom doesn't automatically come with age- it takes life experience and observation from which you can learn a lot.

14. Our childhood, our life experience, our surroundings, form a part of who we are, but we are responsible for who we become.

15. Degrees, credentials, Certificates of Completion and time in the job don't assure competence, without commitment and the right attitude.

LIFE IS

Life is a journey,
Experience and grow through it!

Life can be a bitter-sweet song,
Whatever the song, sing it!

Life is a precious gift,
Share all that you can of it with others!

Life is filled with dreams,
Realize those attainable dreams!

Life is a continuing learning experience,
Study it!

Life is lived one moment at a time,
Treasure each of them, even the tough ones!

Life is a series of mountains, valleys and plains,
You can learn to navigate each!

Life is serving God by helping others,
Do it!

Life is the sum total of your daily choices,
Choose wisely!

Life is a privilege,
But with privilege comes responsibility!

Life is in constant change,
Adjust to the changes!

Life is a series of daily decisions and choices,
Choose wisely!

Life is about today,
Live it today! Yesterday is gone, tomorrow may or may not come!

Life is a series of challenges and opportunities,
Confront the challenges and embrace the opportunities to do good.

Life is like the seashore's wave,
It continues, without pause, breaks up on the shore, then to return to its maker, when life is done!

Life is about times, talents, and things shared,
For it is in giving that we receive!

Life is not a destination or a ladder to climb,
It is a continually evolving adventure!

Life is what you make of it
You determine what it is you make!

THE TWENTY THIRD PSALM; AN OUTLINE OF HIS MANY GIFTS TO US!
(A BRIEF EXPLANATION)

The Lord is My Shepherd	That's His Fatherly Relationship(Our Protector, Our Leader, Our Provider, Our Teacher)
I shall not want	That's His Supply of all our needs (Our physical needs, Our life needs, Our emotional and spiritual needs)
He makes me to lie down in green pastures	That's His gift of peaceful Rest (He gives us inner peace, not temporary respite as the world may give, but Peace beyond understanding)
He leads me beside still waters	That's our daily spiritual Refreshment (A drink of spiritual cool water to the thirsty)
He restores my Soul	That's His Healing of our inner being (He heals our physical body and my spiritual soul)
He leads me in the paths of righteousness	That's His Guidance and Direction (He gives both direction and purpose to our life)
For His Name's sake	That's His Purpose for our life (I am His child and must live to bring Him glory)
Though I walk through the valley of shadows of death!	That's His comfort in our life storms (He walks with us through the hottest flames, the deepest waters, and most violent storms of our life)
I will fear no evil	That's because of His Staff & Shield (We can do and overcome all things with Him, who gives us strength)
For Thou art with me	That's His great Faithfulness (He changes not; Morning by Morning, new mercies we see)
Thy Rod and Thy Staff they comfort me	That's His Protection from our Enemies (We find comfort in His strength and power to meet all foes)
Thou preparest a table before me,	That's His provision of our life's daily bread (Every day a thanksgiving feast- as his creation provides our daily bread)
Even in the presence of my enemies	That's His Re-Assurance when we are surrounded by trouble (Enemies of many kinds surround me, even sometimes I am among the worst)
Thou annointest my head with oil	That's His consecration of our life as His child (Even in our imperfection He makes us pure by the life and blood of His Son)
My cup runneth over	That's our humility, abundant gratitude for His Love and Grace(When we survey the wondrous Cross on which Jesus died for us we are overwhelmed with humility, our greatest gain is but loss)
Surely goodness and mercy shall follow me all the days of my life	That's our greatest Blessing (May the Lord Bless us and keep us, May he make His Face to shine upon us, be gracious unto us, and give us His Peace, now and forevermore, Amen.)
And I shall dwell in the House of the Lord	That's our perpetual Security (He has promised us that whomever believes in Him shall not perish but shall have eternal life with Him)
Forever	That's infinite Eternity(Infinity is beyond the grasp of our human perception, if we were to count the grains of sand on all the Beaches of the world and each grain represented 1,000 years we would not have even begun to measure the love of God and Eternity)

A DECLARATION OF PRIVILEGES

While there are things our forefathers declared as inalienable rights,
Rights granted by divine Providence, and for their denial we'd fight.
And many have died to preserve our rights and freedoms for 250 years,
By each of those who gave their life, their blood, their sweat and tears.

The proclamation declared that each of us has rights, that all are equal,
The right of life, liberty, the pursuit of happiness, and a later given sequel.
To be free to express ourselves, and in such faith or religion as we choose,
These inalienable rights too, to be guaranteed, that we would not lose.

Later four freedoms, our nation proclaimed that we each possessed,
Freedom of speech and of worship, freedom from want and fear, addressed.
These additional rights, guaranteed to each of us, so it is said,
These rights of expression, protection, religion and our daily bread.

Yet, if we think carefully about these rights that they claim and proclaim,
For which much blood has been shed, to maintain freedom's flame.
We must realize that they are neither rights, nor are they guaranteed,
But only treasured privileges, to be embraced, to meet our basic needs.

And while it is true that all are to be on equal footing before the law,
No prejudice, no favoritism granted, that there be equal justice for all.
We are not equal as persons, each is God's creation, different and unique,
Special qualities we each possess, each God given, to create the human mystique.

For life itself is but a gift, entrusted to us for just a little while,
And liberty, like a fleeting butterfly, easily stolen by a tyrant's guile.
And while true happiness may be sought and pursued, it too is an illusory goal,
It cannot be bought or sold at any price, for it is an inner peace, deep within our soul.

Freedom from want and fear, they too can change like the tides of the sea,
Here today, gone tomorrow, it is so much how we feel, deep within you and me.
Freedom of speech too, is not unbridled, that we not destroy one another,
Freedom of worship, does not give us free reign to condemn the faith of our brother.

So as we reflect upon the granted rights that we claim that we own,
These rights are but privileges with responsibilities, not cast in stone.
What we claim then as rights are but gifts, bought at a price, entrusted to you,
Treasured presents, which 'round the world, are enjoyed, by only a precious few.

SECTION III. A DOG'S TALE
(ESPECIALLY FOR DOG LOVERSWHAT WE HUMANS CAN LEARN ABOUT UNCONDITIONAL LOVE FROM DOGS)

A DOG'S TALE, ESPECIALLY FOR DOG LOVERS
(WHAT WE HUMANS CAN LEARN ABOUT UNCONDITIONAL LOVE IN LIFE FROM DOGS)

NOTE: From the time I was a young boy, our family had a dog. We had a number of different dogs. In all, we had a white Spitz, a Chow, a Scotty dog, and a Wire Haired Terrier. For a time we were without a dog. During WWII when my Father was gone, my Mother thought maybe it was time to get another dog. My Grandmother told her about her next door neighbor who had a female dog, and had just had a litter of puppies. The story was, he didn't want them and was going to "dispose of them."

When we went to select one of the puppies, my older brother selected his choice, but I was just taken with another little puppy who seemed so friendly to me. To our surprise, I suspect because my Mother knew how much I wanted the one dog and my brother the other, of all things, she let us take both of them. But they were to be our sole responsibility to care for.

My brother named his dog, who was black and white, "Mike" and I named my red dog "Red." Those were the names of two of our favorite soldiers who came to Sunday dinner with us, during their Gunnery Training at Buckingham Air Field. Mike began to chase cars and in less than a year, was hit by the man with the noisy car. I'm not excusing Mike for chasing the car, but the car that hit him was the noisiest car in town, a 1922 cloth-top Model T. Ford. His back leg was crushed. We took him to the only Vet in the county, Dr. Piper. I remember he told my Mother he'd do what he could for him, but wasn't sure he could or should save him. A few days later he called and said Mike would have to be put down, but he'd wait a day if we wanted to see him.

My Mother worked full time, and my brother and sister had other school obligations. I was pretty much on my own after school, so I rode my bicycle out to see him. An assistant took me back to where he was caged. He had blood spattered all over, but was able to stand up only because he had a large wooden a splint on his back leg. I'm not sure how long I stayed with him. He and I cried a lot and he wanted me to get him out of the cage, but I could only feel him lick my fingers. I went home very sad, but found my Red there to greet me. I never let him out again without a leash on until after my Dad came home from the War, and by then the noisy car man had a better car.

During that time and until after the War, Red was my best friend. We played inside every day when I came home from school. He was always so happy to see me. At night his place was to sleep on a back porch, I'd sneak out when my Mother was in the other room, bring Red into my bed with me, and put him beneath the covers so she wouldn't see him. Then one night she said, "Yes, Red can sleep with you whenever you want, but please keep him in your bed." I did. She told me some years later that every night when she'd come into the bedroom of my brother and I, to "kiss us" good night she would see Red's tail wagging beneath the covers. A wonderful loving Mother was she. A wonderful loving dog was Red, my best friend.

Red lived until he was 15 years old. I was in college when he died. My Mother didn't tell me until I came home because she knew how much he meant to me in those early years. By then I realized it was his time. Many a time in those later years of his life he would fight any dog, large or small, that came into our yard. As an older dog he became beloved and loved by several of his selection of our neighbors, whom he visited each morning (knowing he'd get a friendly reception and a treat when he stopped by for a visit.
When he died of old age, he was very well fed, and had the extra pounds to show it.

My parents never had another dog after Red as long as they lived. Ellen and I didn't get a dog until after Law School and my time in service. In 1958, when we returned to Fort Myers, Ellen and I thought our children should have a one. Our first dog, a little brown dog we called "Kackie", was from the shelter (I had just returned from 2 1/2 years in the Army). He was a fine puppy, loved by our three children

A short time later we secured a thoroughbred female Dalmatian, Tina. This was before leash laws, so Tina had the run of the neighborhood. Since she had papers we let her have puppies with another registered Dalmatian, and Tina gave us a record 13 puppies. It even made the front page of the local paper- a photo of all 13 in a wheelbarrow, Tina standing beside. Because of the joy Tina gave us, we gave them all away and brought joy to friends and family. Tina was very happy, feeding 13 was quite a chore she didn't cherish.

Our next dog was a mutt from the litter of a friend. Her name was Ginger. Ginger, a small dog, lived for 15 years and was loved by all of the family. She brought much joy to each us. Ginger died in Ellen's lap.

Some years before Ginger died we secured a beautiful Old English pup, Maggie. But Ginger was always the senior partner in the dog firm. We discovered later that most Old English were either very calm or crazy. Maggie, it turned out was loving but, crazy.

After several years, we thought Maggie might settle down if she had a male friend. We weren't really looking intently, but one day Ellen and Sandy saw an ad in the paper of someone looking for a good home for a full grown two year old male Old English. Ellen and Sandy couldn't resist and surprised me that evening with Sir Gallagher.

So now there were two big dogs. They were quite a pair. Maggie had one litter of 8 puppies. It was again a nice family experience for the children to observe the birth and help take care of the young puppies. They began to come at midnight, and Ellen and I took turns bringing them out and in, one by one. One of them on Ellen's watch, wasn't breathing. Ellen gave the pup her two fingered version of artificial respiration and the puppy was fine.

We found good home for each of the Old English Pups. Maggie had continual fits of excitement, which only stirred up Gallagher. Several times Ellen fell, as did once my Mother, when trying to restrain Maggie when the doorbell rang, so it was time to find a good home for Maggie, which we did, in the country again. I remember the day we delivered her to the farm of a nice family, and she raced off into the fields in joy.

Gallagher was happy and a wonderful dog for all of the family for ten long years. He was a part of us and we a part of him. Ellen groomed him frequently. In the summer months we shaved his body, because of the heat, but left his full head covered, as the dogs need the shade for their eyes. Oh how we all loved Gallagher. Fortunately, by then Andy and Sandy had married and had children of their own. They loved him just as we did. One of our grandchildren could not say Gallagher so she called him "Hi Guy." That was his name until the day he passed.

Gallagher is the last dog we have had. He died more than 25 years ago. We had lost our son some years earlier, and losing Gallagher as we did, Ellen and I agreed we could not have another dog. At our ancient ages of 84 and 83, we would love, but hesitate to get another dog. However, we have both agreed that when one of us "graduates" the other will have a dog, once again. He or she will be our in-house family member until it's the survivor's time.

So now you know how we feel about dogs. I have said so many times that other than a spouse or family, or the family we choose, a dog is truly the best friend a person can have. "Red" was for me as a young boy so special, and each dog we have had were a "part of the family." We can learn much about love, especially unconditional love, devotion, loyalty and commitment from a dog for his or her "family."

So, what follows are a series of comments and quotes from others about the majesty and love of dogs. ENJOY! I dedicate this to and in memory of some of our best friends and family, Red, Tina, Ginger, Maggie, and "Hi Guy".

WHAT OTHER PEOPLE HAVE SAID:

"Acquiring a dog may be the only time a person gets to choose a relative." *Mordecai Siegal.*

"Thorns may hurt you, men desert you, sunlight turn to fog, but you're never friendless ever, if you have a do." *Douglas Mallock.*

"Histories are more full of examples of the fidelity of dogs than of friends." *Alexander Pope.*

"The reason a dog has so many friends is that he wags his tail instead of his tongue." *Unknown.*

"Blessed is the person who has earned the love of an old dog." *Sidney Jeanne Seward.*

"The one absolutely unselfish friend that a man can have in this selfish world, the one who never deserts him, the one that never proves ungrateful of treacherous, is his dog." *George Graham.*

"Even the tiniest poodle is lionhearted, ready to do anything to defend home, master and mistress." *Louis Sabin.*

"The more boys I meet, the more I love my dog." *Carrie Underwood.*

"Dogs are not our whole life, but they make our life whole." *Roger Caras.*

"Dogs laugh, but they laugh with their tails." *Max Eastman.*

"I think dogs are the most amazing creatures; they give unconditional love. For me they are the role model for being alive." *Gilda Ratner.*

"There is no psychiatrist in the world like a puppy licking your face." *Ben Williams.*

"To err is human, to forgive is canine." *Unknown.*

"If there are no dogs in Heaven, then when I die, I want to go where they went." *Will Rogers.*

"Happiness is a warm puppy." *Charles Shultz.*

"The pug dog is living proof that God has a sense of humor." *Margot Kaufman.*

"Heaven is a place where all the dogs you have ever loved, come to greet you." *Unknown.*

"If I have any beliefs about immortality, it is that certain dogs I have known will go to heaven, and very, very, few persons." *James Thurber.*

"It is no coincidence that man's best friend cannot speak." *Unknown.*

"A dog is the only thing that can mend a crack in a broken heart." *Judy Desmond.*

"If your dog doesn't like someone you probably shouldn't either." *Unknown*

"Dogs are often happier than men simply because the simplest things are the greatest things for them." *Mehmet Murat Ildan.*

"Many of the qualities that come effortlessly for dogs- loyalty, devotion, selflessness, optimism, unqualified love- can be elusive to humans." *John Grogan.*

"A well trained dog is like religion, it sets the deserving at their ease and is a terror to evildoers." *Elizabeth Goudge.*

"A dog can express more with his tail in minutes than an owner can express with his tongue in hours." *Karen Davison.*

"Dogs are better than human beings because they know, but do not tell." *Emily Dickinson.*

"A dog is grateful for what is, which I am finding to be the soundest kind of wisdom and a very good theology." *Carrie Newcomer.*

"Did you know there are over three hundred words for love in canine?" *Gabrielle Zevin.*

"If I could be half the person my dog is, I'd be twice the human I am." *Charles Yu.*

"Dogs live a nice life. You never see a dog with a wristwatch." *George Carlin.*

"A hound will die for you, but never lie to you." *George R. Martin*

"Sometimes I think I like dogs are more than I like humans. The only time a dog has betrayed me… was by dying." *Jose N. Harris*

"The greatest fear dogs have is the fear that you will not come back when you go out the door without them." *Stanley Coren.*

"Dogs are the leaders of the planet. If you see two life forms, one of them' is making a poop, the other one is carrying it for him, who would you assume is in charge? *Jerry Seinfeld.*

"Everything I know, I learned from dogs." *Nora Roberts.*

"Dogs and philosophers do the greatest good and get the fewest rewards." *Diogenes.*

"I have found that when you are deeply troubled, there are things you get from the silent devoted companionship of a dog that you can get from no other source." *Doris Day.*

"No matter how little money and how few possessions you own, having a dog makes you rich." *Louis Sabin.*

"Dogs… do not ruin their sleep worrying about how to keep the objects they have, and obtain the objects they have not. There is nothing they have of value to bequeath except their love and their faith." *Eugene O'Neil.*

"A dog wags its tail with its heart." *Unknown.*

"Dogs teach us many things about being a better person that people don't teach." *Unknown.*

"I always say friends are the family we choose… Is it any wonder that that dogs are called out best friend?" *Unknown.*

"We give dogs time we can spare, and love we can spare. And in return, dogs give us their all. It's the best deal man ever made." *M. Facklam.*

"The average dog is nicer than the average person." *Andy Rooney.*

"If you pick up a starving dog and make him prosperous, he will not bite you: that is the principal difference between a dog and a man." *Mark Twain.*

"Don't accept your dog's admiration as conclusive evidence that you are wonderful." *Ann Landers.*

"Properly trained a man can be a dog's best friend." *Corey Ford.*

"My goal in life is to be as good a person as my dog already thinks I am." *Unknown.*

"Dogs love their friends and bite their enemies, quite unlike people, who are incapable of pure love and have to mix love and hate." *Sigmund Freud.*

"Dogs are the only mammals that will actually stare and look into a human's eyes." *Jerry O'Connell.*

"Dogs are how people would be, if the important stuff is all that mattered to us." *Ashley Lorenzana.*

"A dog doesn't care if you're rich or poor, smart or dumb. Give him your heart… and he'll give you his." *Milo Gathema.*

"A dog can express more with his tail in minutes than his owner can express with his tongue in hours." *Karen Davison.*

"Some of our greatest historical and artifacts we place with curators in museums, others we take for walks." *Alex Caras.*

"I used to look at my dog and think, 'If you were a little smarter me what you are thinking,' and he'd look at me like he was saying, 'if you were a little smarter, I wouldn't have to.'" *Fred Jungclaus.*

"Dogs teach us many things about being a better person… that people don't always teach." *Unknown.*

"We can learn more about true unconditional love, from dogs, that we can from most people, except God, some Moms and Dads, and some best friends. Unconditional love never ends, regardless of the past or present circumstances, or the future promise." *The Author.*

SECTION IV. OBERVATIONS ON FINDING WISDOM AND MEANING THROUGH THE SIMPLE GIFTS OF DAILY LIVING AND A THANKFULLNESS IN FAITH, LOVE, AND GIVING.

A PORTRAIT OF LOVE GIVEN AND RECEIVED*

LOVE never, ever gives up,
Is given and received without conditions,
Requests with "Please", receives with "Thanks,"
Doesn't envy what others may have, and it doesn't have.

LOVE doesn't strut with pride,
Doesn't impose itself or its views on the other,
Gives the other respect for the person they are,
Accepts the other's imperfections, warts and all.

LOVE doesn't force the other to give up their uniqueness,
Is tough, when toughness is called for,
Will generously give or receive a sincere apology,
Shares matters with the other with integrity.

LOVE doesn't keep score of, and resurrect the other's mistakes,
Forgives the other's imperfections,
Doesn't consider the other either lesser or greater than they are,
Always looks for the positives, plays down the negatives.

LOVE doesn't fret over yesterdays "might have beens,"
Always speaks the truth, even if it hurts, but then with kindness,
Lives out today together to the fullest,
And looks to tomorrow with hope and anticipation.

LOVE NEVER DIES, BUT KEEPS ON, KEEPIN' ON, UNTIL THE LAST BREATH.

*Verses written for and read to the wedding celebrants while conducting the marriage of two dear friends, but with much borrowed from the concepts of 1st Corinthians 13.

THE LOVE OF OUR LIFE
(A PARAPHRASE OF PORTIONS OF 1st CORINTHIANS 13)

Nourishment, friendships, mental challenges and physical activity, maintain our physical body and life. But Love sustains and improves our spiritual and emotional life, and strengthens our inner peace in the storms of life that come in each of our lives. Everybody a needs somebody most times.

What is it about real, true and unconditional Love that keeps us going positively? Love never gives up.

Love is not love of self or alone, but is shared with the one, or ones loved. Love accepts self as self is, seeks to make self the best it can be, with the gifts it has. Love cares more for another, or others, than for self. Love seek to always give where there is an opportunity and a need, for the sheer joy of giving and with no expectation of repayment, or quid pro quo. Love doesn't envy what others may have, that it doesn't have. Love doesn't strut with pride.

Doesn't have a swelled head. Doesn't force itself on others. Doesn't seek to change others to suit its pleasure, but gives each his or her own space. Isn't always "me first." Doesn't fly off the handle, but is indignant when fairness fails. Doesn't keep score of the failures of others and joins in enjoying the successes of others. Doesn't revel, when others grovel. Love takes pleasure in learning, knowing and living the truth. Puts up with others shortcomings and idiosyncrasies. Always looks for the positive in others, accentuates the positives, and eliminates the negatives. Never looks back at what might have been, but lives today to the fullest with purpose, and looks forward to tomorrow with anticipation.

Love never dies, but keeps on going to and until the last breath.

A LAUGHING PLACE

Everybody needs to find their laughing place,
Everyone needs to set aside a little laughing space.
Because we all take ourselves and our life too seriously,
So, frequently, look in the mirror of your life, and laugh deliriously.

God gave us senses, Gave us laughter to ease our stress, and that's no rumor,
I'm sure when God planned things, He had a sense of humor.
Ever look at your ears, your toes, your nose- or a giraffe's neck,
So many things, the Rhino's horn, my nubby knees, but what the heck.

Several good laughs a day are good for what ails you,
A funny movie, a good joke, to shake our body through and through.
So find the moments of what it is that tickles the fancy of your funny bone,
T'is better to laugh with others, when you can, or even all alone.

You'll be surprised how wonderfully contagious is spontaneous laughter,
It can take the edge off somber times, to nearly laugh yourself into the hereafter.
Laughter can be a bonding agent, make two strangers as kindred souls,
Seeing another's raucous laugh, we just can't our composure withhold.

Real laughing, is when you shake from your head to your belly,
That brings tears to your eyes, makes your tummy like jelly.
So, regardless of your status in life, or the state of your wealth,
A few good belly laughs a day will do wonders for your health.

Science has proved that laughing brings forth those healthy endorphins,
You'll find that regular laughing will bring you a personality metamorphosis.
Start searching today for the things that make you uncontrollably laugh,
And treasure your laughing place, and laugh so hard, that you rock a seismograph.

A MOTHER'S PRAYER AT NOON

By Harriet McCoy Woolslair (Author's Grandmother, circa 1910)

Dear Lord, the day is long and I am tired
I kneel to ask thy help along the way.
I have travelled far since early dawn
And must go on until the end of day.
So many little things have fretted me
They might have made my judgment err.
May love for them help many blind mistakes I care so much- Lord, hear my prayer.

A WARTIME MOTHER'S EVENING PRAYER*
(Author's Thoughts on How His Mother surely prayed As Father Went to War)

Lord, may my daily labor make me and others glad,
And may I have the eyes to see,
My loneliness since he's been gone from this our home,
Where you have called me at this time to be.

The scent of my supper cooking in clean blue smoke,
The old pans, into the night I daily polish bright,
The kettle's boiling chuckling its little joke,
The stove's red yellow flames lovely light

May I have the vision to take,
The simple joys that around me lie,
Whether I roast, fry or bake,
May my daily labor make me wise.

May my efforts leave me at peace,
When twilight encompasses our earth,
May I have the grace to smile,
And count the effort of the day's good work.

May I love and embrace my children, all three,
As I give each one a good night wish, then off to bed,
May I be thankful, and know their love for me,
Give each one the strength for tomorrow's need, in what I've done and said.

An old love song wells up in my soul,
Yet quiet in my breast,
May I at day's end welcome end of day,
Each night's gift and rest.

And grant me the strength to face each day,
Until My love who's gone to War these years,
I pray to return on the morrow, to I, his wife,
May my labors bless him, my children, and others in my life.

*NOTE: My Father had served in France and Germany during World War I. He was in the trenches of the two of the bloodiest battles of the War for American troops. When the Armistice was declared on November 11, 1918, he and so many soldiers who had given their greatest effort were distressed that they were not permitted to "finish" the War with the German Army. Thousands felt that given the chance they could have secured an unconditional surrender with six more months. "That was not to be."

My Father, as many others returned to this country, dispirited. He lost so many of his friends and "buddies" who were placed in cemeteries at St. Mahil, and Muese Argonne. (80% of my Father's unit were either killed, wounded gassed or died of dysentery, or other disease.) He carried that with him for twenty two years. When Japan struck Pearl Harbor, on December 7, 1941, my Father felt duty bound to return to Europe finally finish the fight, for his friends who had died in WWI, and for the country

At the age of 45, with my Mother, his wife, 35, and three young children, He re- enlisted in the Infantry within 60 days following the attack. He was gone for three and one half years. When he left I was 9, my brother, 12, and my sister 13. My Mother, with courage and fortitude, took a full time job, and kept the family together. We learned quickly to live on little, be thankful for what we had, a hope pour husband and Father would come home. We all had our part in it, but my Father and my Mother were a part of the Greatest Generation.

CHILDREN THROUGH GRANDPARENT'S EYES

God gives us children mercifully, when we are young,
For age saps our energy, strength, and patience, when our spring is sprung.
But age does not steal the loving memories and times we've had,
With our dear children, working through, with them, the good times and bad.

Yet one of the greatest joys that I have ever known,
Is to watch the growth of grandchildren, as they seek to strive on their own.
Without the pressure and stress of the parent's daily grind,
A grandparent's love is complete, and often also blind.

All we see are those growing little ones, so bright and so dear,
Their unlimited futures, how they love us, and we them revere.
Though deep inside, we know they're not perfect in every way,
But then, we don't have to deal with their parent's travails, every day.

We feel quite comfortable with all of this, you know,
Because we had our time in the trenches, wrestling with children's ebb and flow.
Yet, we know, too, that our children must deal with concerns, we never saw,
A different society they face, with so many different things ugly and raw.

So we give thanks for the joys and love each of our children and grandchildren bring,
And likewise, have compassion for the parents, who must worry about many things.
We pray that each might have the wisdom and patience to face each day,
As they guide and direct our beloved grandchildren, along life's way.

And we pray that God might give us the judgment to think twice,
Before we give too much of our unsolicited and ancient advice.
Though wisdom is supposed to come with age and experience, with ease,
They can choose to us listen, then make their own judgment, and do as they please.

THROUGH LITTLE CHILDREN'S EYES

"About that time the disciples came to Jesus to ask which of them would be the greatest in the Kingdom of Heaven. Jesus called a small child lover to Him, and set the little fellow down among them, and said, "Unless you turn to God and become as little children, you will never get into the Kingdom of Heaven. Therefore anyone who humbles himself as this little child, is the greatest in the Kingdom of Heaven." *Matthew 18:1-4 (The Living Bible)*

"One day some mothers brought their babies to touch and bless. But the disciples told them to go away. The Jesus called the children over to him and said to the disciples, "Let the little children come to me! Never send them away! For the Kingdom of God belongs to men (and women) who have hearts as trusting as little children's. And anyone who doesn't have their kind of faith will never enter the Kingdom's gates." *Luke 18:15-17 (The Living Bible)*

If only we could recapture the qualities of our youth,
If only we could retain the childlike joys, the simple truths.
If only we could once again see the world through children's eyes,
The thrill of each day, the imagination and surprise.

A child is not so impressed with an expensive toy,
But is happy with a cardboard box, an old spoon can bring him joy.
He's happy to watch an ant, with his heavy load and toil,
To watch him build his home in the side yard soil.

He doesn't even notice his neighbors have more,
Of the "things" that others have, he doesn't keep score.
For the number of toys to him, neither important nor sought,
But learning and living life, the friends, the family, the things not bought.

And in those around him he has complete trust,
Because he hasn't yet learned, that to be suspicious, you must.
For we teach him you must examine each other's agenda,
Don't trust, or in the end you'll be hurt, this you must remember.

He has a curiosity about just how things work,
He'll study it for hours, to find each little quirk.
His imagination runs wild, building castles in the sand,
Thinking of ancient warriors in faraway lands.

And in his mind he pictures a blanket over a chair,
Is a darkened cave, where he's safe from lion, tiger, or bear.
He lies in the grass, studying the passing clouds in wonder,
Sees an elephant, a dinosaur, a trampling horse amidst the thunder.

And when he speaks, he's honest, truthful, and without pretense,
For he's not built around him the facades we have, that make no sense.
And even when he makes up a story, that he spins to you,
His face shows it all, what he really feels comes right through.

59

He wakes up each day, with a hilarious joy for living,
His enthusiasm is contagious, positive vibrations he's giving.
He leaps from his bed, can't wait for the day to begin,
Races through his day, never waiting to give up at its end.

He is so eager to learn, to observe and create,
His little mind takes it all in, so quickly, never to abate.
But when he grows older, with all the mental barriers we've erected,
He'll learn much more slowly, than his open mind had projected.

To try anything win or lose, to take risks, he has no fear,
He hasn't learned the world praises winners, second best is not so dear.
He'll learn from us, rom great leaps of Faith, you must hold back,
For if you try and fail, your performance they'll attack.

And from us he will meticulously learn to hate,
All the things and people that we don't like and berate.
For to him all people, all colors, all sizes are quite the same,
All a part of humanity, our brothers, the strong, the feeble and the lame.

How I wish for a time when we might become children once more,
When we could trust, be ourselves, not have to even the score.
A time when we could each drop the barriers and the masks,
That separate us from each other, as we pursue life's tasks.

So may the time come when childish simplicity may reign,
That we not look at others with suspicion and disdain.
A time when each of us might see life through Children's eyes,
With joy, with love, with trust, in peace, each day a new surprise.

HOW FAR WILL YOU GO?
(Genesis 1:27; Psalm 8:5; Psalm 107: 1-4a; Psalm 139; Isaiah 43:5-7; Mark 10:45; Lamentations 3:22-23.)Luke 15:11-32 (The Prodigal Son) Romans 7:14-25, 8:1-3

As I stand before Your Judgment Throne Lord, face to Face,
When I have finished the last lap of my life's grueling race,
Though I've tried, I've often failed, to honor Your Holy Place,
I ask then, how can I, broken as I am, see your Amazing Grace?

How far will You go O Lord, to bring me back?
How far may I fall in getting my life off track?
I know, I have failed often what You have taught,
As I stand before Your Glory, my life should go for naught.

What is the time, or where the place, when You say, "He's not worth saving,
For he has again fallen to the Enemy, in his human craving?"
Is there a point when my life is so far in err?
That You will say, "This life is beyond repair?"

Is there anything I have done, that Your love for me will finally cease?
Will you save this sorrowful soul, and unloose the chains for my release?
Then I recall Your Word proclaimed You would take me back in my humble repentance,
That you sent Your Son, to live as a man and die for me, for my death sentence.

I called out to You, to forgive my trespasses, to earnestly hear my plea.
And I heard The Voice of Truth, as You whispered to me.
"How far is it from north to south, how far from east to west?
How far is it from Hell to Heaven, from creation to infinity compressed?"

"How far then will I go? I shall redeem you from the farthest ends of the earth,
From the darkest night, the deepest ocean, for I loved you even before your birth.
I shall rescue you from the wilderness of desolation, yes, even from the Enemy,
I shall by Grace give you New Life, and give you new ears to hear, and eyes to see."

"How Far will I go? As far as from left to right of the Cross My Son's nail scarred hands,
As far as from south to north of My Son's battered feet to His bloodied thorn crown band.
So, be not afraid, I shall bring you back and all My children from near and far,
All who repent, call upon My Name, whatever be their broken lives, wounds or scars."

"For I have created you in My image, just below the Angels, for a purpose and My Glory,
Just as I formed you in your mother's womb to begin your life's earthly story.
As I created you, so will I redeem you, My mercies and faithfulness each morn ever new,
By the life, death and resurrection of My Son, you shall live a life eternal, and renewed."

HUMANKIND (LIVE AND BE BOTH!)

For years, as I have stopped for red light or stop signs, I've enjoyed reading bumper stickers. Some are a joke, some cynical, some promote a candidate, business or a cause, some tell you about the other driver, and some are just there.

But occasionally I note one that makes me ask, "What is that saying to me?" Such was the case last week, when I pulled in behind another car and saw a bright sign. It said: "Humankind, Live and Be Both." I went home to look up "humankind." My New Webster's Collegiate Dictionary under "human," the words human being, humane, humanism, humanitarian, humanity, even humanoid. But no humankind.

So I went back and read the definitions of each word- human: having the characteristics of humans; humane: characterized by kindness, mercy or compassion; humanitarian: one devoted to the promotion of human welfare; humanity: human beings as a group; and humanoid: resembling a human in appearance. What, then, "Humankind, Live and Be Both," what does that mean?

To be human is to be less than perfect. Ancient Scriptures tell us that "The earth, and every living thing is given, and sustained in life by the One who is the Creator of All," by whatever name we choose, The Higher Power, if you will. Scientifically, what a marvelous physical creature is the human being, with scores of parts and organs all working together to keep the being alive. At least four of the major Faiths are based on the premise that on Earth, that the Human, "created just below the Angels," is the one given the special power to create, to reason, and to make choices about our life and those of others, and that that the Human Being was charged with the care of humanity, the earth and all that's in it. But with this gift in this life we make good, not so good, and bad choices, affecting ourselves and others.

The dictionary defines "kind" as generous, warmhearted, sympathetic, understanding, considerate, tolerant, and of helping nature. Maybe, then the bumper sticker means that human, we are imperfect, being kind our aim is to make right choices, to "Live and Do both", all of the above. What a concept!

The bumper sticker "Humankind, Live and Be Both," made me think. I hope that someday my life might have stood for, "ONE OF THE HUMAN KIND-LIVED AND DID BOTH!"

IF I HAD KNOWN

If I had known, I'd not see you again,
So many things I would like to have said to you,
I've rehearsed many times each word in my mind and heart anew.

If I had known I'd not see you again,
When you and I parted that very last day,
I'd never have left, but by your side have stayed.

If I had known I'd not see you again,
I'd have thrown my arms around you, my love to show;
And held you tightly close to me, as if to never let go.

If I had known I'd not see you again,
I would have told you from my heart, just how much I loved you,
Even though I'd told you many times before, it would've been too few.

If I had known I'd not see you again,
I would have told you again, the joy it was to have you in my life, to call you mine,
I'd sing it from the mountaintop, so loud as to cause steeple bells to chime.

If I had known I'd not see you again,
I'd have told you even in our times of anger, my love still flowed,
A love to last forever, beyond life's eternal road.

If I had known I'd not see you again,
I'd have said how honored I was that you bore my name,
That no matter what might happen, I'd always feel the same.

If I had known, I'd not see you again,
I wouldn't have missed that dinner, show or game, for a more "important" date,
All of those trivial things that we permit our daily life to regulate.

If I had known, I'd not see you again,
So many things done and said, undone and unsaid, I wish I'd had the chance,
So many times and words, so poorly handled, I'd better and gently redo perchance.

If I had known, I'd not see you again,
So many "ifs", but after a time I've realized that we can't relive yesterday,
Knowing time waits for no one, and that each sunrise takes us through a new doorway.

If I had known, I'd not see you again,
All the fruitless fretting over missed opportunities of what is past,
But, now I cherish each new morn, knowing new morns will not always last.

Now knowing I'll not see you again in this life,
I trust that you now know, my unspoken words of the treasured life we've had, So I no longer let those missed,
wasted and unspent times, make me sad.

Now knowing that, I'll not see you again in this life,
I've learned to appreciate each moment I have with those close to me,
For there shall come a time, for each of us, when we shall fly away unchained and free.

Now knowing that I'll not see you again in this life,
I shall seek to speak and write the words, and do the deeds, as my inner soul shall tell,
To let flow, express and show all the love that shall in my heart dwell.

Now knowing that I'll not see you in this life, yet in the life beyond that is eternal,
I hope to see you again face to face, to do and say, what I'd like to do and say today,
Not knowing what the tomorrow holds, I shall savor each new day that comes my way.

I'M SPECIAL*

I'm special. In all the world there's nobody like me. Since the beginning of time, there has never been another person just like me. Nobody has my eyes, my nose, my hair (even now, if it's thin, with just a hair here and there) my voice, (my aged ailments) everything about me.

I'm special. Nobody can be found who has my handwriting (thank goodness). Nobody anywhere has my tastes, for food, reading, vocations, music or art. No one see things, others, the world, life, perspective, and faith, just like I do.

I'm special, like no other. In all of time, there's been no one who laughs like me, and no one cries like me, nor has feelings like me. And what makes me laugh and cry, will never provoke identical laughter, tears or feelings from anybody else ever. No one reacts to a similar situation just as I did or would react.

I'm special, I'm solely unique. I'm the only one in all creation, who has precisely my abilities and inabilities. Oh, there will always be somebody who is better at some things I'm good at, but no one – not one in the universe can reach the collection and combination of talents, abilities, feelings, and life and life experiences I have observed. Like a room full of musical instruments, many may excel alone but no one can match the living symphony when all instruments and parts, of my life as are played together. In my whole being wrapped together, I'm a symphony, even if I get off key or tune sometimes. Through all eternity, no one ever has nor ever will. No one will ever look, talk, walk, or think, or do, just like me.

I'm special, I'm rare. And in all rarity there is unique and great value. Because of my great and rare value, I need not try to imitate, nor feel lesser than any other. I am God's creation through man and woman, I will accept, yes celebrate my differences.

I am special. I am the only human being ever like me. And in God's creation of me special, He did so for a very special purpose. My job in this life is to find His purpose for me each day of my life, that no one else can do as well as I, in my place and time in eternity. Out of all of the billions of applicants for my life, only one is qualified, only one has just the right combination of what it takes to be me. That one is me. Because I'm special.

*Adapted by the Author from the Poem "I'm Special", by Elizabeth Anne Richards Shrug.

.

IN PRAISE OF All WORKING MOTHERS

It won't take you long to figure where I'm coming from,
For I lift this in praise of all working Moms.

First, for those who work for career, by divorce or by choice,
For all of the working Moms I lift my appreciative voice.

For those whose husbands or lovers left without a trace,
For those who have to face the world alone, face to face.

For those who have Husbands, but must work for family support,
For those who raise the children, whether they're happy, or out of sorts.

To those who must place their children in child care, five days a week,
To those who get up at dawn, return at dusk, in pursuit of a living to seek.

To those who manage home and work, and are exhausted at bedtime,
To those who grasp weekend the moment with their children, quality time.

These Moms are folks who must function at many tasks, for better or for worse,
Sometimes wife, sometimes employee, sometimes parent, sometime nurse.

Balancing her time between the commands of job and demands of home,
Pulled in all directions, with precious little time in which to call her own.

Yet, the stay at home Mom, works just as surely as the one with career,
The difference is the former spends all her waking hours for the ones so dear.

She does all of the things the working Mom does, only all of the time,
She works night and day to assure that the home life for all is fine.

So, don't misunderstand me, the work out of the home Mom, is really great,
There is something I would like to add about Moms, to be perfectly straight.

The stay at home Mom, works just as hard, focusing all her energies on the ones,
That she brought into the world, involved in every detail of home, 'til day is done.

Twenty four hours, for eighteen years and more, she does the burping, diapering feats,
The boo-boo kissing, scolding, praising, fight mediation, school deadlines to meet.

School visits, little league, trips, science projects, finding lost jackets,
Allergies, sore throats, infected ears, Halloween costumes, and music racket.

Santa Claus lists and gifts, remote control cars, first bras, curfews, driving lessons,
Sweetheart screening, fixing the meals, speeding tickets, teenage obsessions.

The right clothes, monitoring TV and movies, talking things out, and nightmares,
Bathroom and telephone hoarding, driving lessons, and teenage speechless stares.

The above, just a few of the day/night job of the Mom who stays at home alone,
Her job is not as exciting as the career Mom, and often is a drone.

But maybe even more important, because she's in charge of our most precious gifts,
Full time, so let's hear it for the stay at home Mom, and give her a lift.

BELIEVING EVEN WHEN NOT SEEING

I've seen a horsefly, a housefly, a dragonfly, but never seen an elephant fly*,
And, I've never seen an instant miracle, as others claim and testify.
Nor was I struck by lightning, the instant I came to believe,
It was and is a continual searching, a greater knowledge of Him to achieve.

I've never seen a burning bush, nor have I seen the sea divide,
Never seen a man walk on water, nor make the stormy waves subside.
I've never seen a cripple instantly walk, nor a blind man see,
But I've come to learn, I need not see these things, in order to be Free.

So, it was a great comfort to me, when I came to understand and perceive,
That He said "Blessed are they who have not seen, and yet have believed."
For I know that though I may walk through fire, or pass through waters deep,
Though I do not see Him, I shall feel His presence o'er me sweep.

And even though I have not seen, what others claim, he forever changed event,
He gives me courage and strength to press on, when my nerves are spent.
He gives me wisdom, He gives me Peace, that I may know,
He stands beside me, enables me to withstand life's most crushing blows.

He gives my life direction, when I'm lost and in darkened ways,
He gives me Grace, forgives me, when I falter at the end of day.
When I am "in harm's way", He shields and protects me,
He builds up my confidence, takes away my fears and anxiety.

And there are those times, I heard or felt an urge deep within my heart,
Often, at crossroads of life, great or small, must make a choice, this place to start.
And as I've looked, o'er my life, the choices made, I can see His part in all of it,
When I've followed that inner urge to do, t 'was "God's Wink," I must submit.

So, as I've thought through my life, though no dramatic miracles some have seen,
As I've realized there are daily miracles in my life, in His presence, His truth to glean.
That I, as many others, may not have seen, but have believed along life's way,
For we have experienced the miracle of life, and of His guiding presence each day.

Scripture References: John 20:29, Isaiah 43:1-3

*Lyric line from the song "I've Never Seen an Elephant Fly" from the *Dumbo*.

THE CROSSES WE BEAR - JUST A LITTLE INCONVENIENCE

LIFE TRUTH: Taking and accepting the difficult times and circumstances of our life, and making the best of them, and using them positively, for ourselves and others, will not only enrich and strengthen our own life, but may provide an inspiration and benefit to others, far beyond our wildest imagination.

"For He causes His sun to rise on the evil and the good; and sends the rain on the righteous and the unrighteous" (*Matthew 5:45b*)

"If anyone wishes to come after me, let him deny himself, and take up his cross daily, and follow Me." (*Matthew 16:24; Luke 9:23*)

"You shall know the truth, and the truth shall set you free." (*8 John 32b*)

"Consider it a sheer gift, friends when tests and challenges come at you from all sides. You know that under pressure your faith-life is forced into the open and shows its true colors. So don't try to get out of anything prematurely. Let it do its work so you become mature and well-developed, not deficient in any way. (*James 1:2-4; The Message by Eugene Peterson*)

Nearly forty years ago (in 1977), I watched a television program which made a lasting impression on me. It was titled "Just A Little Inconvenience." It was the story of a Captain Timothy Briggs, who had been an American Olympic skier, a graduate of West Point, who had served in Viet Nam. He, as many other soldiers did then, stepped on a land mine, and lost most of his left leg and left arm.

They designed a disabled ski program at the Winter Park Resort, west of Denver, Colorado and from those beginnings other programs have developed at many other ski resorts, all over the country You really must see these folks ski to believe it and appreciate it. I never forgot the story, and will never forget what I have seen with my own eyes.

Our skiing days are now a joy of the past for us. As we went from one resort to the other each winter, I never ceased to be amazed by the number of disabled skiers, and at the super-ability and dexterity of these disabled skiers on the slopes—from the green slopes to the double black diamond (the most difficult) runs. I have seen and spoken with one legged skiers, one armed and no armed skiers, blind skiers, and even paraplegic skiers for whom they have designed boat like vehicles, to come down the steep slopes. I would just stand, leaning on my poles, and watch in admiration and wonderment, as they all confidently navigate the treacherous runs, each after their own fashion and way, according to their own ("little inconvenience").

As I have thought about those inspirational disabled skiers, who now number in the thousands, because of their courage, and the determination and courage of two men, one with but one good arm and one good leg, I realized that there are many people whom each of us knows, or know of, who can inspire us to overcome when (not if) our "little inconveniences" shall come in life. Would that we might have the courage to face these challenges of life, whatever they may be, whatever lies ahead for us, with the same conviction, the same courage and tenacity that others have before us. Would we dare consider our "crosses" whatever they may be, as a gift, to encourage others? Would I have that courage?

As I have thought about this over the years, I have thought of and catalogued a few, of so many, in so many areas of life, who have faced adversity, and turned what seemed a hopeless situation into magnificent victory, and an inspiration to others. In each instance the "Cross" or Crosses these persons have been given to bear, were not asked for.

But in each case, they accepted whatever their lot might have been, not as a defeat, but as a hurdle or challenge to overcome. I would wager that if we could have asked each one about their "little inconvenience," while they might not necessarily characterize it as a "sheer gift" as Eugene Peterson translates James words, and would agree that theirs was a personal struggle, but out of it, they became stronger and more complete persons or as Peterson quotes James" Let it (their cross they bear) do its work on them, so that they became more mature and well developed, not deficient in any way."

Then, I thought about that Man, who lived two thousand years ago, denied, deserted by his disciples and followers, standing alone before all of the power and authority of the Roman Empire, and the Jewish Authorities, and even He, as He hung from a Cross to die, though He cried out as we often do, "My God, My God, Why hast Thou forsaken Me." (*Matthew 27:45-46*)". Yet He also prayed "Father forgive them, for they know not what they are doing." (*Luke 23:34*). And, when He realized He could not, as a human man, handle it on His own said "Father into Thy hands I commit My Spirit."(*Luke 23:46*). "For He who had come to give His life for the ransom of many, He who had come not to be served, but to serve." (*Mark 10:45*).

I thought about what The Man had said to His followers earlier "If anyone wishes to come after Me, let him deny himself, take up His (emphasis supplied) cross daily, and follow me (*Luke 9:23*). And that in carrying your Cross, you will "Know the truth and the truth shall set you free." (*John 8:32b*) This then is what "The Crosses We Bear— Just A Little Inconvenience" is about, overcoming adversity in our lives, with a "can do" attitude, and the knowledge that each of us will at some time in our lives, have a cross or crosses to bear, and that we, as many have before us, can bring victory out of the jaws of defeat, can help others even through our own crosses, just as that Man did, two thousand years ago.

May it be then for you, or those whom you love or know, even when tragedy, loss or burdens which may come from any source or event, that you might remember the call of the Man centuries ago, "Take up your cross daily, and follow Me."

THE CROSSES WE BEAR - JUST A LITTLE INCONVENIENCE

Timothy Briggs, Olympic skier, lost an arm and a leg, in the War of Vietnam, Relearned skiing, on his two remaining limbs, inspired a national disabled ski program, so for others, their own disabilities might be damned, for to him and them, with the badge of courage they wear, the crosses they bear daily, are just a little inconvenience.

Ludwig Von Beethoven was totally deaf through most of his years, yet the sounds of his magnificent music, through the centuries ring, loud and clear. For to him with the badge of courage he wore, the cross he bore daily, was just a little inconvenience.

Helen Keller was born and lived a full life, being both deaf and blind, yet an equal in history, of an inspirational person, would be hard to find. For to her, with the badge of courage she wore, the cross she bore daily, was just a little inconvenience.

As a young lad, Thomas Edison, was deaf, thought to be incorrigible, and thrown out of school, Only to become the world's greatest inventor, did not accept the judgment of others as his rule. For to him, with the badge of courage he wore, the crosses he bore daily, were just a little inconvenience.

Albert Einstein, a German Jew, failed the required exams to graduate from high school, yet he became the most renowned scientist of the twentieth century, his work and discoveries, the antithesis of a fool. For to him, with the badge of courage he wore, the cross he bore daily, was just a little inconvenience.

Franklin Roosevelt, was crippled by polio, as a successful, bright young man, Became one of our country's greatest presidents, projecting wisdom and strength to his people during dark days, throughout the land. Yet to him, with the badge of courage he wore, the cross he bore daily, was just a little inconvenience.

Sir Walter Scott, disabled by disease as a young man in Scotland, transformed literature through his historical novels, by the words of his hand. For to him, with the badge of courage he wore, the cross he bore daily, was just a little inconvenience.

Glenn Cunningham, was severely burned as a young boy, told he would never walk again, only to become one of the world's greatest distance runners, with courage as his lynchpin. For to him, with the badge of courage he wore, the cross he bore daily, was just a little inconvenience.

Joni Erickson Tada, a promising young athlete, paralyzed by accident from the neck down, yet through her life and paintings, with brush in mouth, her indomitable spirit has inspired many, to cast away dark clouds and frowns. For to her, with the badge of courage she wears, the cross she bears daily, is just a little inconvenience.

Bethany Hamilton, still a teenager living in Hawaii, a world class surfer at age 13, was attacked by a bull shark, while surfing, which tore her arm off at the shoulder, within a year she was surfing, now again a world class surfer, a traveling motivational speaker, who openly professes her faith and her positive attitude, each day becoming bolder; yet for her, with the badge of courage she wears, the cross she bears daily, is just a little inconvenience.

Jason Gunter, Fort Myers, Florida, a brave fireman, lost an arm and a leg in an accident. Battling his wounds and life changes, and seeing the plight of those who are injured and in need of help, he purposed to become an attorney, in order to help others having to face difficult times. He did so and his life is dedicated to that cause. At 44, Jason Gunter was one of a few athletes with "Physical disabilities," permitted to compete in the International Iron Man competition in Hawaii in 2009 and again in 2013, when he completed all phases. In both 2014 and 2015, he competed in and won an Iron Man Race. A winner in all aspects of his life, an inspiration who lifts others up, his impact immense. For to him the race of life he continues to run, the badge of courage he wears, and the crosses he bears daily, is just a little inconvenience.

Jessica Cox a woman born with two legs, but with no arms. Now at 26, she is a certified airplane pilot, a black belt Tae Kwan Do master, and travels the country as a cheerful inspirational speaker with a positive attitude, and all who know, hear are by her spirit and her accomplishments totally disarmed. For to her, with the badge of courage she wears, the cross she bears daily, is just a little inconvenience.

Christopher Reeve, a noted actor, was totally disabled in a riding accident, returned to acting, has taken on the cause cure, and mystery of spinal cord incidents. For to him, with the badge of courage he wore, the cross he bore daily, was just a little inconvenience.

Tom Dempsey, born with half an arm, half a foot, determined he would excel in kicking the football, became an NFL kicker of many years, and set the record for the longest field goal of all. For to him, with the badge of courage he wore, the cross he bore daily, was just a little inconvenience.

Patrick Henry Hughes was born with no eyes, and with a muscular joint deficiency, that has never permitted him to walk or extend his arms. At 2 he began picking out tunes on the piano. Through daily work he has as a man in his 30's become an accomplished pianist and musician, and with his singing, his piano and his inspirational speeches of gifts courage, persistence and Faith, audiences he does charm. He has secured a degree in music, played trumpet with the help of his Dad in the college marching band, has written a book and a movie, a made of his life, "I Am Potential", filled with love, labor and inspiration so grand. For to him, with the badge of courage he wears, the cross he bears daily, is but just a little Inconvenience

Abraham Lincoln, whose life was marked by many failures in business, in politics, and in life, yet he persevered, became our most revered president, brought freedom to the oppressed, an end to our nation's greatest strife. For to him, with the badge of courage he wore, the many crosses he bore daily, were just a little inconvenience.

I have named just a few of many thousands before us, who have overcome personal trials, to accomplish great things. These men and women, who gave to and inspired others, not because of, but in spite of the troubles that life sometimes brings. For to them, with the badge of courage they have worn, the crosses they have borne, or now bear, and taken up daily, were and are just a little inconvenience.

May we each take inspiration from Him, from the lives of those we've known, and these referenced accomplished women and men, so that the crosses we may be called to bear, shall not defeat us, nor on us, self-pity descend. May we, as have they, put on our badge of courage, take up the crosses we bear daily, as just a little inconvenience.

For It was two thousand years ago, the Son of Man, was hung from, and died on a cross, far across the seas, He said we shall each have different crosses to bear, and that "Each must take up his own cross, daily, and follow me." He, who bore His Cross willingly, for the eternal life, for the world, all people, for all time, giving history's greatest gift, but for Him, with the badge of courage He wore, giving His life, that others might live, was just a little inconvenience.

JUST LIKE MY DAD

A young boy I know, was passing by, he stopped to visit me one day.
A talkative vibrant lad, I'd always listen to what he had to say.
That day we talked about many things, life, girlfriends and sports,
Talked about his friends at school, having fun with his cohorts.

After we'd talked awhile, I posed a question, just for him,
Asked what he'd like to be who he'd be like when he became a man.
He thought a moment, then said he'd like to be just like his Dad.
Loved his Dad, he was gone a lot, things sometimes hard, made him sad.

And here is what he said:

I want to drive cars aggressive and fast, beat red lights, and look out for cops,
Just like my Dad

I want to cut sharp deals, even if I have to shave the truth, to hit the top,
Just like my Dad

I want to have a bunch of credit cards, so I can get everything I want,
Just like my Dad

I want to learn to party, maybe get drunk at night, frequent the evening haunts,
Just like my Dad

I want to smoke, maybe chew too, and try other stuff, because it's cool,
Just like my Dad

I want a wife to wait on me, I'll do what I must to keep her in line, follow my rule.
Just like my Dad

I'll give my kids money and things, but I'll be real busy, won't have much time,
Just like my Dad

I'll fudge a little on taxes and business, its ok, just to make things right, so I get mine.
Just like my Dad

If things get tough at home, I'll get somebody else, or maybe just leave for a while,
Just like my Dad

It's going to be fun when I grow up, I'll get just what I want for me, nothin' to cramp my style.
Just like my Dad"

Though the story is stretched, yet my friend's, like most boys, looking up to his Dad,
Especially in their younger years, they'll watch every movement, habit and fad.
The way we act, the things we say and do, are indelibly stamped on their little brains,
They see right through us, see what we do, and say, see us as we are, not how we may feign.

Whether our children are young or older, like it or not, we're models for them,
How we treat others, how we do business, whether dishonesty we condemn.
Younger eyes are watching our every move, how we deal with things of life and death.
It's an awesome responsibility, our life lived out, will be our legacy, to our last breath.

THE MIRACLES OF GIFTS GIVEN AND RECEIVED BY RANDOM ACTS OF KINDNESS
(The Good Samaritan, Luke 10:25-42)

Once upon a time, there was a prominent Jewish man, when on the road, who by robbers was beset,
Beaten to near death, everything gone, his money, his horse, his shirt, from this tragedy he met.
As he lay in the ditch at roadside, he could not move or speak, too weak to even cry out,
Bleeding profusely, his face shattered, bones broken from within and without.

Then a distinguished man of the LAW passed, saw him, gave a passing glance, then moved on,
For He had an appointment with the Court, to his solemn duty he was drawn.
Next came a Rabbi Priest, dressed in his finery, on his way to his daily prayers,
He hesitated momentarily, but others were awaiting his religious wisdom, 'twas his barrier.

As the man beset by robbers, lay in the ditch, he thought, "Surely in this place I shall die,"
Just then, a travelling Samaritan man, poorly dressed, considered an outcast of orthodox Jews, on his donkey
passed by.
He, a common man, heard the desperate man's cry, He stopped, and went to him to help and felt compassion,
He, this despised Samaritan, looked into the bloody face, which by now was deathly ashen.

The Samaritan Traveler gave the battered man water, took off his own shirt, tore it in pieces to bind up the
wounds,
Then carefully picked him up placed him on his beast, and did with comforting words commune.
Then coming along side, leading his donkey, he led him to a nearby roadside Inn,
Paid for his room, food and care, and to the innkeeper said, "Take care of him and I will pay the balance, when
soon I return again."

All of these things, the despised Samaritan, whose people considered him a lesser person, did for the beaten
one, for someone of great import, he did not know,
Then the Master asked the question, "Which one of these three men who passed by, did by his actions, mercy
show?"
"He stopped to help, he willingly departed from his plan, he gave what he had to give, with a promise of return, a
random act of kindness he performed,"
In this day and time, would we do the same as he, or would to "hurry down the road" be our norm.

While most times, we and others will not be confronted with such a dramatic event,
Yet from daily life, an unsolicited random act of kindness done, wonderful opportunities doth present.
Sometimes a smile given, a courtesy shown, an uplifting word, a note written will, not soon forgotten,
A moment shared of a little kindness shown to another, could turn a day or a life to good from rotten.

For most of us tender mercies, acts of kindness, can be shared in simple ways,
An opened door, a gentle word or smile, an appropriate embrace, come what may.
May we live each day with eyes, ears, inner senses and observations, opened wide,
That we too, might do a random act of kindness, the opportunity for another, to come along side.

LEARNING TO LISTEN

Listen my children and you shall hear, of the midnight ride of Paul Revere,
Wise counsel, to hear and listen, from Longfellow, words which historians endear.
Friends, Romans Countrymen, lend me your ears,
And from Shakespeare, words about listening intently, without peer.

When Paul and Art sang about "People hearing without listening,"
And "People talking without speaking," there is something vital missing.
Because listening is hearing with sensitivity, discernment and understanding,
If we can learn to listen effectively, with others we'll enjoy great standing.

We need then to learn to listen more than we speak,
For in talking, we don't hear the inner cry of the down and weak.
God gave us two ears and one mouth for good reason,
That we might listen, twice as much as we speak, in all seasons.

For the ability to listen is one of the greatest gifts the Creator gives,
To be able to do more than hear the words of a friend, know where he lives.
But to capture from the words, the deeper meaning of the spirit of another,
Is a Love we can give, and bring us to them, closer than a brother.

So when someone speaks, listen with your ears, eyes, mind and your heart,
For the words may be but a mask of hurting feelings, of a life torn apart.
Seek then to read the face and listen to the body speak, to hear what they truly mean,
Then on your best judgment and wisdom, you must lean.

And having then listened with all of the tools, within you built in,
Choose your words thoughtfully, listening to that Small Voice within.
For having listened carefully, what you say and do in return,
May change a life, your wise words teach, heal and confirm.

LIVE THIS DAY FOR TODAY

"Therefore, do not be anxious or worry about tomorrow, for tomorrow will take care of itself. Each day has enough trouble of its own" (*Matthew 6:34*)

"Come now you who say: 'Today or tomorrow, we shall go to such and such a city, and spend a year there and engage in a business and make a profit. Yet you do not know what your life will be like tomorrow. You are just a vapor that appears for a little while and then vanishes away.
Instead you ought to say "If the Lord wills, we shall live and also do this or that." (*James 4:13-15*)

Today is the oldest you have ever been,
A new day for both women and men.
But today is also the youngest you'll ever be,
Not to be wasted, a day or days aimlessly drifting at sea.

So relish and enjoy today as God's new gift,
Help someone in need give a hand up, a lift.
Then purpose this day to do or say something for good,
Carry it through, even if your motive, by others be misunderstood.

Or take today to meet a current or ongoing challenge, or to help with another's,
For God tells us that at times, we are to be the keeper of our sisters and brothers.
Time waits for no one, like a wisp, it is gone, and has passed you by,
There are no-reruns of a moment of time from birth 'til we die.

Live then for today, it is the only day you have for certain,
We plan for tomorrows, not acknowledging today could be life's final curtain.
No need to carelessly lose it by doing nothing, or something in haste,
T'would be a shame to let today's opportune moments go to waste.

For Life's purpose is not about what we gather, more important are the seeds we scatter,
God's deeds and words sewn are the things that make a life's purpose matter.
A Life of meaning will be measured by what we've shared, a treasured legacy to leave,
The evidence and memory of love, giving ourselves away, did o9ur life's pattern laid out, leave.

MANLY TEARS OF A MANLY MAN

LIFE TRUTH: It is neither unmanly, nor a sign of weakness for a man to show his true feelings and emotions, even tears, for they are manly tears. Through them he expresses feelings that need to be vented and the courage and confidence in being a man- manly tears are ok!

Tears are a part of mankind's life from the beginning of time, from the moment of our birth until our last breath. Tears flow freely for many reasons when we are young. As we grow older, especially for we males, tears are suppressed. They are considered unmanly, a sign of weakness, effeminate, or inappropriate. The Bible is filled with examples of the men considered the Saints of the Bible, have shed their tears, even the Savior Himself.

On the other hand tears of young boys and girls for growing girls and women are considered quite appropriate, to the point that if a woman doesn't cry at one of the times she is expected to cry, she may be thought of as hard or uncaring. Science many years ago discovered that tears release healing endorphins. In other words they are helpful and often times relieve stress, tension and anger.

Because society tells us that men aren't supposed to cry, this may be just a part of why men are generally much more reticent to express their emotions, not only in tears but even in word. And this reticence may well be a factor, among many others, in strained relations in the business world as well as in family life. The result is sometimes that holding in both your thoughts and emotions may result at some point in a total breakdown or "blow off," when the pent up stress just can't be held back anymore.

I have to confess at my advanced age, that as a young man there were a number of times when my emotions were so touched by love, or a kindness, pain, so angered by a situation, or so frustrated with myself or someone else, that the tears wanted to come, but I always suppressed them. Even on occasion watching a very sad movie or story, I would fight back the urge to even let a sniffle, much less a tear flow.

Then I recall the day when my uncle, Dr. Fred Bartleson call upon the family. Uncle Fred was like a brother to my Father, who was considerably older than my uncle, was very strong and composed when he spoke with my Aunt and the children. Uncle Fred was a wonderful uncle to me, being especially kind to me during World War II, in the absence of my father.

My Father was tough, he always had been. He was a tough lawyer with an opponent, and he was a strict but fair disciplinarian as a parent, with us children. He never let himself get too close, lest he show some weakness. He had been through combat in two Wars two World Wars, yet he had a soft heart, which he was reticent to display.

After our visit, when we left the Uncle Fred's home and walked to the car in the driveway, my Father bent over. My first thought was he having yet another heart attack. But his body was shaking. But then I realized he, my tough Father, was crying uncontrollably. I threw my arms around him as I hadn't done since I was a child and held him. I shall never forget those moments. Here he was, my Father, who had always been my tearless strength, and here was I his son comforting him and embracing him as I never had before. Tears welled up in my eyes and ran down my cheek trying desperately to keep my composure, for my Father. After a few minutes, we both composed ourselves and went to the car. I learned in that moment, Manly tears are ok.

My Father asked me to please not tell your Mother about this. I assured him I would not, and never did. For the first time, I realized that well maybe, on rare occasion it was ok for men to cry. I am indebted to my Father for that unplanned but wise and healing lesson- manly tears are ok.

Then in 1971, my beloved sister, Mary Ellen, my parent's first child and only daughter, died at the age of 43 after a five year battle with cancer and multiple surgeries in Fort Myers and at a New Orleans Clinic with what was then an unknown and incurable cancer. Dr. Quillian Jones, Jr. called me at my office from the hospital, advising that she had slipped away, and asked if I would talk with my parents, and her husband. Of course, I would.

I went into my Father's office where he was dictating on his old Grey Autograph, late in the afternoon. When he was dictating I always just sat down and awaited his finish of what he was doing. This time I asked him to stop, that I needed to talk to him. I told him Mary Ellen was gone.
It was almost as if he didn't hear or didn't want to hear me. He picked up the recording device and finished dictating the letter he had been working on. He gently put the recorder in its case, looked at me, again, put his hands over his face and began to quake with tears of sorrow. For the second time I tried to comfort him, and fortunately was able to keep my composure. I told my father then the lesson he had taught me he had taught me- manly tears are ok.

During the days and months that followed, I watched my father cry a number of times. My Mother said that it had to do with his heart attacks, that his emotions were weakened. I knew differently, but did not question her seeing her solid bulwark for 45 years, my father, at a low point. My Father died just a year later. Both of my sons Jay and Andy cried when they heard their Granddaddy had died. I told them- manly tears are ok.

After that, I came to the conclusion in my mind that tears were a sixth sense that God has given mankind in addition to the sense of sight, hearing, speech, smell, and touch. In fact, not only did I come to know that it was good to cry, but I concluded that it was manly for a man to cry then, if only when it was too difficult to hold back the tears.

I learned that tears bring out healing endorphins, as well as enable a person to release the many negative emotions that can take control of our minds and even our physical body. Little did I know at the time that I would have my own very similar time and experience to let the tears flow freely.
Several years later I recall watching on TV then President Gerald Ford, after his defeat to Jimmy Carter in 1976. President Ford openly shed tears of disappointment and release that the battle was over. It was ok for even a President to cry. Since then I have seen other presidents, particularly the latter President George W. Bush shed tears in public and critical times following 9/11, as well as other occasions. If a President of the United States could shed tears, it is acceptable- manly tears are ok.

That was just the beginning of a long and painful journey we shared together for many days, many months, years- a journey down "The River of No Return." I learned personally that the most painful experience a parent can have, for most of us, is losing a child, however it occurs, and it is always unique. As painful as it was, it has helped us over the years to be of comfort to others who have lost children, to have more empathy for all in pain. Sometimes in those earlier years I cried unashamedly with them in their pain because I knew- manly tears are ok.

And yet aside from the painful legacy and memories of our son's death, as well as the deaths of other loved ones and friends, and sharing the grief of scores of others who have lost a child, at any age, we believe God has given us many gifts that have come from this experience including:

- ❖ a much greater sensitivity to the pain and loss of others;
- ❖ a depth of understanding of what a challenge dealing with grief is;
- ❖ when the inner intuitive voice tells us to speak up or write a note, make a call or visit, give a smile, an affirmative word- and to do it without fear of feeling it was out of place or might not be understood as we might have intended it;
- ❖ an appreciation of loved ones around us each day;
- ❖ realizing that each day we have is a gift, that neither life nor anyone else owes us anything;
- ❖ and what the truly important things in life are- love, living each moment even the painful ones, knowing that the light of day follows the dark of night, and the sheer joy of doing something good or nice for someone else (even a total stranger or maybe particularly a total stranger);
- ❖ to tell frequently tell our friends and loved ones how much they mean to us;
- ❖ that bottled up anger, jealousy, bitterness, envy, any of the negative emotions that attack each of us from time to time, need to be let go quickly, that bottling them up will only hurt ourselves;
- ❖ to use wisely and share generously each day our time, talents and whatever tangible things we may possess from time to time, knowing that we take nothing with us, when we depart this earth;
- ❖ that when our time comes to graduate, that our life might have stood for something that will leave a positive legacy for those who have known or followed us;
- ❖ And, the gift lesson that has been confirmed and firmly etched in my mind and heart, that manly tears are ok.

The gift of tears then is our sixth sense (since it is physical), and intuition our seventh sense. Tears are the given sense to express the host of emotions we experience, a relief valve, a healing sense for what life has for us and a humility and recognition of our humanity.

So, I am thankful and thank God for the wonderful life that I have been given, a beautiful and loving family, friends, the many extended years that I have been blessed to have, and I thank my earthly Father, and My Heavenly Father, for teaching me the lesson that Manly tears are Manly, and are o.k. It takes some element of courage to let them flow when they need to flow, and not worry about what others may think. And may other men, women and child learn the lesson that took fully half of my life to learn.

MANLY TEARS OF A MANLY MAN

The tears of the infant come with a shrieking cry,
The anxious parent seeks desperately to know why.
The may be tears of pain, hunger, anger, or fear,
Or just the comforting warmth of mother's touch and voice to hear.

The tears of the young child come often, and express many emotions,
Jealousy, anger, frustration, fear, or a skinned knee in need of a lotion.
But they come freely in whatever the child feels,
These tears that express the moments of his early ordeals.

But as the young man grows older, he's told not to cry,
It's not good, not being a "man," tears show weakness, it's sissy, that's why!
We are carefully taught that real men should never show their emotions by tears.
It is not manly to show our emotions, our pain, our joy, and fears.

And as we grow to manhood, then, we've learned to bury all within,
Keep it all inside, share it with no one, nor let them know, let no one in.
Even the pain, the insecurity, rejection, failures, the broken relations,
Guard it with your life, preserve your dignity, always display outward, calm and patience.

Imprisoned in our dignity, surely we're the only one who hurts and feels this way,
Not one who is a Man, shows these hurts and feelings that we shan't display.
If only there was someone like me, who would listen and share, really hear,
If only I could feel whole, not less of a Man, in letting go what's inside, through my tears.

Somehow we must recycle these lessons we Men have been taught,
That we have feelings we've held in that need to come out, and what it has wrought.
To know that God gave us each senses and emotions to use and express,
That our deepest joys, our fears, our inner troubles might be addressed.

For we need to know when we Men are deeply troubled, our eyes glisten,
There is a need for release, to share, a need for a friend to listen.
To bury, deny, and to conceal the deep emotions and burdens we feel,
For it will only grow like a cancer within, make us ill, get worse, to deny what is real.

As I've grown older, looking back through the years and experiences I've known,
Many seeds of joy, love, thanks, and relief yet also anger, pain, failure have been sewn.
I've gown know that some life's times need the tears of joy and pain be shed, with no shame,
That rather than weakness, tears reflect care and passion, an inner strength to remain.

It is in our words, our touch, our listening, feeling, God's gifts, reflect that we care,
Tears of joy, of grief, of loneliness, of love, of compassion that we share.
Outward expression of this caring, love and compassion can't be wrong,
Rather than weakness, they reflect our commitment is strong.

If only this simple truth could be learned by we men, early in our years,
That in times of great love, grief, pain and joy, we too can shed our Manly Tears.
For our tears, our feelings are part of our inner being, no matter what others may say,
I've come to know that God gave us and added sense of tears, and Manly Tears are ok.

A SPECIAL BLESSING FOR YOU

May there always be work for your hands, and the mind and heart to do,

May your purse or wallet always have a coin or two.

May the Sun always shine on your window pane,

May a rainbow always follow your storms and rain.

May the hand and hug of a friend always be near you,

On cloudy days may you see the rays of the Son's Light, shining through.

May your heart be filled with gladness and courage to start anew,

And, may your life be filled with blessings to cheer you.

MIRROR, MIRROR, ON THE WALL (WHO'S THE FAIREST ONE OF ALL?)*
(A View as Other's See Us)

"Mirror, Mirror, on the wall" is what we see, what others see?
Some envision a vibrant, muscular handsome man to be.
Others, a woman of striking beauty, with flowing hair,
Some see what they judge ugly, of no worth, or utter despair.

Some see the image of confidence, some see pride,
Others see too skinny, some see too fat, yet we wonder what's inside.
Some see scraggly or balding hair, a wrinkled face, a fading life,
Others see leathery skin, imbedded lines of worry, and scars of strife.

Some have looked so many times, they scarcely see anything at all,
Others see too light, or too dark, one too short, another too tall.
Some dare not even give their image a passing glance,
Others stare at the beauty or revulsion, as if in a trance.

But oh, what an instructive lesson, it would be,
If we could see the outer and inner image, that others see.
It might be humbling, encouraging, shocking, devastating or great,
More important, what God sees, for He Knows your every thought,
"He doesn't miss a move you make, knows every step you take." **

*The Wicked Witch, in the Walt Disney movie, "Snow White and the Seven Dwarfs" (1937)

**"Mark well that God doesn't miss a move you make; He knows every step you take." (*Proverbs 5:21 The Message, by Eugene Peterson.*)

MOTHER THOUGHTS*
By Harriet McCoy Woolslair

Often as she walks she needs me, Little Toddler by my side.
Baby Feet will strangely falter, Baby steps might need a guide-
Paths are rough and might be lonely Often tread on marsh or stone.
Heavenly Father, help me to teach her, How to walk aright alone.

Still she needs me near for counsel, grinning school girl, straight and tall.
Times are hard- Life's lessons harder, (I'll be near if she should call.)
Things worthwhile she might pass over, in this glittering, gay today.
"Heavenly Father, help me show her Better things along the way."

Life and love are beckoning onward She must hurry on her way.
Bur, as when we walked together Prayers for her at close of day.
Always in my thoughts I follow Tho' her path leads far from me.
"Father guide her, bless her, help her: little girl that used-to be"

*Circa 1910 (My Grandmother with four young children living in the wilderness, early Buckingham, Florida.)

MOUNTAINS AND VALLEYS

When we climb life's mountains, we look forward to the top,
And in life's climb, we often grow weary, and stumble on the rocks.
But it's good to look back at where we've been, lessons learned from our mistakes,
To see in perspective our failings and our victories, viewed in our journey's wake.

And when we descend to the deepest valleys down below,
It's sometimes only then, when down on our back, we see the Son, and Heaven's glow.
For these are times of reflection and appreciation of what the good times did portend,
These are times of learning, times of renewal, the meanings of life to comprehend.

So whether we are scaling, up mountain cliffs, or slipping to the depths,
Each are times of growth and learning, as we pause to take our breath.
Life is a struggle either way, but to both extremes, we need to give thanks,
For what we learn from each, for the quiet times, as we travel between life's riverbanks.

OUR LIFE PASSIONS AND WHOSE OX IS BEING GORED

LIFE TRUTH: The height, depth and length of our passion for or against a cause or issue, is often determined, by our own experience, the experience of those around us, how that experience has affected us or those close to us, positively or negatively, our closeness to and observation of events, and how we view the result of those events experienced or observed.

OUR LIFE PASSIONS, AND WHOSE OX IS BEING GORED

Our view of things is oft' determined by our present or past space,
What we've experienced, endured, or observed, puts our focus in place.
So it is, that one whose son or daughter was wounded or died in Iraq,
Views the War quite differently than one whose son went, and came back.

Similarly, one whose daughter, son, or friend is strung out on crack,
Views drugs differently than one whose family escaped the pain of smack.
And one whose loved one has been riddled with or died with a cancer,
Has a greater passion for the need to find the cancer cure's answer.

It was the woman, whose young daughter was killed by drunken driving,
Who founded MADD, and committed her life to this striving.
So, one who's "been there" sees an issue as more critical and more clearly,
When it has affected or taken a friend, or a special someone, loved dearly.

To one the same cause may be slight as a pimple, to another a painful boil,
One remains silent, the other acts to assure the squeaky wheel gets the oil.
For the height and depth of our life passion, is often its impact upon us,
Whether we seek redress, a cure, or whatever solution seems just.

What's important to us is determined by our life, who and where we are,
Whether a cause, a problem, an issue, or life observed, is near to us or far.
The River of passage may be to us deep or stormy waters, or a shallow ford,
'Twas Martin Luther who aptly wrote, "It makes a difference whose ox is being gored."

PARK YOUR GUNS AND BAGGAGE AT THE DOOR

"Come unto Me, all who are weary and heavy laden, and I will give you rest. Take my yoke upon you, and learn from Me, for I am gentle and humble in heart, and in Me, you shall find rest for your souls." (*Matthew 11:28-30**)

When my son, Andy was young, had just turned three,
A full blown cowboy suit, for his birthday, brought him glee.
He proudly wore it to Church, entered his class, hoping to play cowboy wars,
His teacher gently said, "Andy, please park your guns and baggage at the door."

In life, we often have excess luggage we carry, and baggage to bear,
Some we chose, some we didn't, some by chance, for to care.
But these are often issues of excess, for which we have no need,
That baggage, kept in our life, will only unbearable burdens breed.

At times, we all need respites, from the cargo which is our daily load,
'Lest in time, the weight become too heavy, for our very life being's abode.
Then, in need of a place of rest, to cast off the shackles too long we've bore,
There is a time and place to trust a Friend and "leave our guns and baggage at the door."

There is a Gentle Friend who knows us well, yet He's not within our sight,
Who calls out to us, "Trust Me! Come unto me! Lean on Me! Even your darkest night.
My yoke is heavy, my burden light, I'll be your Bridge over troubled seas,
You who are heavy laden, let it go, I'll carry your baggage, give you rest, and a Peace that sets you free."*

*With no disrespect to the *Words of The Gentle Friend*, but with a credit also to Carole King (*You've Got a Friend*), Paul Simon (*Bridge Over Troubled Water*), and Bill Withers (*Lean On Me*), in case their words are more familiar to you- all of the lyrics of these songs are about special friends (friends of the heart), none of whom can compare with our Gentle Friend, yet the words of the lyricists too have the message of turning over or letting go of our excess baggage and " Trust me, and leave your guns and baggage at the door".

SOMETIMES

Sometimes I'm in a great rush to achieve or get somewhere,
And Often, I find, I don't know where I am when I get there.
Sometimes, life is in such a rush, I just want to stop and get out,
It's then, in His frantic world, I wonder what it's all about.

Sometimes, I'm really focused, have many goals to achieve,
I'm so organized, have it all together, or so I believe.
But then sometimes, nothing seems to fall in place,
At those times it seems whatever I do, I'll fall on my face.

Sometimes the days go so well, oh how I enjoy,
All the lessons of life, I so readily employ.
But then, sometimes, it seems that nothing goes right,
Absolutely nothing comes together, try as I might.

And sometimes, I've found it important the right words to speak,
But at other times, I know 'tis best, my silence to keep.
Sometimes are the times when people, ideas, and love I must embrace,
But there are sometimes, when I must let go, their release I must face.

Sometimes the big things that had seemed so important to me,
I found in time were inconsequential, would wash out to sea.
Then, Sometimes, I realize the loves I'd come to take for granted,
Were and are to me, most important, my greatest commitment demanded.

In all of life, then, I've learned, there is a sometimes for everything,
The highs and lows of life, Bells of gladness and sorrow to ring.
So it is, then I must learn from each of my sometimes, in joy and in strife,
To appreciate in love all of these sometimes, that are a part of our life.

THE "ENTIRE" PRAYER OF SERENITY (EXPANDED EDITION)
(Philippians 4:4-13)

God Grant me the Serenity to accept those things I cannot change;
The courage to change the things that I can;
And the wisdom to know the difference.

Enjoying one moment at a time; accepting hardship as the pathway to Peace.
Taking as He did, this sinful world as it is, not as I would have it.
Trusting he will make all things right, If I surrender to His will;
That I may be reasonably happy in this life, and supremely happy with Him forever In the next.
By Reinhold Niebuhr

GOD GRANT ME THE SERENITY TO ACCEPT THOSE THINGS I CANNOT CHANGE.

❖ that you would grant to me the Peace and Serenity to accept the events of my life, the people, circumstances, and events over which I have no control or cannot change, may I see these times through Your eyes of wisdom and clarity, not my own blurred vision, that I may see life clearly, even those things that are not a part of Your Master Plan.

THE COURAGE TO CHANGE THOSE THINGS I CAN.

❖ knowing that you are a God who has loved the whole world, but that your Will is not always done in the world by people (including me) and events, so that there is need of change, and that you will give me the insight, courage and discernment to change those things, under my control, in need of change, for good;

❖ using my best efforts to have an impact on the people, events and circumstances which may need change,—which even though I do not have complete control, I may, with Your guidance have a part making those changes for the good.

AND THE WISDOM TO KNOW THE DIFFERENCE.

❖ that You may give me the wisdom that comes with life and experience and insight, given only by You—to know the differences in these three situations in my life, and to respond, to act, or decline to act as may appropriate to the people, events or circumstances.

ENJOYING ONE MOMENT AT A TIME, ACCEPTING HARDSHIP AS THE PATHWAY TO PEACE.

❖ that I might have the vision of the whole scheme of things in life and in my life, to know that each moment and each day is a gift from you;

❖ that I may understand that all that I am, all that I have and all that I am capable of being are but gifts from you for a time- to the end that I may live out each day, not fretting over what is past, nor worrying about what may come tomorrow, and enjoying each moment with the enthusiasm as if it were my first and the commitment as if were my last;

- ❖ that I may come to understand that hardship, pain, loss and failure are each a part of life, for as your Son taught us "The sun and the rain shall fall on the evil and righteous alike", and that if we are to emulate Him we must "take up our Cross and follow Him;"
- ❖ that I may come to realize that people and events are not always fair and just, but that You will make all things right in Your time, even if not my time;
- ❖ that I may rejoice in You- even in the difficult times, for it is out of life's storms that I become stronger, more patient, and gain endurance;
- ❖ that when my Faith is tested, I might understand that if I am receptive, I may learn more about what are truly the important things of life, and how I might help myself and others in dealing with life, as it;
- ❖ that I may discover the truths of life that You have for me, and will set me free from the shackles of fear, greed and self.

TAKING AS HE DID, THIS SINFUL WORLD AS IT IS, NOT AS I WOULD HAVE IT.

- ❖ that I may come, as did your Son, even with His perfection, to take the imperfections and failures of myself and others, and all things in the world, and not expect them to always be as I would have them be;
- ❖ that while I will always strive for perfection, though perfection is not possible in this imperfect world that I will seek excellence in my life in serving, not judge the imperfections of others, lest I also be so judged by You, seeking always to bring about the best in myself and others.

TRUSTING THAT HE WILL MAKE ALL THINGS RIGHT, IF I SURRENDER TO HIS WILL.

- ❖ that I may come to realize that I must fully trust You, my Father and my God, in all things, and surrender to Your will;
- ❖ And that although I am unable to see that time now, You will, in Your own Time and in Your own Master Plan of Eternity, make all things right and just, and at that time there shall be total Peace in the Valleys of the of Living, when Your Son returns;
- ❖ that even though I know that all things that happen in this world are not good, that all things will, in Your time, work for good through You, and Your Son;
- ❖ that with this knowledge, I may be content in this life, and through seeking to love You, my family, my neighbors and myself;
- ❖ that may I and all of creation come to know and receive that Peace and Serenity that only You can give that is beyond all comprehension, and my own understanding;
- ❖ that I may know, and be set free of all anxiety and worry about tomorrow, in the knowledge that through You, He who came to serve and gave His life for my failures, and the failures of the world;
- ❖ that I can survive both in times of plenty and times of need, and that Whatever I have, wherever I am in life, that You can and will grant to me the strength to face and endure all conditions and all things, through You, the Lord of Life who created me;
- ❖ that I may rest in the promise that I and all who know You, or have not knowingly rejected you, and seek to serve you, who are repentant of their known and unknown transgressions and failures, are forgiven by You, will be at Peace with You, in the Eternal Life to come.

- ❖ And, that others may see a glimpse of You in my life as I strive to fulfill all that You have planned for my life to be.

AMEN! And AMEN!

- ❖ If it be Your will, receive these prayers, and Lord may it be, for all eternity!

BEAUTY IN THE EYE OF THE BEHOLDER

They say that wisdom comes with age,
If that be so, then I should be an enlightened sage.
One thing I've learned, though as I've grown older,
Is that beauty truly is in the eye of the beholder.

We look for beauty in the wonders of nature,
Or in the supple female body, with just the right curvature.
Sometimes we find beauty in the lope of a graceful animal,
At other times in something packaged large, sometimes small.

Others find beauty in the magnificent art of the great masters,
While someone else, discovers it in what seems thrown together plaster.
One will tell you fine art is only to be found in the strokes of Impressionism,
But if he speaks to a Dali enthusiast, there'll be between them a great schism.

The truth is that we can find beauty in any person, animal, plant, or thing,
For the stonecutter, beauty is found in a rock, for another a sunset makes the heart sing.
One may see beauty in a red faced newborn child, another in a bearded crippled old man,
And admiring affection will transform a child's messy painting to a Gauguin.

How is it then, that in beauty and grace, we have such contrasting views,
Observe the same artistic work, one sees junk, another marvels at the strokes and hues.
There is then artistry in all things, on surface or within. Each is God's or Man's creation,
Its appeal or not, is governed by whether heart and mind join with eyes in adoration.

It is love though, that truly opens the eye to find the beauty in anything,
For love looks out and in, finds good and beautiful, makes a pauper into a king.
So beauty is subjective, depends upon what is in the perceiver's heart and mind,
Enables the eye to see through all imperfections, 'tis fallacy when it's said love is blind.

GOD, "IAM," HE IS THE GREATEST

"For God so loved the world, that He gave his only begotten son, that whoso ever believes in Him, shall not die but have everlasting life. For God sent his Son into the world, not to judge the world, but through Him, we might be acquitted of all of our human flaws and saved, to eternal life." (*John 3:16 – 17*)

FOR GOD	The Greatest Living Being, forever and ever
SO LOVED	Greatest Love to the most unfathomable Degree
THE WORLD	The Greatest Number and Universe Expanse
THAT HE GAVE	The Greatest Act of Sacrifice
HIS ONLY BEGOTTNE SON	The Greatest Gift Ever and Human Miracle Ever
THAT WHOSOEVER	The Greatest most Extensive Invitation
BELIEVES	The Greatest Challenge to Man, with yet the Greatest profound simplicity
IN HIM	The Only Living Being Who was and is Wholly God and Wholly Man
SHALL NOT PERISH	The Greatest and Only Eternal Rescue
BUT	The Greatest Difference Ever
HAVE	The Greatest Certainty
ETERNAL LIFE	The Greatest Future Destiny Imaginable
NOT TO JUDGE THE WORLD	The Greatest Forgiveness and Grace
BUT HAVE EVERLASTING LIFE.	The Greatest Miracle.

THE LONGITUDE AND LATITUDE OF ATTITUDE

LIFE TRUTH: While we don't always have a choice about the circumstances in which we find ourselves, in life, we do have a choice as to how we respond to every circumstance. Our attitude is the most important thing in determining each situation's final outcome.

THE LONGITUDE AND LATITUDE OF ATTITUDE

We can sail a skiff, either with or against the wind,
It is how we set the sail that really matters, in the end.
For with the wind in our sail, we can go either way,
North or South, East or West, with a slight tilt of the rudder, to stay.

Yet, we also need a centerboard, to keep our sloop from sliding, and aright,
Else a howling wind, will capsize our craft, and cast it out of sight.
It's not the strength or direction of the breeze, that determines our course,
But the set of our sail, and strong hand on the line and tiller, whatever the wind's direction or force.

And when the time comes, that the wind is too strong, for us alone, we need to let go,
For then, we can't handle without a Greater Help, when the foul tempest's gusts blow.
In those times, we release our mainsail, as the winds pass through the mast, in the breeze,
Only to begin again, reset our compass, to a new setting, and with a new wind, to seize.

So it is with life, we need a deep centerboard, to keep our life's ship from going awry,
That we be grounded in strong principles, give all our effort, with our Captain at our side.
And with His strong and steady hand, guiding ever so gently, our tiller and rudder,
That our minds, hearts, and actions, stay His course, and not be filled with useless clutter.

So, also, it is in life, whatever fair or foul winds blow, we have a great deal of latitude,
In choosing, how we deal with life's storms, what will be the direction of our attitude.
It is we, who set the tenor of our soul's thoughts, actions, and how we respond,
Whatever be the gale, to choose a positive attitude, or to wallow in pity, envy, bitterness, or the sea of despond.

THE MASTER WEAVER'S MASTER PLAN

Listen to the faint, rhythmic hum of the Master Weaver's busy looms,
Spinning the minute seconds of our lives, 'til the vision of a lovely flower blooms.
Interlacing the fabric of each life, one with the other, every moment, without cease,
Connecting the patterns of all life, through all time, designing The Great Masterpiece.

HE deftly works the thread of each breath of human life, until it's time is complete,
Never before, and never again, does HE fashion a portrait, just like ours, so unique.
Using the bright strands, yet also disfigured and broken filaments, each in its own time,
Knitting them all together into the grand motif, of HIS Master Plan Design.

For Eons HE patiently weaves the brilliant, the plain, and flawed shreds, a part of each life,
We can feel HIS presence, in times of joy, pain, success, failure, peace and strife.
HE is with us, as we walk thru the valleys of shadows, yes, even in our darkest days;
HE will in His time re-create all aspects of our life's journey, as sewn together, in HIS perfect way.

Yet, not 'til life's end, will we fully understand, each thread, by HIS hand, had its part,
Every strand, borne from whatever source, HE fits in, to add richness to HIS art.
By HIS gentle Hand, carefully integrating each life together, with HIS shuttle's levers,
Creating a magnificent artistic tapestry, authored by, and bearing the matchless signature of

THE MASTERWEAVER.

SPENDING THE GIFT OF EACH DAY'S LIFE

The song's lyricist proclaims, "Love is better the second time around,"
But, alas, in life, there's but one of each special minute and day, I've found.
For there are no "mulligans" to re-live my today on another tomorrow,
Nor, is there any re-run of yesterday, on which I can today borrow.

So, true it is that each moment of each day is spent but once, before passing,
It only appears once in history, and is not long in lasting.
And as the proverb says, "we shall not pass this way again,"
What goes down today, tomorrow is past, done, has been.

The seconds, minutes and hours our life's clock is wound but one time,
And, we know not when our ship's last midnight's eight bells will chime.
All that we own for sure is this instant, this day, and this hour,
A passing moment in time, spent as we will, 'ere, sunshine, dark, or stormy shower.

So, while we may do more, learn more, give or receive more, on one day or year than another, Each one is
priceless and irreplaceable, perchance difficult to choose one from the other.
Conversely, we need to take for ourselves each day a time of respite, reflection and rest,
To appreciate the moment, prepare for each day's next challenge or opportunity that presents its test.

Seeking always to maintain balance in all aspects of our life,
In all seasons, those of growth, testing, teaching, sharing, loving, losing, peace and strife.
Yet always keeping close to our heart, in the core of our being,
Those things most important, love, integrity, humility, family, faith, purpose and meaning.

Begin and expend each day then knowing, this very day is but a passing gift,
Each moment will come and go never again, as the grains of sand in the hour glass sift.
Knowing today is God's unique present, a gift to us, to waste or use wisely, so that at its end,
We have done justice, loved mercy, walked humbly with God, for we shall not pass this way again.

*With credit to a Proverb (sometimes attributed to Stephen Grellet, 1773-1885) " I expect to pass this way but
once; any good thing therefore that I may do, or any kindness I may show to any fellowcreature, let me do it now;
let me not defer or neglect it, for I shall not pass this way again."

THE RACE OF LIFE*

In many ways our life is like a variable distance Faith race,
We must discipline our minds and bodies and confront our weaknesses, face to face.
Not designed as a short sprint, where we run the distance as fast as we can,
Carefully measure the course, to finish victorious, the path we run, within HIS plan.

Each will run his or her unique course or pathway they will complete,
To some, a lengthy race, to others but a short dash in which to compete.
So each must run his own distance, not knowing precisely its end, making his mark,
Each runs as in a relay, others past, setting our standard of excellence to impart.

In training preparations we must pursue, before and after our race is begun,
We build our knowledge, our skills, tenacity and endurance all in life's hot sun.
Our training, by the way we live our life, that we might well finish the course,
Striving our best, as we are endowed and able, empowered by the Greater Force.

There will be times when we will forge ahead, as well as times we fall behind,
Though our daily fortunes may vary, we keep our ultimate goal in mind.
Inspired by the agility of other runners, alongside us, those before us, those we've passed,
Encouraging others in their race, who've grown weary or feel outclassed.

Running life's race, we'll encounter hurdles, success, failure, joy and pain,
Yet we work hard, to run well, finish the route before us that our efforts are not in vain.
So at journey's end, we have kept the Faith, finished the course, fought the good fight,
Then, pass life's baton to other runners, leaving our mark, our Eternal Goal, now in sight.

* Scripture references (*1st Corinthians 6:19, 9:24-27; Philippians 3:13,14; 1st Timothy 3:13-14; 2nd Timothy 2:3-5; 4:6-8*)

THE CHANGING TIMES OF LIFE*
(Ecclesiastes 3:1-8, 11)

Life looked at through the microscope of day to day,
May seem to you, either out of control, or a boring picture portray.
Yet, if we were able to stand back, and see our life as a whole,
'Tis a passing parade, swinging between ennui and ecstasy, mountain and pothole.

So while life may appear to you, either a difficult journey, or an endless plain,
That the challenge of exciting things, happen to others, for us it's just the mundane.
Into each life, at some time, both rain and sunshine shall surely send,
Life has storms and calm, it's not a question of whether, but of how and when.

So, it is with the times of our life, there is a time for everything,
There is a time for work and a time to recreate, a time to hum, and time to sing.
There is a time for precision, and a time to be loose,
There is a time for explanation, and a time for no excuse.

There is a time to eat, and a time to fast,
There is a time to give away, and a time to amass.
There is a time to be angry, and a time to forgive,
There is a time to exist, and a time to live.

There is a time to be silent, and a time to speak,
There is a time to be bold, and a time to be meek.
There is a time to push away, and a time to embrace,
There is a time to strike out anew, and time to retrace.

There is a time to look, and a time to turn away,
There is a time to question, and a time to pray.
There is a time to be certain, and a time to have doubt,
There is a time to speak softly, and a time to shout.

There is a time to climb mountains, and a time to descend,
There is a time to be independent, and a time to depend.
There is a time of plenty, and a time of need,
There is a time to root up, and a time to seed.

There is a time to love and a time to hate,
There is a time to stand up, and a time to lie prostrate.
There is a time to hold on to, and a time to release,
There is a time for our wars and a time for our peace.

There is a time to contest, and a time to accept,
There is a time to let pass, and a time to intercept.
There is a time to laugh, and a time to cry,
There is time to be born, and a time to die.

And though most of life is spent between these extremes,
There are daily swings of the pendulum, through which we find what life means.
Yet 'tis often in the times of trial and stress, that we grow the most,
That we learn the important lessons of life that will be our guideposts.

The test of our learning and wisdom, then is to know what time, for us, it is,
That we take each time of our life, live it fully, with nothing to miss.
And knowing what time it is, that we appropriately respond,
Knowing that others through time, have been where we are, since man's life first dawned.

As we look at our life, then and see each day as much the same,
May we realize there are daily swings and challenges that a life will claim.
May we be thankful for the times of joy, and learn in the times of sorrow,
With the assurance, that better things are coming, in God's time, on His tomorrow.

May we take the challenge and opportunity of each day, He will later our mettle refine,
For we are told that HE will make everything beautiful in its and His time.
For HE, in HIS wisdom, has placed eternity in each human's heart,
Because HE knows the beginning to the end of time, to its ending, from its start.

*A revisit and different expansion of Solomon's times and our times (appearing Section V of this book "A TIME FOR THE MANY SEASONS OF LIFE.")

THE LOVE OF OUR LIFE*

Nourishment, friendships, mental challenges and physical activity, maintain our physical body and life. But LOVE sustains and improves our spiritual and emotional life, and strengthens our inner peace in the quiet eddies, and in the storms of life that come in each of our lives. We all need somebody to love, and somebody who loves us, most times.

What is it about real, true and unconditional Love that keeps us going positively?

❖ Love never gives up.
❖ Love is not love of self or alone, but is shared with the one, or ones most loved.
❖ Love cares more for another, or others, than for self.
❖ Love doesn't envy what others may have, that it doesn't have.
❖ Love doesn't strut with pride.
❖ Doesn't have a swelled head.
❖ Doesn't force itself on others.
❖ Doesn't seek to change others to suit its pleasure, but gives each his or her own space. Isn't always "Me first."
❖ Doesn't fly off the handle, but is indignant when fairness fails.
❖ Doesn't keep score of the failures of others and joins in enjoying the successes of others. Doesn't revel, when others grovel.
❖ Love takes pleasure in learning, knowing and living the truth. Puts up with others shortcomings and idiosyncrasies.
❖ Always looks for the positive in others, "accentuates the positives, and eliminates the negatives). (from Johnny Mercer.)
❖ Never looks back at what might have been, but lives today to the fullest with purpose, and looks forward to tomorrow with anticipation.
❖ Love never dies, but keeps on going to the last breath.

*The Inspiration of 1st Corinthians 13: 1-8a.

ARTISTIC VIEW OF LIFE FROM THE SUNSET*

At this evening's sunset, near water's edge, I beheld God's miraculous creations anew,
A veritable kaleidoscope of colors appeared, and silver linings as if the angels drew.
Beauty beyond description, in nature's open amphitheater, colors like none I'd ever seen,
All the colors of the spectrum, reds, orange, yellows, blues, indigo, violet and greens.

There was also cobalt blue, yellow ochre, emerald green, every hue and shade,
Distant thunder, nimbus clouds arise, and nearby pink cirrus, as if The Heavenly Artist made.
A red and golden causeway, stretched across the water, it appeared as if the road to paradise,
And as I watched, the sun's manifold colored rays reaching skyward slowly fade, the pink clouds became, as edelweiss.

The shade of night slipped quietly in, then comes the darkness, that brings out our innermost fears,
Yet, we need not be anxious, for on the morrow, a new day is coming, soon to reappear.
It is the cycle of the earth, and the cycle of life, just as the seasons come and go,
And I saw in the bright and vivid colors, the light of joy, of happy times I've known.

Beauty, even in the storm's dark clouds, for as I weather them, growth and strength will come,
And, in the golden bridge, I saw the direction I should follow, to complete life's run.
It was as if the crossing was a path to heaven's gate, to the new world, on the Other Side,
Yes, even though I'll encounter tempest storms, my hope within, need not subside.

In the silver linings, I saw the assurances of His promises, which I know to be true,
That though in our lives, we'll see storms and rain, yet also sun and beauty too.
And, if we follow the golden span, that links us with Him, when we say to life, "Shalom",
We'll know He waits for us, His children, with open arms, saying "Peace unto to you My child, welcome home!"

*Revealed to the Author many years ago when visiting a friend in his the high rise apartment, just the day before he was called home.

WISDOM DISCOVERED THROUGH LIVING AND GIVING*

INFORMATION is data gleaned from living and nonliving things, history and events,
KNOWLEDGE is retained information learned, can have great value, or make no sense.
WISDOM is skilled Art of living, knowing Truth, thru experience, seeing what's in store,
It is valued knowledge in perspective, assured by Eternal Truth, now and forevermore.

WISDOM begins as we begin to see life's not solely in us, our status, or what we've got,
Aware life can have meaning in sharing our life, what we have, with those who have not.
With three gifts each are endowed, a unique amount of time, treasure and talents,
One of our life's tasks is to hone all, as on loan tools, giving of each with grace and balance.

WISDOM listens to the quiet inner VOICE of TRUTH, as our life's compass of morality,
Perhaps the dawn of WISDOM, is that we are as leaves of grass, in our own mortality.
It is then we come to know that each moment of each day is but a gift, a valued treasure,
Rejoicing in the good and learning from the difficult, both part of WISDOM's measure.

WISDOM hears the cries of the children, the hungry, the hurting and the downtrodden,
It responds to the cries for help to the needs where they are, that they not be forgotten.
It knows that it cannot be all things to all people, that TRUTH gives each special gifts,
Our purpose here to give ourselves away, giving those who are down a needed lift.

WISDOM sees more clearly, the living of life, and foresees there is an end to life.
That a noble life lived is one finding purpose, joy and peace, even if peppered with strife.
WISDOM seldom arrives early, and often follows arduous labor, struggle and pain,
It's then we view life with greater reality and humility, when ego and vanity are drained.

WISDOM remembers always that we own nothing forever, but merely possess for a time,
And that all are not allotted equal portions, but whatever we receive, our goal is to refine.
It grows and uses wisely, the three gifts we tenant, abundantly sharing of each,
With those in need, our impassioned causes, as each comes within our life's span reach.

WISDOM knows, when life is done, it's not measured by what we've won or heaped up,
But how we've shared, and left in love, what we had, to help others, from our given cup.
For just as the breadth, height, and worth of an old tree is not determined 'til its cut down,'
So may our life's legacy be gauged, "A valued life, well lived, a life's labor, well done."

** References for Wisdom in Life: (1st Chronicles 29:14-16); We don't own anything (Psalms 82:3-4); Take care of the needy and fatherless (Proverbs 27:19); Sudden inheritance goes quickly (Micah 6:6-8) Mercy, Justice, Humbly walk with God (Malachi 3:7-10) God Pours out Blessings (Matthew 25:31-40) Giving, Unto the Least of These (John 3: 16-17; John 8:32b) God so loved; Know the Truth (Roman 7: 18-25, 8:1-3) Wretch that I am, No Condemnation (1st Corinthians 13) The Love Chapter"; Galatians; 5:13-14; 6:2, 7-10; Peace Philippians 4:4-13 (James 1:2-4; 2:14-18; 3:1-10) Pain Thanks, Faith &Works.

WORRY - LET IT BE!*
(*Matthew 6:25-34*)
Written By "Grandpa"
For special ladies

"In my times of trouble, Mother Mary speaks to me,
Singing words of wisdom, Let it be, Let it be!"
So wrote and sang the Beetles, nearly fifty years now past,
But this ancient healing message of letting go our anxiety, will surely last.

The ancient Teacher, taught us worry does nothing to solve the things that trouble,
Benefits no one, and often merely breaks us down, turns our life into rubble.
Worry, comes from a German word, "*vergen*" which means to strangle, or choke,
But to one who lives life strangled by worry, as to what may be, is clearly no joke.

Worry begins almost as a droplet of water, just a single innocent thought,
Gradually develops into a continuing stream, from that one thought, wrought.
And if we let it, it will become an obsessive raging flood,
That will dominate of our lives, 'lest we seize control of it, and nip it in the bud.

Logically, worry about what is past is folly, for it's gone and done,
We have no way to change yesterday, there just is no time re-run.
But we can correct what we can, learn from our mistakes, and do it differently next time,
But we can't re-live even a moment, nor retrieve a hurtful word spoken, not in a lifetime.

And, worry about tomorrow, next year, or some day in the future, is also futile,
Worry is wasted energy, never productive, as things daily change, meanwhile.
For we may find in our worry about what tomorrow brings, the worry of anticipation,
Is, more often than not, much worse than our mind's wildest realization.

So, if we deal with just the known problems and concerns that stand before us today,
We'll find tomorrow's challenge will find tomorrow's solution, along the way.
If we focus upon and tackle only what we have to do now, at any rate
And give it our best, we'll have an amply full and generous daily plate.

It may help our angst, to know that while we can completely control a few things,
There are other matters, in which we may have some say, but not resolution bring.
There are yet many more situations, over which we have zero dominion or deliverance,
May these truths ease our anxieties, and may we have the wisdom to know the difference.

Worry never passed a test, paid a bill, or cured or helped sickness or disease,
It never finished a job, slew Goliath, or defeated Hercules.
In all of history, worry never accomplished a single thing,
But to make us less effective, and to our doubts cling.

So, when worry comes to knock at your mind's door,
Simply say, no thanks, I have no need of you anymore.
Knowing that worry has nothing to offer or benefit you,
That things will go better, without adding worry, to your life's milieu.

*Another Expression and Writing of "Worry, Let It Be," appears in Section VI.

THE GREATEST VOYAGE

LIFE TRUTH: We need not fear what lies beyond our life's horizon, the promise is it will be a place of joy and peace.

Some years ago, I was asked to do the eulogy for a longtime friend. As I began to think about his life, and about his passage through life, and into the next life, thoughts and ideas began to surface about the analogy of sailing, and specifically sailing beyond the horizon. This was not a new idea that of sailing to the other side, as Tennyson had said it masterfully and eloquently in his writing called "Crossing the Bar." Here is the way he put it:

> Sunset and Evening Star, And one clear call for me.
> And may there be no moaning of the bar, When I put out to sea,
> But such a tide as moving seems asleep,
> Too full for sound and foam, When that which drew from out the boundless deep
> Turns again home.
> Twilight and evening bell, And after that the dark.
> I hope to see my pilot face to face, When I have crossed the bar.

Having had a brief, but enjoyable encounter with sailing some fifty years ago, the parabolic idea of sailing, with the sailboats being our bodies, and the sailing around our "bay" as being our lives here on earth, and we who do the sailing, being our hearts, minds and souls, came naturally to me. The analogy of the sailboat being our bodies was not original with me either. The Apostle Paul described our bodies, as the temple of the Holy Spirit.

HE said it this way:
"Do you not know that your body is a temple of the Holy Spirit, who is in you, whom you have received from God? You are not your own, you were bought at a price. Therefore honor God with your body" (*1st Corinthians 6:19-20, New International Version*)

By the same token, when a ship sails beyond the horizon of our human sight, the "soul and heart" of the vessel still exists, it is not "gone," it has just passed beyond our human sight. Likewise, when a child is born from and through the birth canal the Mother's womb, the child lives before it is born in one dimension but in a traumatic and often painful birth passes into a new life, so too, when we pass from this life, "through the valley of shadows of death," in an often painful new birth, we are born into a new life, a new adventure, which will be our "Greatest Voyage."

As originally written and published, this poem was entitled simply "The Voyage" to the other side, that we need have no fear, and that our Captain has prepared a place for us. This then, I wrote for my good friend who died.

We presented this poem at the International Famous Poet's Society in September 2003, and were graciously rewarded, as well as a designated "Poet of the Year for 2003."

We now call it, "The Greatest Voyage." When diagnosed with cancer twelve years ago, revised it to its present structure with a renewed interest and insight into this life and beyond from that and previous experiences. Even now at seventy seven, and with an ample share of old age health problems, I have no fear of the future, whatever it may hold.

As we all know this life is but for an uncertain time. Each day is a gift. Biblically the extension of life is "as for the days of our life, the contain three score plus ten (seventy years) or eighty years if we have the strength." (*Psalm 90:9*). As you can see at eighty four I am working at best "overtime", and at worst "borrowed time." This life, as short or as extended as it may be, is in effect preparation for how and under what conditions we will spend eternity beyond this life.

Now, if I have my "druthers", I'd just as soon delay my voyage for the immediate present, and not leave loved ones and friends, as I have sometimes expressed it "on the next train out." I'd rather defer leaving my loved ones and friends for a time, not only because of what grief or loss they may feel, but also because I believe there is yet some unfinished business for me on this side of the River. On the other hand, I am ready when HE is.

I do not fear death or what lies beyond and actually view it with anticipation, with the assurance that we have, neither you nor I need fear our "Greatest Voyage." I believe that, from what Scripture tells us, that HE will be incredibly Forgiving of our shortcomings and failures (which are many), through the ONE HE sent, if we have truly done from day to day the best that we can muster for that day, where we are and what we are, but upon realizing where we fall short, being repentant. His standard for us is set forth in Micah 6:8 "This is what HE demands of you O Man and woman, only this, that you do justice to others, that you seek and love mercy, and that you walk humbly with your God." This is where it begins and we'll never do it with perfection but may we strive for excellence, as we are able as we are endowed.

So to me, our future holds incredible new adventures, a new life, a new spiritual body, new horizons, far beyond our wildest imaginations, when our time shall come, all as ordained by the One who created, gives and sustains all life as we know it on earth.

While I would like to defer my voyage for a time, and not leave those I love, especially for the pain they will feel, hopefully but for a time, I am ready when He is, whenever my voyage may come.

We have also been privileged to recite the poem at a number of other friend's services including classmates, coaches, clients and friends. May they each now, and may you, be blessed. Sail on my friends. Life is good! God is good! And what lies beyond this life will be good!

THE GREATEST VOYAGE
(A Parable of Continuing Life)

Revised August 2006, and September, 2008, July, 2016.
(First Published and read at the International Famous Poet's Society Convention,
September, 2003)

Some time, some day, just how or when, I cannot say,
I shall unbind my moorings, set my course, and sail away.
And just as the shade of night slips in, at the close of day,
Silently, on a quiet, gentle breeze, I shall BE, yet beyond this life's horizon, but be not afraid.

And as the skiffs that are anchored 'round me, move in rhythm, to and fro,
Some time, some day, in that certain moment, my final wind shall blow.
Ah yes, there will be some who've known me who will feel dismay,
Those who will miss my familiar vessel, and sailings, around our friendly bay.

Some whose sailing ships of life have been anchored near mine, for many years,
Will grieve my last passage, and cry out, "He's gone!", and shed their tears.
But grieve not long, for I have begun my greatest voyage, a new adventure,
Bound for the Promised Land, a safe harbor, sheltered from life's storms, and secure.

Near journey's end, I see brilliant lights, and sense my CAPTAIN, has made a special place for me,
A beautiful home, a haven of rest, down by the water's edge, bounded by HIS Crystal Sea.
And when I arrive, I'll be greeted, by the ones I once knew, who've sailed this route before,
This new course, uncharted by we living, into a new dimension, to His peaceful shore.

Then I shall dock my skiff, near those I've known, and close to HIM, for eternity,
Cleansed, and bathed in joy, as I await those cherished ones, who have loved and grieved for me.
Knowing that they too, shall one day, when they are called, loose their moorings, and sail away,
And, we shall live together, with our CAPTAIN in new bodies, clothed in HIS Peace, forever and a day.

THE PASSAGES OF LIFE

LIFE TRUTH: We Can't Re-Live Yesterday- We Only Pass This Way Once, So Live and Give of Your Best

"Heaven and earth shall pass away, but MY words shall not pass away." *Matthew 24:35*

"It's like this: When I was a child, I spoke as a child and thought and reasoned as a child does. But when I grew up I put away childish things. Now I see all things imperfectly as in a poor and clouded mirror, but then we shall see everything with perfect clarity. All that I know now is partial and incomplete, but then I will know everything completely, just as God knows me now. There are but three things that shall endure eternity, faith hope and love, and the greatest of these is love. *1st Corinthians 13:11-13*

"I expect to pass this way but once; any good thing therefore I can do, or any kindness I can show to any fellow creature, let me do it now; let me not defer or neglect it, for I shall not pass this way again" *Proverbial saying attributed to Stephen Grillett (1773-1855)*

"The world will little note nor long remember what we say here, but we shall never forget what they did here." *Abraham Lincoln (Gettysburg Address)*

"Life, so they all say, Is but a game, and they let it slip away.
Love, like the autumn sun, Should be dying, But its only just begun.
Like the twilight on the road up ahead, They don't see just where they're going, All the secrets in the universe, whisper in our ears, all the years.
We may not Pass this way, again." *Seals & Crofts*

In 1973, Jim Seals and Dash Crofts, wrote and sang, a then popular song entitled "We May Not Pass This Way Again". The message of the song was that we live only once, so we should live each moment, take life's opportunities as they come, listen to the inner voice, not wasting any of the time we have. Not a bad message!

Two thousand years ago, Jesus of Nazareth, in His "Parable of the Fig Tree", which appears in three of the four Gospels, concludes, "Heaven and Earth shall pass away, but MY words shall not pass away." He was saying that nothing on this earth remains the same—everything and everyone one changes, and passes away. Only the truth He spoke would remain. He said it quite plainly "You shall know the truth and the truth shall set you free." (John 8:32b) For He was and is the Gatekeeper for Eternity-- the Way, the Truth, and the Life. (John 14:16)

In an address given, September 30, 1859, before he became president, and at a time when dark clouds of civil war hung over the nation, Abraham Lincoln, quoting an earlier wise man said, "And this too, shall pass away."

In the nineteenth century, words attributed to Stephen Grellett, said that we should do whatever good we can while we are here, for "I shall not pass this way again." So, the idea that nothing remains constant, everything we know, including ourselves, even life itself, is in the process of continuing change, and according to Scripture, everything, save three things, including you and I, and each moment in which we live is changing, from moment to moment, day to day, and year to year. We are truly a work "under construction."

The opening words of Charles Dickens book "A Tale of Two Cities", are, "It was the best of times and the worst of times." So too, at some time, we may look back and find even some of our worst of times, were times of learning and growth, and in that sense, may also have been some of our best of times. Passages is a fictional account I have written, but which I believe may bear some lasting truths about our time maybe about all times, our circumstances and their passage. May "Passages" help you to consider this, even in your best of times and worst of times, the latter of which someday may turn out to be the best of times.

THE PASSAGES OF LIFE

An ancient King asked that his Wise Men to study and write,
A few short words that would be wisdom for all, for all future times, in sight.
Something that would be appropriate for all occasions, whatever may come,
Words that would encourage one person, chastise another, be an elixir to some.

They pondered for days, the sage words that would be enshrined on the palace wall.
Words that would be instructive, words that would, at special times, be meaningful to all.
After many hours of reflection, they agreed on the words that they would say,
Their six words of wise counsel, "AND THIS TOO, SHALL PASS AWAY."

The puzzled monarch asked, "How is it that these simple words, did you, after much deliberation, choose?"
"How did you arrive at your decision, what great scholar's writings did you peruse?"
They replied, "After careful consideration, the one constant in our life, is that of change,"
"Nothing in life remains the same, even the mountains imperceptibly move, though it may seem strange."

"For following the light of day, gradually comes the dark of night,
And following the doing of wrong by one, yet another will be doing right.
After the death of one generation, comes the birth of a new,
And after the scorching dry heat of the midday sun, comes the next morning's dew."

"An infant is born a babe, yet, all too quickly, to a child does change,
Then a child with childhood ways, does soon for adulthood, his young life exchange.
Both man and a woman progress through this life, through its many stages,
Too soon, to become old, to pass on and become a product of the ages."

"So, these six words tell us that nothing, nothing save our Creator, ever remains the same,
That each of us, and the world around us, what was yesterday or yesteryear, we cannot reclaim.
These words give us the humbleness and gratitude we need, in our hour of glory and pride,
"Yet in our darkest times, tell us, that this difficult hour we now endure, shall not always abide."

"And, we know that whatever comes in this life, save our legacy, will not eternally last,
Beyond the moment or the hour, for on each tomorrow, a new day shall be cast.
So we can accept even the painful times, for it's in them we learn and grow, though their fire may sear,
Enjoy, relish and be thankful for the good times, when and where they may appear."

"Knowing that each moment of life, is a gift, and we shall not again this way pass,
May we then savor all our life's experience, just as each grain of sand, passes through the hour glass.
And, whatever time we may be in, not forgo any good thing for others, we may do,
For we shall not pass this way again, and knowing all of our numbered days, are so few."

The King responded "May these six words enable all my people to taste the beauty of each day,
Yes, all of the joyful, sorrowful, and untroubled times, before we begin the climb of Heaven's stairway.
And, as we look back, we can see that from all times good and troubled, can come great good,
That having rushed our life through, had envy, discontent, and worried our time away, we'd missed the living of so much our life that we should."

And yet, as profound and sage as the King's Wise Men's chosen words were,
There are three things that for time immemorial, will our soul's heart stir.
These three shall never pass nor change, this our Creator Word guarantees,
They are Faith, Hope and Love, and Love which comes from God, is the greatest of these.*

*1st Corinthians 13: 13, "And now these three remain: faith, hope and Love. But the greatest of these is Love."
(NIV)

ALL THAT LASTS IS WHAT WE PASS ON!

LIFE TRUTH: We bring nothing into this world as we enter, and we shall take nothing out when we leave. And few of us ever know the day of our leaving until it has arrived. Whatever we've said or not said, done or not done while we are here as well as whatever we possess when we leave stays behind. All that lasts is what we pass on. When our life ends, we will leave a legacy. What will your daily and life legacy be?

"And He told them a parable, saying "The land of a certain rich man was very productive. And he began reasoning to himself, saying "What shall I do, since I have no place to store my crops?' And he said, 'This is what I will do: I will tear down my barns and build larger ones, and there I will store all my grain and my goods. And, I will say to my soul, "Soul, you have many goods laid up for many years to come; take your ease, eat, drink, and be merry.' But God said to him, 'You fool! This very night your soul is required of you; and now who will own what you have prepared? So is the man who lays up treasures for himself, and is not rich toward God." *(Luke 12: 16-21)*

"For we brought nothing into the world, so we cannot take anything out of it. And, if we have food and covering, with these we shall be content. But those who want to get rich fall into a temptation and a snare and many foolish and harmful desires which plunge men into ruin and destruction. For the love of money is a root of all sorts of evil, and some by longing for it have wandered away from the faith and pierced themselves with many a pan. . . . Fight the good fight of faith, take hold of the eternal life to which you were called. Instruct those who are rich in this present world not to be conceited or to fix their hope on the uncertainty of riches, but on God who richly supplies us with all things to enjoy. Instruct them to do good, to be rich in good works, to be generous and ready to share, storing up for themselves the treasure of a good foundation for the future, so that they may take hold of that which is life indeed. *(1st Timothy 6: 6-10, 12, 17-19)*

"Do not lay up for yourselves treasures upon earth, where moth and rust destroy, and where thieves break in and steal. But lay up for yourselves treasures in heaven, where neither moth nor rust destroys, and where thieves do not break in and steal; for where your treasure lies, there will your heart be also. *(Matthew 6:19-21)*

Have you ever had an "epiphany"- a life truth, come to you from an unexpected source? Some years ago, my wife handed me an issue of the Family Circle magazine she bought at the grocery store, and asked me to read an article she had marked, written by the famous horror story writer and author, Stephen King (The Shining). I still get the willies, when I think about the movie "The Shining."

It seems that, one evening, Stephen King, while alone, on a dark lonely road (sounds like one of his novels), had a serious accident. As he lay on the side of the road, not knowing whether he would live or die, bleed to death, or if anyone would find him before he died, he began thinking about what is important in his life.

Here are some of his thoughts, as recounted in the article that came to him as he lay bleeding and broken on the side of the road. "We come into life naked and broke. When we go out, we may be dressed, but we are broke. (We take nothing with us into the next world). Warren Buffett, broke! Bill Gates, broke! Tom Hanks, broke! Stephen King, broke, not a crying dime!" (See 1st Timothy 6:7). (In other words, no matter what we made, possess or control while we are here—when it comes time to graduate) "It's going to be a quarter past getting late, whether your watch is a Rolex, or a Timex." (See 1st Timothy 6:8).

Stephen King then muses "Sooner or later- the only three things you can call your own, your body, your mind, and your spirit. So, I want you to consider making your life, one long gift to others. Why not? All you have is on loan anyway. ALL THAT LASTS IS WHAT YOU PASS ON!" (emphasis supplied) (See 1st Chronicles 29:14-16).

King continues "Giving ISN'T (emphasis supplied) about the receiver or the amount of the gift. IT'S FOR THE GIVER (emphasis supplied)... to improve oneself... Giving is a way of taking the focus of the money we have (and ourselves) and on and putting it back where it (the focus) belongs- on the lives we lead, the families we raise, the communities we nurture, and nurture us. A life of giving- not just money, but of time and spirit- repays." (See 1st Timothy 6:9-10-17-19). Wow! Did he get that right or what?

King concludes, "It helps us, to remember that we may be going out broke, but right now we're doing ok. Right now, we have the power to do great good for others." (Now, or at our passing, or our "graduation.") "So I ask you to begin to give generously. I think you will find... you gave and got more than you ever had, and did more than you ever dreamed of."

All of this from Stephen King, possibly the greatest story writer since Edgar Allen Poe. Who would have thought it? Sometimes God has to hit us between the eyes with a 2 by 4, (like the old mule) to get our attention. Stephen King got a whack, both physically and spiritually and got the message, that night when he lay in that ditch, on a dark and lonely road. He heard it loud and clear! Have you heard the message? Has a 2x4 hit you between the eyes? What is really important in our life? Is it what we accumulate or the positions or power we've attained? Or is it family? Is it what we have done with our lives? What have we given of ourselves, and our riches, to others in need? What will we leave behind as our legacy? All questions that go to the very purpose of our being here.

The Gospel of Luke (Chapter 12) records a parable of a rich man, who hoards and stores up all of his riches—so he can relax and retire and "take his ease, eat, drink, and be merry." The parable concludes "But God said to him, "You fool! This very night your soul is required of you; and now who will own what you prepared? So is the man who lays up treasure for himself, and is not rich toward God."

Did you notice that in this short five verse parable by Jesus about the rich man, the word "I" appears six times, and the word "my" two times? That was no accident! We need to think more than just about "I", "Me", and "My". Both the parable, and Stephen King, tell us that we need to do good with what we have, while we are here. And doing good means, not only taking care of those persons God has personally entrusted to us, but in helping others as we can. In this way, we are "being rich toward God."

So what will be our legacy? What will we leave behind? It is our last chance to leave, as a part of our life, something that will be enduring, something that will help others, in whatever way our heart, our experiences, our soul shall deem best. Think about it! That's what "All That Lasts, Is What We Pass On" both from our life lived out, as well as what we leave behind, is all about.

But it goes beyond our lifetime. What about when we "graduate"? Surely we should make provisions for our loved ones. But the Psalmist gives us wise counsel about knowing the extent and duration of our days, "Surely every man walks about as a phantom; surely, they make an uproar for nothing; He amasses riches, and does not know who will gather them." *(Psalm 39:6)*. Am I suggesting that your children, grandchildren, nieces or nephews, are going to "blow" your money so it ends up in the hands of people you don't even know?

Not at all! Hopefully, whatever we leave to family and loved ones, will be managed and spent wisely, maybe even according to the wise and prudent standards, hopefully, we have lived.

But the Psalmist's words do give us pause to think. Do they have the same principles of what is important and frugality that you have had? Recently, it was reported on a financial radio program that someone had gathered statistics that reflect that seventy per cent of the inheritance that the average person leaves at death, will be spent within fourteen months. The person presenting the program did not give the authority of the statistics, but at least, it should prod us to consider, leaving a portion of what we leave behind, to our church, synagogue, or charitable organization in which we have confidence, or a cause which we have a passion for, a portion of what we leave behind. Maybe a tithe (10%), maybe more. You decide! But at least consider it!

ALL THAT LASTS IS WHAT WE PASS ON!

Two thousand years ago, a parable was told, about a rich man, that teaches you and me,
That our goal in our life, should not be our own pleasures and accumulating riches and money.
For if we direct our greatest energies on hoarding our riches and power for the morrow,
Who knows, there may be but for us only today, and no tomorrow, to our sorrow.

We bring nothing into this world, and surely we will take nothing out,
So, we need to focus our lives on what we do while here, on what life is all about.
The only time we have for certain, is this very moment, of this day,
God only, knows when we'll hear our last trumpet sound, and be called away.

What is important then, is not what we have, or what we spend, you see,
It's how we learn to share and help those who are more needy than we.
And, giving's purpose is not only for what we've taught, or given a lost soul solitude,
But, also, about growing in ourselves, a thoughtful mind, a giving heart and generous attitude.

For when our life is over, and when all has been said and done,
The value of our life will not be what we have, or the races we have won.
Our true measure, will be, the lives we've lived, the good we've shared, and left behind,
The tenor of our legacy, to those who follow, will be the tie that us to them binds.

And, with those tangible things with which we've been entrusted, while we're here,
While surely, we should make provision for those in life that we've held dear.
The Psalmist says we know not how, what we've had for a time, will be used, and by whom.
That sometimes, the "things" we leave, will be sewn in wild oats, and be gone, all too soon.

So, in addition to the lived legacy that each of us will leave behind,
Maybe we consider, giving a portion to noble causes that lesser ones may yet achieve.
Knowing that all that lives on in this life, as well as into the life beyond,
Is how we've lived and left this life, for All That Lasts, Is What You Pass On!

NO TIME

LIFE TRUTH: We live in a fast forward world. Slow down, take time, to smell the roses in your life.

In the 1970's, a then popular rock band, known as The Guess Who, had a hit song, entitled "No Time". A part of the lyrics said: "No time for the gentle rain, No time for the watch and chain, No time for revolving doors, No time for the killing floors- You need not wonder why, there's no time left for you, No time left for you."

It's true! If there was "No Time" in the 1970's, it's even more so today, many fold, in spades, in the twenty first century. There just isn't enough time in the day, to cover all the bases, to get it all done. Instead of 24 hours in a day, we need at least 36, for starters.

And then we're also full blown in the electronic age now with "ever-smarter" smart phones (surprisingly only came out in 2007- but today there are many, many millions in use throughout the world). Then there is Facebook, Twitter, and successors, the latest social media areas. As for me, all I do is a desktop, only a Jitterbug phone, don't do any of other social media. So I remain an outsider, a recluse from the electronic world. And yet recent discoveries have brought to social media hackers, who can destroy your computer or your credit in a minute, even the national security, so we constantly seek better protections.

Even a few decades ago, only a few businesses had computers and fax machines. Today, any business without the latest electronic equipment, telephone systems that require answers to countless questions before reaching a human being, is in the dark ages. Now, if you don't have a smart phone you remain in another world. Through the Smart Phone we can stay in touch 24 hours a day, never more than a second from our family, our friends, our business, even those people we don't want to necessarily be in touch with, and the latest news and information all for 124 hours a day. Anything you put on e-mail, Facebook, twitter, or any of the social media is open to the world. There is no privacy, no confidentiality.

Does it ever bother you that when you're having even a causal conversation with someone, their phone rings, and you get "I have to take this message, or this text?" Guess I'm old fashioned.

That reality of today, then, was the impetus for the "no time" that follows. While I don't believe it is autobiographical, maybe my children would disagree. But, if it speaks to you, where you are, resolve to change your priorities—for to reference the title of another Seventies song, made popular by Seals and Croft, "We Shall Not Pass This Way Again." Don't let the times of your life in the real world pass you by, they will be gone before you know it! Trust me I'm there at 84, but never give up.

NO TIME

There's been just no time to do all I'd like to have done,
My life's been a "rat race", I've been constantly on the run.

No time for my family, when duty calls,
No time to relax at home, as the night falls.

No time when the cell phone rings, instant messages, calls to make,
A fax coming in on my hand held computer, for heaven's sake.

No time to spend an hour, listening to my beloved spouse,
Got to make more money, to pay for cars and things, and house.

No time to read with my daughter when she was four,
'Cause I knew the creditors would be knocking at the door.

No time to help my son fix his broken bike,
Even though there's nothing better, I'd have liked.

No time to take my wife out on that special date,
I really intended to, but well, it was always too late.

No time to sit with my family and watch the afternoon rain,
But I've got to make that business meeting, just the same.

No time to go to my son's Little League baseball game,
I'd already scheduled a business golf match, what a shame.

No time to attend Annie's first recital of piano and dance,
Just so happened, had an important business trip, just by chance.

No time to be thankful, for what I've got,
A loving wife, normal, healthy children, and that's a lot.

No time to take that exciting planned family vacation,
No time to travel to an exciting theme park, in the nation.

No time to kneel, and thank God for all of my blessings,
Nor to mention all of my failures, that need confessing.

As I look back now, after twenty five years,
I see I never had the time, to share in their joys and tears.

I had no time to spend with those who matter,
I've been too busy, no time for family small talk, and idle chatter.

119

No time for anything now when you have 20 text messages, 15 voice mails, to take care to,
No time to spend with just for me and for you.

Now, my children are gone, to live their own adventures and lives,
They have no time to spend with me, and I wonder why.

Then, I realize that in taking care of business first, I must insist,
How much of my life has passed me by, how much I've missed.

I pray that my children, and those beyond, will not spend their lives, the way I did,
Too busy, chasing business, even if in different areas than, and as Dad and kid.

So learn from my experience, leave time for the important, don't busy your life away,
For all of those treasured moments lost, you'll wish you had back some day.

There is no time to re-live, the times that are our past,
Only those times we've really lived, will in our memory last.

IT'S OK- EVEN IF YOU DON'T ALWAYS FEEL OK

LIFE TRUTH: Man (and woman) are created in and live in an imperfect condition, so all will at some time have insecurities about themselves, though we'd like not to let them show. So it's ok, deal with it. Try to overcome them, and know that others have them too, you just don't see them because they hide them as we do!

Dr. Thomas Harris wrote a bestselling book in 1967, which became a household word, "I'm OK, You're OK." The book dealt with the question of how we feel; about ourselves, and those around us, (OK or not OK).

In this life, we are always imperfect, that is the human condition, and that's "OK". Those of us of the Christian Faith, believe we are made "Ok", by the death of a Man upon a Cross, two thousand years ago. We all, often do, say and think things we are not proud of, often don't do the very things we should, and do the things we shouldn't. As a result, we don't always feel OK about ourselves inside, but because everyone one around us seems OK, we believe there is something wrong with us.

We pass a friend on the street and say, "How are you?" They respond "Fine" or "Great". They return the greeting, "How are you? "Good, have a great day!" we respond. We both proceed on, sometimes thinking why can't I really be OK, like him? The truth is neither of us is being honest! What do you think would happen, if instead you responded "Well, if you have about two hours to listen, I'll really tell you how I am!" Just try it and you'll probably find your "friend" will be taken aback, and will seek the quickest exit. But, because everyone else claims to be OK, we think something is wrong with us, if we don't feel OK.

And today there are so many more things to worry about. TV brings to us new medicines today for illnesses that we have that we didn't know existed. We have these new diseases but rather than in words they give them to us in acronyms- like OAB, ED, RLS, and COPD to name just four- but there are enough to cover the alphabet many times over.

Fortunately, we are in good company. The Apostle Paul didn't feel OK about himself. To the contrary, he wrote "For that which I am doing, I do not understand, for I am not practicing what I would like to do, but I am doing the very thing I hate... For I know nothing good dwells in... for the wishing is present in me, but the doing good is not... Wretched man that I am! Who will set me free from this body of death?" *(Romans 7:14-15, 18-24)* Did I mention this was the Apostle Paul speaking of his own condition?

IT'S OK, EVEN IF YOU DON'T ALWAYS FEEL OK!*

One of the issues of life, on which we need, for our feelings to allay,
Is whether, we are, in so many areas of our life, really, OK.

The daily ebb and flow of the tides of life, that swing and sway,
At times we show an outward face of content, as our inner feelings, we hide away.

In our mind and heart, we feel sick or inadequate, yet dare not these emotions display,
Thinking we must appear confident, all together, a positive image to convey.

Our need then, is to look inward and outward, knowing others too this same game play,
They too, have their own, though different insecurities, wonder quietly, if they're OK.

Each of us then, needs to impress on our lives, this, new, yet old concept, to inlay,
That no one is always all together, all perfect, all knowing, all confident, along life's way.

Strive each day to give life the best we can, anticipate tomorrow, worry not for yesterday,
Knowing that while we're not always whole, neither are others, from day to day.

So, then, we accept ourselves, as we are, and with quiet assurance, approach each day,
Realizing that for the moment, even though our thoughts and actions, may be in disarray,

Confident, that in all our life and times, we are human, that our doubts will fade away.
And that to have our secrets, or open anxieties and questions, is quite OK,

For there is The One in control of all things, hence, we need not dismay.
Knowing that He seeks, but does not demand perfection, just our best, in life's daily fray,

Assured, there is a Peace past understanding, only He gives, that keeps our fears at bay.
Faith that He always loves us, as we are, He is always with us, never to betray,

So, just know in your heart of hearts, whatever be the time, or whatever be the day,
That wherever we are, whatever the threat or hurdle in life, we're ok.

*A STUDY IN TWO LINE IDENTICAL END WORD RHYMES, BUT THAT'S OK!

Scriptural References: Micah 6:6-8; *John 14:26-27,16:13, Philippians 4:4-13*

THE RIVER OF NO RETURN

LIFE TRUTH: Troubled times will come to all of us, seek the help you need, and know that this too shall pass, that god is with you, at your side in troubled times.

My eldest son Jay, died October 28, 1980, 36 years ago. The memory and moments of that day, and the weeks and months, that followed, are burned in my mind, as if they happened yesterday. Yet, at the same time, the times surrounding his death, also seem as if they happened in another life, another time. Anyone who has lost a child understands that, because life never is, never can be quite the same. We are different people!

We expect to lose our parents (our past), and even our spouse (our present), but we don't expect to lose our children (our future), a future in which we place our hopes and dreams, dreams that their life will be even better and more fulfilling than ours, and that they may reach their greatest individual potential.

My son, Jay, and his death, left us three legacies: one of unimaginable pain, grief and loss, another, wonderful memories of times lived and loved, as well as a third, priceless and unexpected gifts (which I describe in the next following, "Blessings Come Forth").

"The River of No Return" was written two years after Jay's death, in commemoration of his passing. In it, we seek to describe where we had been in the previous two years, and some of the passages and phases which are a part of all grief recovery. God sent to our family a Man, a man who we did not know at the time, but who ministered to us in our time of trouble. He came one evening, shortly after our son died. He said "My name is Dolph Allen. Someone told me you need help and asked if I'd come."

It seemed rather strange, and I wasn't sure why at that time, I didn't know him. But I responded "I don't know you but you've sure come to the right place." I soon knew why I invited this stranger into my home at night.   He was a minister and Pastor, highly educated, but he was to everyone just "Dolph." As you first met him you felt as if you'd known him for a lifetime.

We thank God for his coming into our life. He became our counsellor, our helper, and our minister for years. Yes and he was like a brother for the remainder of our life until his death in 2015. Imperfect as he was, as we all are, I now know from whence he came and where he is this day, and forever.

We wrote the words that follow just two years after our son's death, when Ellen and I went to a place together for several days, alone with each other, to gather our thoughts and lives for the future.

THE RIVER OF NO RETURN

I was cast into the cold and raging water,
Suddenly, without warning, it's beyond belief.
I thrashed about and denied it could happen,
Yet, it was I, in the River of No Return- Grief.

No shortcuts, I must begin at the beginning,
And pass through its treacherous course.
Battered by its many jagged rocks,
Guilt, Anger, Doubt, a host of others, and Remorse.

In those early days, I am numbed by the cold,
By the shock of the loss of my precious Loved One.
Scores of friends rush to the River's bank, casting out lifelines,
But nothing can return my beloved, but lost, Son.

These friends want so desperately to help,
But scarcely know what to say.
Then, some who have lost as we, enter the troubled waters,
To reassure us, they understand, for they too, have passed this way.

The days become weeks, the gaping hole is still there,
I cry out to God "Why? What have You done?
What have I done? When will the pain stop?
When will this journey end, this terrible River run?"

And then one day I see a ray of sun,
A day when things seem better, to all black.
Then, just as suddenly, I am dashed again on the sharp rocks,
Of Depression, Despair, Pain, it has all come back.

Again, one day I see a glimpse of truth,
That many others have been here before me, are here now.
I am not alone in this River, and must finish its course,
And yet, I am still filled with hurt and doubt.

Then another insight one day comes to me,
I can neither get out, nor turn back, I must pass through.
I cannot bury the hurts, the past, those dark corners,
At last, I truly know what I must do- to pass through.

So, onward I go, knowing the River will have more raging rapids,
But I shall work my way through, one day by one.
For as I do, I find there are those moments of Peace, quiet eddies,
When I feel again the joy, like warm rays of the sun.

Two years now, that I've traveled this River of Tears,
While I know life won't be the same, I must let go the past.
To become stronger, more loving, caring and understanding,
To reach out to touch those who've also been in this River cast.

I must tell them, each one, to have hope and heart,
The River of Grief is hard, and when it seems you just can't take it.
Reach up for inner strength, and accepting Faith, reach out for help,
For as others have before you, you can, and will, make it.

And as I look back down the River's path I've gone,
I was puzzled, and wondered why I did not drown,
Then, I realized, I was not alone, buoyed, carried, directed
By the God of Love, and through others help, was lost, but now am found.

BLESSINGS COME FORTH, EVEN OUT OF HARD TIMES!

LIFE TRUTH: Out of the trials in our life, though we can't always recover things that are lost, many blessings may come to us, if we are receptive to them.

Some twenty five years ago, I was asked to speak at the dedication of a Memorial site, for the now Golisano Children's Hospital, at a quiet site established to remember the children who had died. It is a place of serenity and peace for the families of those who have lost children, brothers, sisters, and grandchildren.

(Touched by that moment in time and those seeking a respite from the damaging blows of a child who is injured, ill or who has died, several years ago Ellen and I were moved to assist in providing a Chapel, a place of peace and rest for those families seeking peace, prayer and quiet. Not yet completed as we write this we hope to be privileged to see it upon completion of that marvelous facility in 2017.)

It was, at the same time, a somber occasion, because each one of us there had lost a young loved one, but it was also an occasion to find peace, and an occasion of remembrance of the love of a life lived and loved.

At the outdoor site twenty five years ago, as we had lost our son ten years before,, and in thinking about what I might say to these people, whose loss was much closer in time than mine. And, the passage of time (ten years at that point) does dull the pain, so that likewise your sensitivity to the pain my not be as sharp as in times past.

I felt I needed to be honest with them, not give them meaningless platitudes, yet give them hope, as we, Ellen and I were walking proof, that they can and will get through this time, and to tell them that even though we cannot bring back our lost loved ones, that if they would be open to it, many positive things can result from their loss, and their lost child had for them some beautiful gifts and legacies, which they can treasure. Not that they wouldn't prefer to have things the way they were, to have their child back, but that neither I nor they had that choice.

As I began to reflect again, I knew that even ten years later, the loss is never completely over, and life is forever changed. Grief or loss in life leaves its scars, yet in some ways it is like losing a leg. Life is never quite the same, but you do adjust and learn to live with the change.

However, I had also come to know that from our loss many good things had come, not because of it, but almost in spite of it. That if we are open to God's quiet teaching that he will show us ways in which we can become better, stronger, and more caring, compassionate people.

In all events, it is our attitude that will make the difference. Particularly in the early days, we must not be hesitant about asking for help, from whatever source we may find it. We must decide, that with God's help, to consciously find good things from, and make good things from the trials in our life. We can choose how we will respond to crisis and troubles. And, if we choose to find and create good out of our hurts and hard times- "Blessings Will Come Forth".

I believe this writing naturally follows "The River of No Return" looking back now, after all of these years. A lot has happened and we have received and continue to receive many blessings, even out of our greatest loss.

BLESSINGS COME FORTH, EVEN OUT OF HARD TIMES!

It was just 35 years ago, all my life was going so well,
Then, in an instant, what was joy, turned into a living hell.
For on that day, I received the news, that my Son was dead,
The shock, the unbelief, how to tell my wife, spinning in my head.

"My Son, My Son," from the depths of my Soul I cry out,
All of those terrible feelings, the pain, guilt, and the doubt.
Wrack my body and my soul, can anyone understand?
What I feel inside, I think my weeping shall never end.

Days, weeks, months pass, the cavernous hole, still there,
The loss, the questions of what if, and why, it's all so unfair.
Then one day, the thinking becomes so clear, in my sight,
I can't change, turn back the clock, to a day before that one dark night.

I then realize that I must purpose, for myself, and those I love, to make a choice,
Whether 'tis better to be angry, feel pity, or let healing be my voice.
How grateful I am, I chose to seek the positive road for my life,
For, to have chosen anger and self-pity, would have bred cynicism and strife.

The recovery was irregular, seemed interminable, ever so slow,
But out of the ashes of our hurt and loss, yet a new life would grow.
Not that I wouldn't trade all that I own, just to hear my Son's voice,
I must accept that such a trade, is neither an option nor a choice.

For out of my loss, I have found a depth of sensitivity, I never knew,
To the pain and loss of others, the things they've gone through.
And I've learned to treasure each memory and day that I may live,
To focus on the present moment, to find what is it, today, that I may give.

I've come to know, how important are the people who come in my care,
And express my Love to them openly, things before I wouldn't dare.
I've learned that the greatest thing each of us can give or receive,
Is our Love and Compassion, share others joy, and their pain relieve.

Yet another Blessing came forth from my loss and my pain,
Was to find and focus on the truly important things of life that sustain.
The priorities of my life are now so different than they were before,
All of the past ideas and goals of success, aren't so important anymore.

And I've learned that though death may one day steal our loved ones away,
Death cannot take away the precious memories, we treasure each day.
Even though twenty years have passed, these treasures are crystal clear,
The love and life we shared, each day, each week, and each year.

So, I've found that even through the loss of my beloved Son,
He has left me many gifts, which I could not have on my own won.
For how much richer and meaningful is my life, even in his death,
How much I've learned, from His gifts, and may it continue 'til my last breath.

And yet with all the Blessings from the ashes that have come unto me,
There are yet many questions, the answers, to which I cannot see.
But a Man once came to me, HIS Providential message to confide,
"You shall have all the answers when you meet Him and him on the other side."

A PROPHET IS WITHOUT HONOR IN HIS OWN HOMETOWN
(Luke 4:16-24)

LIFE TRUTH: Sometimes those who know us best, may appreciate our efforts least, sometimes because they know us best, and see our shortcomings too, sometimes because our efforts have become too easy to come by, sometimes because they are growing up, and, sometimes because, well, who knows why?

It has been said that an expert is a person who is at least twenty five miles away from his hometown, wears a blue pin stripe suit, smokes a pipe, and carries an attache' case. While the suit adds richness and professionalism, the attache' case connotes knowledge and importance, the pipe smoker can give the appearance of being wise, but the most important part of this definition is "at least twenty five miles from his own hometown" factor. There is something to the adage "Familiarity breeds contempt." Those who know us best, and have seen our worst, as well as our best, often see through our best presentation, and tend to remember our worst.

Many people who have had children have experienced what their children view as a "dumbing down" of their parents, as they reach and pass through their teen age years. These are the same children, who a few years earlier, saw their parents as the fount of all knowledge and wisdom. While as parents we may never recover the awe of our children we held at their tender years, if we are fortunate, as they and we, grow older, they come to see us as, well, not as "dumb" but "flawed, yet doing the best we can.

At eighty four, I'm wondering how long it will be until my children must assume the parental role for me. So concerned have Ellen and I been about this change in circumstances, we have written a letter to our children, telling them, that while, at the moment, we are hopefully still thinking clearly, "Don't pay any attention to what I tell you then, when it comes time to take control, and please do what they have to, just do it!" Again, heaven help them!

The phenomenon of "a prophet being without honor in his own hometown" is not new, and is clearly exemplified in the Gospel of Luke, with the Master himself. Here is the way he put it "Truly, I say to you, no prophet is welcome in his own home town." *(Luke 4:24)* When He returned to his hometown of Nazareth, not only did his neighbors not accept Him as a prophet, his own family thought He was insane. It got so bad the "home towners" gathered as a lynch mob, and planned to take him up to a cliff and throw him off the cliff. *(See Luke 4:16-34).*

So, if you have had or have trouble in "your home town" at home, or with friends, or family, and those who have known you well, accepting your authority and expertise in some area, while complete strangers readily accept your credentials, without hesitation, take comfort, YOU ARE IN EXCELLENT COMPANY!

A PROPHET WITHOUT HONOR IN HIS OWN HOMETOWN

That a cobbler's children has no shoes to wear,
That a barber's son lives with shaggy, unkempt hair.
That a lawyer who represents himself, has a client, who is a fool,
That a doctor whose child is always sickly, is the rule.

But One who was greater than all of these in re known,
Said, "A prophet is without honor in his own hometown."
What He meant in part, was familiarity breeds contempt,
For those who know us best, our best efforts are often misspent.

There are many reasons why this might be so,
Maybe because with those closest to us, only our love we bestow.
Or maybe it's because to be objective, with these, is most difficult,
To give friends and loved ones, wise advice, and expect the desired result.

Or maybe, it's because, our human frailties, they've often seen,
So that our advice and prophecies, are viewed with our homegrown backdrop, with less esteem.
Or maybe, it's because it's easier to speak with another not so well known,
Rather than with the one, with whom so much of our life has been thrown.

Or, maybe it's uncomfortable for them, to fully confide,
In one, from whom their failures, they'd rather hide.
Whatever it be, it seems to be an almost universal law,
It's often tough to give advice, to those persons, to whom we closest draw.

Even though we may find they don't hear the best advice we've ever given,
They discover the same truth, comes from a stranger, seems to them God-given.
Just be happy, if they finally get the solution to their issue right,
Even though the memory of your same counsel is far out of sight.

This is not to say we shouldn't share with loved ones our best advice,
Because the wisdom we share, may well change their life.
But whatever we say, must be with all gentleness and care,
Words carefully chosen, not to just correct, but to repair.

So don't feel discouraged, or like a failure you've been,
When you can help others to see the truth, yet not your own kin.
For if this be the case, join the club of the greatest One of all,
The Master, the Prophet, without honor, in His own town hall.

GRANDMA'S BOOK OF LIFE*

My wife Ellen, is not only my wife (now 62 years), but my best friend, my love, my helper, my support, my defender, and has given me always unconditional love. She is, in short, my life. But, she is also chief cook and bottle washer, unlicensed fixer upper and carpenter, unlicensed philosopher, and along with many other titles, she is to others, "Dear Friend" "Mom" and "Grandma." To me, she's "My Best."

We were blessed to have each of our six grandchildren, now all full grown adults, live nearby, so that we were able to watch them grow up, almost day by day. During that time "Grandma" has been a veritable storehouse of practical wisdom for them, which she was not hesitant to impart to the grandchildren on a regular basis.

A number of years ago, one of the grandchildren began to kid "Grandma" a bit about her proclamations and affirmations about life, and how to behave. After hearing one of her pearls of wisdom, he/she said "Now that statement is found on page 65 of "Grandma's Book of Life." From that point on whenever Grandma gave advice, the grandchildren, the children or I will say "And, that is on page 32 of Grandma's Book of Life."*

Yet all have always appreciated her advice and folksy wisdom, and even now as adults, come by to get Grandma's take on a particular situation. Maybe that will be yet another book, "Grandma's Book of Life Part II." It will sell a million copies.

*A "goldie oldie", our youngest grandchild is now 29, the oldest 35. Haven't heard a one of them tease her again about that since they have been adults.

GRANDMA'S BOOK OF LIFE**

She's a wonderful lady, my beloved Grandma, and oh so wise,
In old, but valuable common sense, she'd win the prize.
She's always willing to give that unsolicited, but sage advice,
From Grandma's Book of Life, that wisdom, without a price.

Always be thoughtful, in all the things you do,
Always be truthful, it will pay rich dividends for you.
Always respect your parents, because they've loved you so,
They have given so much of themselves, more than you now know.

And always give life the very best that you can,
Whether it be in school, in sports, in life, or the race you ran.
And even though you won't always win the race,
Give to it all that you have, in whatever test, you face.

Prepare each day for the worst, but expect the best,
And approach each task, with confidence, with fervor and zest.
And in whatever you do, be precise in how you measure,
For then you will find, what you produce will be a treasure.

And, take time to enjoy each day, as life passes through,
Else you may miss so much of living, important to you.
Always keep your sense of humor, and at yourself, even laugh,
For even in your successes, will be many mistakes, and many a gaff.

And, when you love, be certain of the one you select,
Is the one to live your life with, and not easily cast off or reject.
Be happy with who you are, and with the talents you are given,
For 'tis the unhappy person, trying to be who he isn't, his efforts miss driven.

When they look back over all the things they've been taught,
Lessons in life, no book could teach, nor at any price be bought.
They shall never forget that unwritten book- Grandma's Book of Life,
For she and her book have prepared them, for life's joys and strife.

**Written 20 years ago- still good and true today.

SECTION V. HAPPY DATES AND DAYS FOR US.
(To My Anna with Love)

A LIFETIME LOVE COMES AROUND, BUT ONCE IN A BLUE MOON (50)

NOTE: My wife Ellen and I at this time have been married 55years. On our 50th wedding anniversary we had, what to us was a big celebration a 5 course meal with 120 guests, our pastors, family and friends. Before Ellen and I were married we had "our song" and it was blue moon, as it was sung by the velvet fog, Mel Torme, because his rendition was popular when we were early dating in 1951.

There were probably better recordings by Frank Sinatra and Ella Fitzgerald and others but Mel Torme's version was our song. Not that I had a voice for singing but we'd drive down old US 41 taking her home and with one arm on the wheel one arm around her (don't tell the grandchildren) I would sing the song, I thought, and she told me that I sang it just as well as did Velvet Fog (Mel Torme). We were in love!

For our 50th Anniversary, our children planned, and we had a nice dinner party, with 120 guests, champagne, and a five course dinner. (Our wedding night dinner fifty years before was in Sarasota, at Morrison's Cafeteria in Sarasota, Ellen in a new white suit, hat and corsage, me in a double breasted suit of my Father's that was a bit tight. (People did stare- Think they knew?)

The 50th Anniversary Party was themed around a number of events of our courtship and marriage including the song Blue Moon, "our small motel by a wishing well" (from the 1950's song A Small Hotel)   honeymoon at "Azure Tides," on Lido Beach in Sarasota Florida. Other themes were our children, my time in the Army service, and other notable dates and events- each table was named for an event. And as dinner was served, Ellen and I went to each table with a Mike and described the significance of the table's theme in our life.

So special were those three days of our honeymoon, that we went back there, frequently when our children were younger. The family always enjoyed it. Ellen and I decided to return for our twenty fifth anniversary. It was still there, quaint, seemingly clean the same terrazzo floors. I believe there were not the same beds, and there was a pleasant odor so we enjoyed it. We returned again for our thirtieth anniversary, and it was not quite as nice, but still tolerable. We spent more time on the beach and in restaurants then.

Then on our fortieth anniversary we decided one more time. To my surprise when I called it was still "Azure Tides." I was so pleased. We made a reservation for two nights again. Ellen and I drove in with great anticipation, but were not delighted with the then condition. When the lady at the desk gave us the key, we noticed only a few old cars there, (one up on blocks) and the place was badly in need of paint and repair. I placed the key in the door, and opened it widely. The odor was overwhelming. We looked inside, closed the door, returned to the office and gave the lady the key. We were sorry but we couldn't stay. I paid her for two nights and we left. So much for trying to re-live your younger days! The place was forty years older, but then so were we.

We found another place, many years younger, thought we were many years older, down the road and had a pleasant time at Lido Beach once again. We dared not go back there for our 50th anniversary, and haven't been back to Lido Beach since then. Our 50th anniversary party was our celebration and it was wonderful.

Do you know what a Blue Moon is? I didn't either when I sang with such melodic voice for Ellen. But I decided some years later to research what Blue Moon really meant. I knew simply that it was something that was exceptional unusual. According to the most recent definition, a blue moon is the second full moon within a calendar month. Now the average span of the moons is 29.5 days, so with no months more than 31 days, obviously the first full moon must be on the first or second day of the month, and the month must have 31 days.

So, if say in the month of July, a full moon occurs on July 1 or 2, you will have a Blue Moon on the last of the month. So as you see a Blue Moon is rather unusual and rather exceptional.

Ellen and I have always felt our relationship, our marriage and our life together has been so blessed and so exceptional, that even then 62 years ago as now 62 years later it is a Blue Moon marriage. The following verses I wrote down for our 50th wedding anniversary and among many things, we read the verses together and sang the song to each other together. Here are both the verses and the lyrics (there is no music CD as of this writing.)

A LIFETIME LOVE COMES AROUND BUT ONCE IN A BLUE MOON
To My Anna with love

A Blue Moon is the second in a month to be a full moon,
And for young lovers, it can never come too soon.
'Cause a blue moon is one that doesn't come very often,
But, a Blue Moon is a time when lovers' hearts will soften.

Since the cycle of the moon is exactly twenty nine and 1/2 days,
To have two full moons in one month, God must search for ways.
For its then that a lover's mate, that once in a lifetime arrives,
That one, he needs, for his heart's life to survive.

So be aware when your one true love comes by you,
The one, who will love you, your whole life through.
That the love of a lifetime, comes but once in a Blue Moon,
Know that she's the one, 'ere it be at early morn, night or noon.

Looking back over these years, though it may sound strange
There is not one moment with you, I'd choose to change.
For t'was fifty years ago, you were my bride, and I your groom,
How blessed I've been, God gave you to me, once in a Blue Moon.

So, on this Blue Moon night, it is only of thee I sing,
I prayed you'd say yes, so that June wedding bells might ring.
So I renew my vow of love to you again, from June to May,
And, if I could sing, here is exactly, what in my song, I'd sing and say-

BLUE MOON

Blue Moon- you saw me standing alone,
Without a dream in my heart,
Without a love of my own.

Blue Moon- you knew just what I was there for,
You heard me say a prayer for,
Someone I really could care for.

And then there suddenly appeared before me,
The Only one my arms could ever hold.
Then I heard someone whisper, please adore me,
And when I looked the Moon had turned to gold.

Blue Moon- now I'm no longer alone,
Without a dream in my heart,
And with a love all of my own.

136

YOU'RE STILL THE ONE* (55)

Ellen and I celebrated our 55th anniversary on June 4, 2009. Wonderful times and wonderful years. We both are thankful for each day together, and wonder just why we have been so blessed to have found each other, and shared so many years together.

In the months and years, before June 4, I had listened to National Public Radio as I took my early morning, 5:30 or so, 3 mile walk. (Now, at 84, the distance of walk is somewhat less). But I've found that recently the news is so depressing that I began walking slower and slumping over as I walked. Then several weeks before June 4, I found a new station, FM Radio Station, 92.5, playing only Classic Rock of the 1960's and 70's. I love it, and it has caused me to pick up the pace in my walk, even catch myself dancing to some of the music. I know a passerby must think I'm a nutty old man. That's ok.

Then, about a week before our anniversary, I was walking and listening and heard the song I recalled from the late 1960's with lyric line, "We're Still havin' Fun, 'Cause-- You're Still the One." By Orleans. I danced all the way home and knew right then how our 55th Anniversary Day would begin.

I wrote the following verses for Ellen, and gave her the CD for our anniversary. Little did she know that I had already placed the CD in the chamber of our Radio, with CD. Since I always awake earlier than Ellen, I made the coffee, and when she arose and came into the kitchen, I turned on the CD rather loud and said "Let's dance." Oh how we danced, just as we did when our three children were in High School in the early 70's, just like we did before we were married. Even danced to the next song On the CD, "Dance With Me."

After that, both of us were just a bit winded, sat down in the Kitchen, poured a cup of decaf coffee for each of us, and I read to Ellen my rendition of "You're Still The One." She cried and I teared up a bit too. I always do when she does, but these were good tears, tears of appreciation, tears of love, and tears of joy. With 153 years between us, (as of now we have 167, oh how quickly time passes, when you double up!) we enjoy the simple life. Our 55th Anniversary was all that it could be and more, that morning, and She's Still The One, these 62 years later! Thank you Lord for yet another day.

YOU'RE STILL THE ONE!*

It was 58 years ago that I met you,
Never dreamed then I'd get you.
But we we're still havin' fun,
'Cause you're still the One.

For three years thereafter, it was back and forth,
From when you left Long Island, way up north.
But we we're still havin' fun,
'Cause you're still the One.

We married on June 4, of Fifty Four,
Neither ever knowing, there'd be so much more.
We we're still havin' fun,
'Cause you're still the One.

Three years rolled by, just you and me,
Then came the children, like 1,2,3.
Yet we're still havin' fun,
'Cause you're still the One.

In all these years we've had good times and hard times,
Most sweet as honey, a few like lemons or limes.
But we're still havin' fun,
'Cause you're still the One.

Looking back, our love has deepened and grown, thru' the years,
Strong in the many days of joy, even in the heartbreak tears.
Yes, we're still havin' fun,
Cause you're still the One.

Whatever lies ahead, we shall not fear,
Our bond of love is everlasting, unique and dear.
Whether we be here or there, we're still havin' fun,
'Cause forever, you're always still the One.

*With credit to Orleans hit song (You're Still The One)

138

I HOPE YOU'VE HAD THE TIME OF YOUR LIFE

Some folks will probably think Ellen and I are peculiar, some things we like are weird. Some of the things we enjoy don't seem to fit what we profess and believe about life, about God and His plan for us and for everyone.

But from one of the most difficult days of our life, we found that in all times, and especially in the hard times, we need to laugh, we need to have a sense of humor, laugh at ourselves, and our plight at the times, laugh with, but not at others. It was during that time after we lost our son Jay that Ellen and I both were at the bottom of the pit. (But, as I've told so many times elsewhere, more times than some would like to hear, while losing our son was the most difficult time of our life to date, a time we wouldn't wish on anyone, and an event that I would even today give everything I "possess" or have "possessed" in this life, to give Jay another chance, that is not an option- BUT from that life- changing event, God has entrusted to us so many wonderful gifts- gifts that we try to share with others).

For months I managed my days by going to work, sometimes sitting in my car in tears before going in, and dealing with other people's problems. It was not only a distraction, it was healing, because we all are given crosses to bear, but each our own, each different kinds, different sizes, different times, and for different reasons. But in those times of "Cross Bearing" we need to follow the Master's words "Take up YOUR Cross and follow ME." So that's what we've tried to do.

In Ellen's case she was at home alone with her pain, our children were grown, just out of the nest, married and lived away, so there were frequent times of loneliness and depression for Ellen, even though she and I talked by phone several times a day, and I always came home for lunch, and dinner, that we be together.

Ellen was ironing and watching TV one day, and one of the Peter Seller's, "Inspector Clouseau" movies came on. She suddenly discovered she could laugh and it felt really good. Good endorphins flowed. Good endorphins can come from laughter, and sometimes, yes, even from tears

She told me about her day, and I said we both loved to laugh with those movies, so we ordered the entire series on VHS. We also got laughs from the ridiculous humor and satire of Mel Brooks, so we invested in Young Frankenstein, High Anxiety, and several of his other movies. Ellen got out one of the movies most days, and when she felt the "gray cloud" coming in, she'd pull out one of the Movies. We watched them, over and over, often in the evening. So much so, that even today, we can exchange dialogue from both actor's movies and have a "light moment."

So ok, we like weird stuff- but only for the fun in it. And after all Scripture also tells us "To everything there is a season, a time for every purpose under heaven, a time to weep, and a time to laugh, a time to embrace, and a time to refrain from embracing; a time to keep, and a time to throw away; a time to be silent, and a time to speak. (Ecclesiastes 3:1-8). We try to pay attention to the RIGHT time for things.

We don't take the comedy as life serious. But even the comedy sometimes has a good important message.
Another series, more recently, that somehow, by chance, we became interested in is the nine year series of "Seinfeld." Our family doesn't understand why we enjoy it or the comedy so much. I'm not sure I understand. Nor am I especially an admirer of Jerry Seinfeld, personally, nor certainly any of the characters in that TV comedy, or even some of the subjects the episodes covered. However, Ellen and I do find a certain humor in the ridiculousness of the vanity and selfishness of all of the characters, each as persons whom we'd most like not to be like. Heaven forbid!

So much are we fans that we have purchased not once, but twice, the entire nine year series of the Show, having worn out the first set. Once again we can exchange with each other a quip of the dialogue to the other- and each have a chuckle during the day. I know it must irritate sometimes our friends and family, when we share an "Inside" quip. We consciously try not to do that, but we do have an occasional slip. So we find this comedy often as our time to laugh together.

All of which gets me to what follows. There is a song, parts of which are played on several episodes of Seinfeld (especially the very last episode.). A man, and a guitar. It's hard to catch the lyrics for old folks with less than good hearing, but for years, I didn't know what the song was, the tune was catchy, maybe from repetition, the one thing that I could usually hear was "It's something unpredictable, but if in the end it's right. I hope you've had the time of your life." I liked that.

In a different way, it kind of sum up what I think many of us hope life may be- always unpredictable, but in the end its right- and our hope is that we and those we know and love "might have had the time of their life." Good times, joyous times- even though with it also come the hard times, but if in the end it's right- and if we get our life ship on the right course and stay with it hopefully we'll "have the time of our life." God has blessed me in so many ways, and so many gifts, at so many times, but the one I have treasured most is my dear wife, Ellen, all of my children and their families, and the friends He has placed in my life, the opportunities He has given to me, with regrets only for those to do some good I have missed or pulled away from. Even though I too often let opportunities to do some good slip through my fingers, and even though I fail Him miserably sometimes, I know that by His Grace, there is forgiveness.

Not until very recently did I think about, wonder about what that song was and who it was. All I had to do was go to the master mystic "Google" and found it. The song is "I Hope You've Had The Time of Your Life" and the artist (some would question the appellation and the artistry) is Green Day. I had heard of Green Day, my grandchildren sometimes spoke about Green Day, but never knew who they were, or what they played. I simply knew the repeating lyric lines of the chorus. Now knowing the song and some of the song's lyrics I've found on Google, are not necessarily some I would treasure, but I did find the chorus of the song interesting and maybe it had a message there.

So borrowing from the title of the song and even the tune, rhythm, and parts of the written verses, I have written what follows for Ellen in honor of our 58th anniversary. God willing, I sang it to her, as I have written it for her, and will read and sing it to her, early in the morn of Our Day, if not our green day.

But I give credit to Green Day, who have been most successful, having sold combined, more than 60 million records. I hope that they have been blessed by their success, and use the success and the blessings wisely and share it bountifully, in their own time. And, I hope that Ellen will like it, and that God will be understanding, of my human frailty and imperfection.

I HOPE YOU'VE HAD THE TIME OF YOUR LIFE*

We've reached another turning point, a fork stuck in the road,
Time grabs you by the wrist, and directs you where to go.
Recall the memories, photographs of the times of joy and pain,
With all the bumps and strain we've had, I'd do it all again.
It's something unpredictable, but in the end it's right,
I hope you've had the time of your life.

Yes all the many things we've done, in rainstorms and the sun,
With all the laughs and love we've shared, I deem it all as fun.
Yet once a special time passed by, I don't look back and sigh,
We treasure all the times, and never wonder why?
It's something unpredictable, but in the end it's right,
I hope you've had the time of your life.

So what 'er tomorrow holds, It's mysteries to reveal,
I hope you've felt as I have felt, our love each day's more real.
We don't know what lies ahead, we embrace every day,
But learned to take each rising sun, as God's gift sent our way.
It's something unpredictable, but in the end it's right,
I hope you've had the time of your life.

And when our days are done, the passing from this life,
I trust that God shall grant, that you'll still then be my wife.
We'll be with ones we've known before, at peace, no pain, and grim
A place where love and light will rule, until the end of time.

IT'S SOMETHING UNPREDICATABLE, BUT IN THE END IT'S RIGHT,
I KNOW IN OUR HEAVENLY HOME, WE'LL HAVE THE TIME OF OUR LIVES.
IT'S SOMETHING UNPREDICTABLE, BUT IN THE END IT'S RIGHT,
I KNOW IN GOD'S NEW HOME, WE'LL HAVE THE TIMEs OF OUR NEW LIVES.

*With credit to Green Day.

DRIFT AWAY*
(ANNIVERSARY 59)

Day after Day I'm old and used,
I see Your light through the mist and rain.
My attitude, is what I choose,
Even this ole age pain,
That's like a chain.
*Oh, Give me Your hand, Love, and hold me tight
I want to get lost in Your Love tonight- and Drift Away!

Beginning to think- how I'm a losing time,
I've had my laughs, when I'm amused.
How I need you- I need to remind,
I'm counting on you- to carry me through
**Give me your hand, Love, and hold me tight,
I want to get lost in Your Love tonight- and Drift Away!

And when my mind is free,
I know Your Love can move me.
And when I'm feeling blue,
It's Your Love that always soothes me.
Thanks for the Joy, You've given me.
***Oh, give me Your Hand and hold me tight,
I want to get lost in your love tonight and- Drift Away.

I want you to know- I believe in You,
I want get lost in Your Love tonight- and Drift Away!
Your Rhythm of Life and harmony,
Oh Take me, Take me- Take me-Drift Away
You help me along, Makin' me strong.
*So give me your hand, Love, and hold me tight
I want to get lost in your love tonight-and Drift Away!

*With credit to Mentor Williams and Dobie Gray, *Once **Twice, ***Thrice

I LOVE YOU JUST THE WAY YOU ARE*
(ANNIVERSARY 60)

What began, as your personal pleasantness and my attraction to your outer beauty,
You were from the start, exciting, friendly, easy to talk to, sometimes insecure, never snooty.
A here I was, nineteen, immature, small in stature, just a student and former sports star,
You accepted me, and I you, don't change a thing I WANTED YOU JUST THE WAY YOU ARE.

And as time went by, we came to know each other as friends, sweethearts, and soul mates,
You waited patiently, while I deferred my commitment, like a skating kid on roller skates.
Yet I knew inside, you were my one and only, you were truly my lucky star,
Even then, don't change a thing, I LOVE YOU JUST THE WAY YOU ARE.

Then came our blessed day, we committed to each other for life, for better or for worse,
Each knowing little about, but sharing a wonderful life together, now treasured, each chapter and verse.
Our lives through sickness and in health, thick and thin, bonded together with an endless love's reservoir,
I love you then, through all the years, I LOVED YOU JUST THE WAY YOU ARE.

You've been my partner, my teammate, my lover and my muse,
Always put me first, none of my many changing life needs, did you ever refuse.
Through all times together and apart, you've been my faithful one, from near and far,
In all that time, I wouldn't change a thing, I LOVED YOU JUST THE WAY YOU ARE.

You've always been my confidant, my lover and my life's soul friend to keep,
Our love today, a smile a glance, a word, a shared laugh, a touch a hand held, each soul deep.
You've always been and shall be, my bright and shining morning and evening star,
You surely know after all this time, don't change a thing, I LOVE YOU JUST THE WAY YOU ARE.

And now in the twilight, we treasure each day together a gift, our time together here, not unending,
But whatever comes, and when our life and memories will give us needed strength unbending.
And when the day comes in this life when you and I must say for a while, au revoir,
I'LL LOVE YOU THEN, JUST AS NOW, I'LL LOVE YOU JUST THE WAY YOU ARE.

*To my Anna, with credit to Billy Joel, "Just the Way you Are"

WITH SIXTY ONE YEARS OF LOVE SHARED

On the day we were married, we never thought we'd make it to sixty one,
That many years together was way beyond our vision of things to come.
But here we are today, and we're still having fun,
We've seen life is a learning journey, not just a short run.

We've passed through many times of both rain and sun,
So many memories shared, yet still our race of life at the moment not yet done.
May God give us the days, that we might leave nothing undone,
But we've loved, wept, laughed all with joy, no regrets, none.

Been blessed with three loving children, a daughter and two sons,
And six caring grandchildren, all totally different, every one.
Today we five great grands, (one pending), three little girls and two little sons,
Each beginning life's journey, exciting times ahead, nothing to shun.

There is nothing either of us could have separately achieved or won,
That could compare to our full life lived together, nothing left undone.
I could never have asked for the blessings, you've given my life here, under the sun,
Because we've had an incomparable life together, each with the other, our only one.

TIME AFTER TIME
(UPDATED FOR 62 YEARS LATER)*

What good are words, I say or write to you?
They can't convey to you what's in my heart.
If you could hear, rather and instead,
All the many things I've left unsaid.

―――――――――――――

Time after time,
You've heard me say that I'm So Lucky To have been, loving you.
So lucky I've been,
Your love has had no end,
Every day, the whole years through.

**I've only known, what I've known,
These passing years have shown,
You've kept our love so young, so new-
And time after time
You've heard me say that I'm So Lucky To have been loving you.

*(With due credit to Jimmy Styne and Sammy Cahn, for their popular song "Time After Time," (1947)), beautifully sung by Frank Sinatra and others. Sung to Ellen on the morning of June 4, 2016

**Repeat.

TILL THE END OF TIME (2017-OUR SONG FROM HERE TO BEYOND THE BLUE)

NOTE. Ellen and I have just celebrated our 62nd anniversary. We long ago learned from health and from life that every day we have, especially together, and even when one of us has left for beyond, we are truly blessed with each day that we have. Not in our wildest dreams in earlier years did we even consider we would have this much time together. So as I write these words, not in anticipation of but in the event either of us might "graduate" before our next anniversary—I want this one song to be "on record" for her.

The song is a "goldie oldie," as have all of the songs we've "re-done" since our 55th. Mostly Oldies that both of us knew in our younger years and even listened to in our three years she waited patiently for me to pop the question. She didn't know then but later I told her that being old fashioned, I didn't think I deserved to marry her until I know what I would do with my life, and how I would hope to support her and our family to be.

The song "Till the End of Time," was written in 1945, by Buddy Kaye, lyrics, and composer Ted Mossman, who designed but did not originate the music. In fact, the melody music was an adaptation by Mossman of Frederic Chopin's Polonaise in A flat major, opus 53. It was then called the "Polonaise Heroic." It was and is a beautiful haunting melody, written in 1842. Interestingly, it was written a time of revolt in what is now Poland , and was said to have been written about overbearing Czarist leaders—which Americans could identify with the Nazi leaders in Germany.

"Till The End of Time" was sung for the first time, early in 1945 before the War ended the following August. I recall when it came out and heard it on the radio then. By that time I was 12 years old and took a shower each evening and sang popular songs I knew. Back then I could hear the lyrics and tune once and know them. Today, I can't memorize or remember worth-- well you know. At 84 I am a bit older and by now have my brain storage cells filled with 84 years of life. It's all there I just can't bring it up my brain's computer.

It was first recorded by and became the theme song of a young Perry Como. Other recordings the same year were by Doris Day, Dick Haymes, and Ginny Sims, all of whom I recall. It was an extremely popular song, high up on the Hit Parade, during the year.

Hollywood, not to be outdone, made a movie about Frederic Chopin, early in 1945, titled appropriately, "A Song to Remember." While historically the movie is not completely accurate, it portrays Chopin as a Polish Patriot in freeing Poland from the Czars. Under his renewed patriotism he writes and performs his greatest works including the patriotic "Polonaise," at continuous concerts to raise money throughout Europe for Poland's freedom cause. The movie ends sadly with Chopin a young 36 by giving his life's toil and labor to raising the money for the patriotic cause, and dying of Tuberculosis. Back then we could connect that with the many servicemen who gave their life and limbs for the cause of freedom.

As WWII was still raging in Europe (until the Nazi surrender in May 1945 and in the Pacific (until August 1945), it was very popular with American audiences, American actor Cornell Wilde was nominated for Best Actor and seven other film and musical awards. I recall hearing it often played on the radio and pianists playing the "Polonaise". A member of my class in both Junior and Senior High School Scott Hough, who was a piano prodigy, played the Polonaise frequently at various functions to the delight of students and adults alike.

I could not play the piano, but loved to sing "A Song To Remember," and if the Lord be willing, I shall sing and present to Ellen at our next anniversary, with new lyrics and a new title "A Life To Remember." But knowing that for certain is beyond my pay raise. I'm very blessed to take each day one at a time.

A LIFETIME TO BE REMEMBERED*

Till the end of time,
Beyond the time of our lives are through,
When There's Heaven there, Beyond the Blue,
I'll go on loving you.

Till the End of time,
Beyond when darkness disappears,
I'll be there for you to care for you,
'Til eternity appears.

So take my soul in sweet surrender,
And tenderly say that I'm,
The one you've loved and lived for
Till the end of time.

*With credit to Buddy Kaye and Ted Mossman.

SECTION VI. SEARCHING FOR TRUTHS AND TREASURES IN PROSE
AND VERSE FROM THE PAGES OF THE HOLY BIBLE "THE WORD."

NOTE: The separate items in this Section will have the related Scripture references at the top of the page in the heading, followed by an explanation in poetic verse- amplifying what the Scripture says. In some cases, though not all, there are prose study comments.

So this Section is then, a "Light Study Session," of selected Scripture passages which we found of interest and with special meaning. It is not a comprehensive study of the Bible or any Book of the Bible, but we hope arouse your interest in help in understanding these selected passages from Scripture.

We hope also, that taking selected Scriptures for study, it might encourage your read to continue a further Study of THE WORD, in its unending teachings and lessons in this life, the past, present and beyond this life. The items listed in what follows are in some chronological order beginning with verses from Genesis and ending with a passage from The Revelation.

The first item is designated "In the Beginning," is from Genesis. And what follows is first from the Old Testament to and through the New Testament. Our hope is that you might find this meaningful, and maybe arouse your interest to look further into THE WORD. And, of course, you may want to first refer to the related Scripture, reading them as they appear with each unit or selectively.

IN THE BEGINNING - PREFACE
(Genesis1:1, 26-27; 3:1-5; Luke 15:17-20, 22-24)

"In the beginning God created". Think about it. In the beginning of everything, even beyond what we can imagine, God was there. And then consider, everything that has been, is now, and will be in the future, for all time, is at the very least spawned by God's creations, if not directly created by God. God created life, God created the universe, the galaxies, the earth, and even the smallest plant and animal life on earth.

And to think, that not only did He create everything, but that He created it all, in balance, in context with everything else, so that the earth rotates on a precise axis to the sun, so that the temperature of the earth, in context to the sun, is maintained, so that life will continue, that the power of the revolution of the earth (gravity) keeps our feet on the ground, that the human body is made of thousands of different parts, which work in harmony to enable us to exist and perform as we do.

(I realize the preceding sentence is a mouthful- hard to fully grasp.) Oh, how wonderfully complex we and are, and the wonderful world we live in IS!

We could go on for hours about the miraculous marvels that exist in concert, orchestrated by "The Great Supreme Life Orchestra Conductor" that the symphony, enabling the cycle of life, to continue. It is enough to blow our minds just to try to conceive of a God so powerful, a God so omnipresent, a God so omnipotent, a God of time and eternity, a God so caring, to create all that Is. And then to consider that the God who created- Was "Here" or "There" even before time and infinity began, IS "Here" now, and Will Be "Here", for all time and Infinity to come, unchanging. HE WAS, HE IS, AND HE WILL ALWAYS BE.   "

By contrast, then, when we consider how small, and seemingly insignificant we are, in the whole scheme of things, that alone is enough to send one into a permanent state of depression. That is, until, we consider the care that he has for each of us. He knew each of us, even before we were born, knew that each of the billions of people He has created, each wholly unique. He knows our every thought and movement. He knows every hair on our head. (Read Psalm 139). And, even in spite of, and not because of, what He knows about each of us, He loves us, with agape love, beyond what any human is capable of, and forgives us, of our daily failings.

He loved us enough to send His Son to live with us, and to die for us. (John 3:16-17). I reckon that only those who have given up a child of their own to death, can even begin to understand the magnitude of giving away, freely, the life of One's Child. And, even though He knows every thought we have, everything we do and say ever step we take, He doesn't give up on us. (Psalm 139). And, even if we lie down with dogs and get fleas, or lie down with pigs and have the odor of the sty, He doesn't give up on us, and He takes us back, warts and all, with open arms. (The Prodigal Son, Luke 15:11-32).

These then are the things I think about when I read, or hear, the words, "In the beginning- God- Created". It gives me a great deal of inner peace and security, about yesterday, about today, and about whatever may come tomorrow, and beyond. I hope that it will also give you a peace about your life, and your future, too.

IN THE BEGINNING
(Genesis 1:1,26-27; 3:1-5, 24; Luke 15:17-20,22-24)

In the very beginning of existence, when there was but a void, God was there,
He created everything that is, or has been, from galaxies to flowers, so fair.
For He is the Alpha and Omega, He was and is the ultimate, beginning and the end,
He created it all, the light, the darkness, the water, the air, and life itself, He did send.

To Him, but an Artist's brush stroke, whether in an instant, six days, or six million years,
God created, brought into being all that was, is now, and all that will in the future appear.
And He created us in His image, gave us a mind to choose, both woman and man,
A wondrous complex being are we, for a lifetime, a time to Him, but a grain of sand.

Then God entrusted to us dominion over his world, every corner upon which man stood,
He said "You will have control over all of my garden, for what I have created is good."
But as the first Adam, in Eden, we have departed from His direction, in many ways,
In caring for His world, self-serving, and hurting others, by what we do and say.

So God sent down His only Son, who walked and lived among, us as God and Man,
To teach us anew, to help us understand, how we are to live, according to His Plan.
The message, that though we may bear the legacy, the burden of the first Adam's sin,
He would still love us, guide us, overcome our failures, and help us to follow Him.

He, the Creator of it all, abides with each of us, from our first life's breath, until our last,
The God of the second chance, always takes us back, though we have our wild seeds cast.
He, who never changes, hears our every prayer, and gives us freely, His eternal Grace,
He will never turn His back on us, and awaits our return, to meet Him face to Face.

THY WORD, A LIGHT UNTO MY PATH
(Psalm 119:105, John 1:1-5, 14)

Thy Word, is a light in the darkness, a lamp unto my feet,
A light unto my path, when each stumbling block of life, I meet.
Thy Word, is my direction, my compass, and my guide,
Thy Word, assures me, that in all times, You are at my side.

In the Beginning, as time began, thy Word was there,
It was with God, was of God, with whom nothing could compare.
Through Him, I AM, Thy Word was spoken, All things were created and made,
And, in Him, by the Light of Thy Word, a life was in each being, inlaid.

In Thy Word, He gave to the world His Light,
Ever present, in a world of darkness, pointing to the right.
Thy Word was, Thy Word is, Thy Word ever shall be,
Our guide, the source of truth and life, for all eternity.

Thy Word, in time became flesh in Christ, who lived as and among man,
To show us the path of truth and the way, across history's eons span.
We, then, through Thy Word, written and lived, in the One's life story,
Resplendent with love and grace, we can perceive Him in all his glory.

Thy Word, Thy Life, from the Beginning, a Light unto my path,
That shows me the road I must travel, to shun Evil's wrath.
Thy Word, Thy Way, is my passage, a Lamp unto my feet,
That I may pass thru my life's dark valleys, barriers, and snares, until I, my Maker meet.

THE BLESSING
(Genesis 25:19-34, 27:27-41)

Four thousand years ago, there was a man named Esau,
The son of Isaac, Esau, a burly man, who had something in his craw.
Fort his youngest brother Jacob, whom his Mom always loved the best,
Had tricked his Dad, Isaac, took Esau's inheritance and bequest.

Not only that but Jacob also tricked his blind Father, and got Esau's Blessing.
He put on his brother's clothes, cooked Dad a meal, never his deceit confessing,
Yet what hurt Esau the most, was not the loss of the land of his inheritance,
But that his Father would not bless him or affirm him, under any circumstance.

The pain of his Father's rejection, followed Esau all of his life.
He lived as a man of anger, his mind and heart filled with strife.
Until one day years later perchance would Esau and Jacob meet,
Jacob was contrite, sorrowed by what he'd done, fell at Esau's feet.

Only then did Esau's life of pain and rejection begin to heal,
His Father's blessing and approval withheld, the love he needed to feel.
If only Esau's Father, would have given him the affirmation he refused to say,
To tell his son Esau he loved him, his life had great value, and said "You're OK!"

May we then learn lessons from this ancient story of long ago,
There is one thing each child, yes, each person needs to know.
That we are God's unique creation, like no other, special to Him,
We need to be affirmed by someone's cup of love, is filled for us, is filled to the brim.

Our need for approbation begins with an inner need to please our parents,
And for parents to withhold that affirmation, plants bitter seeds to ferment.
But our need to have another's Blessing, extends far beyond our home,
For we need that assurance of family, workers, and friends to know, we're not alone.

Each of us then has a lifelong need, from the date of our birth,
To know that we among all others, are a creature of worth.
We need to affirm those around us, that they may know,
That they too, are unique and special, our blessing on them, we bestow.

A priceless gem that we each own, and may give or receive,
Is the unconditional blessing telling another that in him we believe.
And out of our Blessings, surely great things will flow,
For the Blessing gives life meaning, assurance, it is the leaven for the dough.

PROVERBS WISDOM FOR LIVING, DAY BY DAY*
(Just a Taste from Proverbs 27, Selected Verses)

Do not boast about tomorrow, for you do not know what a day may bring forth
Let another praise you and not your own mouth; a stranger and not your own lips.
(Proverbs 27:1-2)

Wrath is fierce, and anger is a flood, but who can stand before jealousy?
Better is open rebuke, than love that is concealed…
Faithful are the wounds of a friend; but deceitful are the kisses of the enemy
(Proverbs 27: 4-6)

Oil and perfume make the heart glad, so a man's counsel is sweet to his friend.
Better is a neighbor who is near than a brother far away.
(Proverbs 27: 9-10)

A constant dripping on a day of steady rain, and a contentious woman are alike; he who would restrain her
restrains the wind, and grasps oil with his right hand…

Iron sharpens iron, so a man sharpens another.

He who tends to his own fig tree will eat its fruit, and he who cares his master will be honored.

As in water face reflects face, so the heart of man reflects the man.
(Proverbs 27: 15- 19)

The crucible is for silver and the furnace for the gold, and a man is tested by the praise accorded him . . .

Though you pound a fool in a mortar with a pestle, along with crushed grain, yet his folly will not depart from him
(Proverbs 27:21-22)

Know well the condition of your flocks, and pay attention to your herds; for riches are not forever; nor does a
crown endure all generations.
(Proverbs 27: 23-24)

*Giving you just a little taste to whet your appetite.

WISDOM FOR LIVING, DAY BY DAY
(Reference the Scriptures of the preceding page)

From the mouth and the pen, of an ancient king, a wise old man,
Come timeless words of wisdom, that will, the eternal test of time stand.
For He tells us n relevant and practical terms, the way we should live,
To use daily, the mind, the heart, and the senses, that God did to each of us give.

He says, do not boast about what you will tomorrow, or next year do,
For we don't know what the rest of the day holds, until it is through
And do not praise ourselves, for the mighty things we think we have done,
But let the acclamations of your accomplishments, come from another one.

Wrath, anger and jealousy, he counsels, will overcome us like a flood,
For these emotions will bring us to evil, may even lead to shedding of blood.
And, it is better to display, by what we do, and to tell others of our love
By withholding, our most precious gift is wasted, no matter how well thought of.

And even the gentle, truthful, yet painful words of a friend, are to be revered,
Much better than the pretentious kisses, of the pseudo friend, who is insincere.
For sweet as honey, is the wise and gentle counsel of a genuine friend,
A friend who is near, is better than a faraway brother, who does his good wishes send.

A contentious spouse, is like the steady dripping of raindrops on a rainy day,
Better is the spouse, who like apples of gold, speaks a chosen word, knowing what to say.
He who tends his fruit trees will enjoy the fruit, he who honors his boss will be rewarded.
But he who cheats and dishonors his master, will, in time, be entirely discarded.

Know the condition and extent of your colleagues, your flocks, and of your goods,
Or any one or all may be lost, even before you know it, as you should,
For your wealth is not forever, fleeting as a wild bird, must be cared for like a friend,
It can be quickly lost, though slowly won, leaving you with nothing, in the end.

The crucible molds the silver, just as the furnace tests the gold,
Just as man's mettle is tested in times of success, will his principles fold?
And some who are foolish, you can pound to grain, as with a pestle in a mortar,
It doesn't change his chemical elements, his folly, which will give no quarter.

And, just as a pool of clear water, reflects the image of our body, our outer face,
So too, our inner heart reflects the depth of our love of our neighbor, the human race.
And, just as iron strengthens iron, and three strands of hemp, strengthens a rope,
So too, men bound together in a common purpose, strengthen their common hope.

So much more wisdom, in the pages of Proverbs, from one, who did it all, in ages past,
So read it daily and carefully, learn from his experience, a knowledge that will last.
Yet even he, the sagest of us all, concluded, that all is vanity, when all is said and done,
That young and old alike, are dependent upon, and must, one day, for our life lived, stand before the Holy One.

NOTE: THE FOLLOWING THREE ITEMS ARE FROM SCRIPTURE, FROM THE SHAKER HYMN SIMPLE GIFTS, AND FROM MUSIC THE "SHAKER" HYMN WRITTEN BY ELDER JOSEPH BRACKET BRACKETT, AND THE CONTEMPORARY CHRISTIAN SONG UNDER THE TITLE "THE LORD OF THE DANCE" WRITTEN IN 1963 BY AN IRISHMAN NAMED SYDNEY CARTER WHO DREW THE MUSIC FROM ELDER BRACKETTS SHAKER HYMN, AND THE VERSES FOLLOWING BY THE AUTHOR RFEFER TO KING DAVID'S DANCE HIS RETURN TO JERASULEM, UPON RECOVERY OF THE ARK OF THE COVENANT.

(See further information on the music of the Lord of the Dance in the Preface of this book as relates to1944 Musical Appalachian Spring)

(The three items are tied together by substance and title under the heading of "The Lord of the Dance')

THE LORD OF THE DANCE

"David again brought together out of Israel chosen men, thirty thousand in all. He and all his men set out for Baalam of Judah to bring up from there the Ark of God, which is called by the Name, the Name of the Lord, who is enthroned between the cherubim that are on the Ark… David and the whole house of Israel were celebrating with all of their might before the Lord, with songs, and with harps, lyres, tambourines, sistrums, and cymbals. And David was dancing before the Lord with all his might, and David was wearing a linen ephod. So David and all of the house of Israel were bringing up the Ark of the Lord, with shouting and the sound of the trumpet… Michael the daughter of Saul looked out the window and saw King David leaping and dancing before the Lord, and she despised him in her heart." (2nd Samuel 6:2, 4-5, 13-16.)

THE LORD OF THE DANCE
(First Published 2002 By the Author)
(2nd Samuel 6:2, 4-5, 13-16; Psalm 30:11-12; Ecclesiastes 3:4.)

The Word tells us that life's times can have jubilation, and a time to dance,
Though the dance may, at first, feel awkward, we need to give it a chance.
For if we don't ever go to His dance floor, we may never come to know,
That our dance of life, danced to a NEW song, will make our heart glow.

The type of music to which we dance in life, is our choice,
Whether our song and dance in life is somber, or one with jubilant voice.
We can choose a dance of anger, a dance of resentment, or one of sorrow,
Or, we can choose a dance of rejoicing, with gusto, as if there is no tomorrow.

So, dance with abandon, and dance through life with joy,
That your dance of life, will inspire others, this dance, to employ.
That they may see, your mirthful steps, as you dance through life,
While the music of the dance, is played, with earth's strings and fife.

Choose as your partner in life's dance, HIS HOLY SPIRIT in you, exuberance in living.
Let your loving spirit and body glow, with the joy of HIS, and your giving.
Dance, then, with the ONE, from who, the very breath of all life, gives,
That others may know, and see in you, that HE, in your heart lives.

Dance through your life, with ecstatic and childlike glee,
Let the LORD OF THE DANCE, live in your life, and HE shall set you free.
Seeing your joy, will bring in others too, to dance HIS dance, upon life's stage,
That the music of the LORD OF THE DANCE, may continue, to the end of the Age.

SIMPLE GIFTS
*Music and Lyrics by Elder Joseph Brackett (1848)

"Tis a gift to be simple, tis a gift to be free,
Tis a gift to come down there where we ought to be.
And when we find ourselves in a place just right,
T'will be in the valley of love and delight.
When true simplicity is gained,
To bow and to bend we shan't be ashamed
Till by turning turning we come 'round right.

LORD OF THE DANCE

Music Tune By Elder Joseph Brackett and Lyrics By Sydney Carter (1963)

I danced in the morning when the world was begun,
I danced in the Moon and the Stars and the Sun.
I came down from heaven and I danced on earth
At Bethlehem I had my birth.

Dance, Dance wherever you may be I am the Lord of the Dance said He!
And I'll lead you all, wherever you may be, And I'll lead you all in the Dance said He!

I danced for the scribe and the Pharisee,
But they would not dance and would not follow me.
I danced for the fishermen, for James and John,
They came with me and the Dance went on.

Chorus

I danced on the Sabbath and I cured the lame,
The holy people said it was a shame!
They whipped and they stripped and they hung me high
And they left me there on a cross to die!

Chorus

I danced on a Friday when the sky turned black,
It's hard to dance with the devil on your back.
They buried my body and they thought I'd gone,
But I am the Dance and I still go on!

Chorus

They cut me down and I leapt up high.
I am the Life that'll never never die!
I'll live in you if you'll live in me
For I am the Lord of the Dance says He!

Dance, Dance wherever you may be I am the Lord of the Dance said He!
And I'll lead you all wherever you may be, For I AM the Lord of the Dance said He!

WHERE YOU LEAD I WILL FOLLOW
(Ruth and Naomi)
(Ruth 1:1-17)

It is an axiom of life that for some is difficult to swallow,
That there are those who will lead and those who will follow.
Yet even the one who leads well, must have had a mentor to follow, to light his way,
One that shows him the right roads to take, the lighted paths along "The Way."*

Leadership comes in many forms, sometimes a mere presence, sometimes of command.
Yet respect and willingness to follow another, must be earned, doesn't come on demand.
For some, leadership qualities are quiet and by example, yet readily visible.
For others, it's actively taking charge, either way, for those who follow, it is indivisible.

So, it was long ago, in the land of Moab, lying just north of the Dead Sea,
That there are important lessons of leadership, love and loyalty, for us to see.
It was there a woman named Ruth, who spoke to her deceased husband's mother,
Who had a loyalty, respect and a love for this Naomi, like no other.

And Ruth said "Where you go, I will go. Where you lead, I will follow.
You are my guiding light, and without you, I am incomplete and hollow.
Where you lodge, I will lodge. Where you die, there also will I die.
You shall be my beacon star, it is you that I shall stand by."

"And may the Lord keep us together, 'til death do us part.
Your people shall be my people. Your God, my God, with all of my heart."
Would that each of us have such a loyalty as Ruth to our family and our friends,
That they might know they could depend on us from the beginning to the very end.

In Naomi, we see a mentor, quiet leadership, unconditional love, and unfailing loyalty,
In Ruth, unconditional love, unwavering commitment, a role model for you and me.
This kind of life too seldom seen, to be emulated, finding the one to attach our star-
A spouse, a friend, a parent, but choosing carefully, who we follow to places afar.

Who then is your mentor, the one you will follow, the Leader in your life,
The one upon whom you can depend, and follow in times of joy, trial and strife.
Choose ye this day, a FRIEND, who will be the ONE you will follow and observe,
And may the King of Kings, as with Ruth, be the ONE leader that you will faithfully serve.

*In the early days of the Church, Christianity was called "The Way."

A PSALM OF PEACE
(Psalm 23)

Oh God, my Father in Heaven, you are my ever present mentor and guide,
You provide all of my needs, and You are constantly at my side.

When I am frazzled and confused, you calm my heart, like soft flowing waters,
You restore my mind from my fears that come in the night, my most dreaded marauders.

You show me, the ideals and the paths I should follow to do the right thing,
You relieve and refresh my body and my soul, as would a warm mineral springs.

And even in the dark valleys of shadows of my life, when pain, danger and death seem so near,
I know that You are with me, my Guide and my Sustainer, there is nothing that I need fear.

I need not be anxious about anything, from my circumstances, or harm from others,
For You are always with me, will always be my Friend, closer than a brother.

Your wisdom and strength, will, from all outside forces be, my rod of protection,
My Inner Peace, my Saving Staff, when I've fallen in the pit, or lost my direction.

You provide for all of my needs, even when my demons are nearest me,
You anoint me with the knowledge of Your promise that I am with You for eternity.

My appreciation of Your Love for even me, overflows, is beyond what I can express,
For I know that even in my life's failures, you have provided for my redress.

In all of these wonderful things, Your Mercy shall be with me all of my days,
I shall dwell with You, and You, be in my Soul, forever, as I seek to follow Your ways.

LEARNING TO WAIT UPON THE LORD

I waited patiently for the Lord
He turned to me and heard my cry. He lifted me out of the slimy pit, Out of the mud and mire.
He set my feet upon a rock,
He gave me a firm place to stand. He put a new song in my heart, A Hymn of praise to our God.
Many will come to see and fear, And put their trust in the Lord.
(Psalm 40:1-3)

LEARNING TO WAIT UPON THE LORD

It's taken me the better part of my lifetime to learn,
To indelibly upon my heart, my mind and soul, this lesson to burn.

That our God hears and knows my every action, word, thought and prayer.
Even before my cry, he knows my need, takes me from my despair.

Yet slowly I've learned these many years, as upon His answer I wait,
That I must be still, be patient, even though now, I'm in an anxious state.

For He controls all life, the planets and stars, are under His command,
And He is the Rock of my life, on Him alone, I can confidently take my stand.

With the assurance that He has a life course set for me, my daily path to chart,
With this knowledge, I can be at rest, with the new song He gives, in my heart.

It is a song of praise and thanks, that dwells deep within me, to sing,
"Be still my soul, listen and wait upon the Lord, for he guides my life in everything."

May others come see and hear in my life, or that of others, this new song,
That we each can have the Peace only He gives, which will sustain us all the day long.

IN HIS OWN TIME
(Psalm 73)
(Some Answers to the Why Questions of Life)

As I look around and see what is going down,
I hear the cries for justice, and I don't like the sound.
From the top on down the dishonest seem to win,
It seems like the best way to succeed is do the big Sin.

All across life's landscape, I see bad things happening to the good,
The bad guys win, the good guys lose, each of them more than they should.
The hypocrites seem to gloat over their ill-gotten gains,
While the down and out seem to suffer with their continuing pains.

With their ostentation, the wicked prosper, while the righteous are dying,
Makes those who strive to be honest, wonder if it's really worth trying.
I see their gold necklaces and chains, obnoxious actions, loud cursing voices,
They, curse, profane and defy the Father of Light, with their selfish choices.

I cry out "Why God? it isn't fair! Where, Oh God is the justice,
When the evil prevail so often, and the good fall into the abyss."
"My God, Oh God of Justice, Where are You? Why have you forsaken us?
Has this madness always prevailed? Or only in our generation been thus?"

Then I began to reflect upon what these greedy ones have lost, and have,
Their things, their instant gratification, phony friends, are their salve.
Yet they have often missed the really important things of life,
Of loving families, and trusted friends, helping others in strife.

For neither material things nor transparent faux friendships, inner peace bring.
Nor do they have the joy of loving, being loved, that make the heart sing.
For when their end comes, all their riches, left behind, will bring them no peace,
Leaving other behind to fight over their spoils of life, which will never cease.

I thought about those who've truly revered You, gave their lives and time,
Their laborers in the fields of service, whose lives will forever You enshrine.
For those who have served others will be feted, will get their reward,
Rather than those who've served only self, who live and die by the sword.

And the God of Justice, will make things right in His own time,
To Him, a century, like a grain of sand, with Justice by His measure, not mine.
And those who have prospered by trampling over the lives of others,
The Author of Life, will know all in their greedy hearts, their acts upon their brothers.

So I vowed to continue to do my best, to fight against injustice and wrong,
To do what I can to make the voice of Grace and Mercy ring strong.
To leave the time and the place, for bringing perfect justice, setting all things right,
To the God of my Salvation, who shall, in His own time, turn darkness into Light.

YOU KNOW MY EVERY THOUGHT
(Psalm 139)

You know my every action, You know my every thought.
You know me inside out, my coming and going, every battle I've ever fought.
You know everything about me, things others have not conceived, or know.
You know my loud crescendos, yet also as the faintest song my heart sings pianissimo.

You wrap Your arms around me, protect me from the winds of storm.
You lay Your Hand upon me, to give me comfort, and keep me ever warm,
The knowledge of the depth of Your Love is beyond what I can comprehend.
You follow, and are with me to the ends of the earth, however blows the wind.

If I go to the heavens, or beneath the earth, You track me down and follow me there.
And if I go to the remotest distance to hide from You, even then You still care.
You stand beside me even in the darkest night or in the brightest light of day.
You are with me in my valiant moments, even when my feet are made of clay.

I am Your creation, you formed my every part, my DNA, my every gene and cell.
You wove the tapestry of my whole being in my mother's womb, sewn so well.
I marvel at the complexity of this mind and body, so wondrously and mysteriously made.
You knew me even before I was conceived, You heard my mother's wish, as she prayed.

You held me in your hand, even before I was a child, when I was but a single cell.
You knew all that I could or would become, and even in that knowledge, yet loved me well.
You know each step I take from my infancy, throughout my life, until the day I die.
My name and life indelibly printed on Your Mind, 'til I come home, bye and bye.

How precious is the thought that You are with me all my days.
For this gift Lord, I want to follow You, and seek to do Your ways.
May I be your instrument, yet be a person who gives freely and lives in peace.
Yet, may I confront those who deny and embattle You, without surcease.

So look deep into my thoughts and heart, and know all of my defects.
And if You find greed, bitterness and anger, wash away each of their effects.
And help me to follow daily, the path that You would have me go.
That I may be Your faithful sower and seeds, of love and kindness sow.

I WILL LIFT UP MY EYES
(Psalm 121)

I will lift up my eyes and my heart to Heaven, to Him, who through eternity sees,
When I want to give thanks for blessings, or when all earthly help brings no peace in me.

For He is all powerful and knowing, He who created the stars, the Heavens and the Earth,
It is He, who is the giver and sustainer of all life, He, who is Lord of the Universe.

And though I marvel at His greatness, it is more than I can comprehend or express,
He knows me, inside and out, my deepest inner thoughts, will provide all my redress.

He is with me, insignificant as I am, night and day, even when I hide from sight,
He never sleeps, and hears my desperate cries for help, in the noonday sun, or dark of night.

God is my Protector from all that is within me or without, from life's daily blows,
He shades me from the hurt of painful words, shows me the way, when I do not know.

In His presence, nothing shall ever defeat me, or strike me low,
And He accompanies me on each day's journey, in and out, as I come and go.

He will give me the strength to do what I should, refrain from what I should not,
He will be by my side in this life, and the next, forever, whatever may be my lot.

THE NUMBER OF OUR DAYS
(Psalm 90:1-6, 10-17)

Father in Heaven, You have given birth to all living things,
Since the dawn of Universe, joyous life from your Heart rings.
From the Beginning, to this day, and then to all eternity,
It is You Who gives and sustains Life, for all to worship and see.

For You have the Will and the Power, to breath all life into being,
And, to turn it back to dust, by Your very Word Decreeing.
Time to You is endless, a thousand years is but a watch in the night,
And to You, a year is but a millisecond, a mere flash of light.

A human lifetime, for You, is like a morning's bright blade of grass,
Yet, by evening, it has faded away, its uniqueness and beauty have passed.
So while we are yet young, to us a year seems as an eternity,
Our each day passing slowly to us, but only a moment, a breath, to Thee.

The days of our life are marked by a number of heartbeats, say seventy years,
Or with good fortune, and strong bodies and minds, maybe eighty to bring cheer.*
Yet we should not pride ourselves in the number of our years, too soon to fly away,
For each day of our fragile life is as the prima donna's dance, the pirouette of ballet.

Since we know not exactly how many years, or the moments, which shall be ours,
Teach us to use each of our numbered days wisely, for Your Glory and Power.
Let us sing songs of joy and be glad in one and all of our days,
And, may we honor and praise You, each of us, in our own way.

And may we sing your praises and for joy, even in our days of travail,
Knowing that You watch over us, that Your love for us, will never fail.
Then at the end of our days, may You will look fondly on the work of our hand,
That it might be acceptable in Your sight, and meet Your every command.

*As we write this HE has already eighty and four more plus years. I am thankful for each and every day, and seek to follow HIS WAY.

YOU
(Psalm 18:1-3; Psalm 78:35; Psalm 121; Isaiah 40:28-31; Matthew 11:25-30)

YOU are my strength, when I am feeling weak,
It is in my weakness, You are the one I seek.

YOU are my help, when I am down and heavy laden,
I know that you will carry my load, for light is your burden.

YOU are the wind beneath me as I seek to stretch my life's wings,
You are the song that gives me joy, makes my heart sing.

YOU are in the darkness of my night that calms my fears and lets me rest,
That I may be renewed, and begin each day with a new zest.

YOU are in the Son/Sun, that gives me warmth, my light and my life,
That sustains me daily, through my spiritual mountains and my valleys of strife.

YOU are my heart, when mine has turned hard and cold,
YOU give me the will to overcome, make my timidity bold.

YOU are my senses, when I do not feel the pain,
YOU teach me to be sensitive to another's day of rain.

YOU are my eyes when I am not perceptive and cannot see,
Blinded by my vanity, doubts and anger, I do not perceive.

YOU are my voice, when I cannot speak the right word,
YOU form the images of love, from the depths of my soul stirred.

YOU are my ears that I may not just hear, but listen and discern,
To hear other's silence of isolation, the groans of agony, a soul, at point of no return.

YOU are my outstretched hands, when I've folded them across my chest,
Withholding my affirmation, You reach into my heart and draw out my best.

YOU are my legs and feet that I may hasten to go where I should,
And not tarry, hold back, or hide, pushing me on as only You could.

YOU are the one to whom I owe my life, am indebted for all that I am,
It is You who gives my life purpose, and maps my future diagram.

YOU are the genesis of all that I have, all that I am, and am capable of being,
YOU provide all of my wants, and all that I may be needing.

YOU are my alpha and omega, my beginning and my end,
YOU know my strengths and forgive my weaknesses, love me, lead me, and be my friend.

167

IT'S ALWAYS BETWEEN YOU AND HIM, ANYWAY

"Mark well that God doesn't miss a move you make, for He's aware of every step you take." (*Proverbs 5:21, The Message.*)

All people are sometimes unreasonable, Illogical, offensive, and self-centered,
Let it go, and forgive them, even yourself, anyway!

If you are generous or kind,
Some may accuse you of grandstanding, seeking praise or ulterior motives, Be generous and kind, anyway!

If you are successful (even with humility), by the world's terms,
You may win some new false friends and some real ones, "keepin' on, anyway!

When most of your world is swimming downstream,
And your heart of hearts tells you it's right to swim upstream. Difficult as it may be, despite derision or mockery,
Keep swimming upstream anyway!

When you fall short or down, get up, even if you fall again, just know, no matter how many times you fall,
You aren't alone, the race "ain't over 'til its over," no matter what "they say," So keep on getting up keepin' on, again anyway!

If you are honest and prudently frank,
Some will think you stupid, others take offense, Be honest and prudently frank anyway!

What you spend years building,
Something or someone could destroy it in an instant, never, ever give up! Keep on Building or Rebuilding, anyway!

If you find your life's meaning, peace, and serenity, some may be suspicious, jealous, others resentful,
Pursue your life's meaning with peace and serenity anyway!

The good you did yesterday, do today, or may do tomorrow,
Some will never say thanks, question your motives, or forget the following day. Keep on doing good, anyway!

Give each day to and in your world the best of yourself,
Knowing for some it may never be enough,
Know you'll be replenished, and keep on giving the best of yourself, anyway!

For you see, summing up, when life's journey is at its end,
It never was about or between you and them,
He doesn't miss a move you make, He's aware of every step you take,
Because it's all always been, always will be, between you and Him anyway!

WISDOM FOR LIVING, DAY BY DAY
*(Proverbs 27, Selected Verses)

Do not boast about tomorrow, for you do not know what a day may bring forth
Let another praise you and not your own mouth; a stranger and not your own lips (1, 2)*

Wrath is fierce, and anger is a flood, but who can stand before jealousy? Better is open rebuke, than love that is concealed… Faithful are the wounds of a friend; but deceitful are the kisses of the enemy (vs 4-6)*

Oil and perfume make the heart glad, so a man's counsel is sweet to his friend. Better is a neighbor who is near than a brother far away (vs 9*)

A constant dripping on a day of steady rain, and a contentious woman are alike; he who would restrain her restrains the wind, and grasps oil with his right hand… Iron sharpens iron, so a man sharpens another… He who tends to his own fig tree will eat its fruit, and he who cares for his master will be honored… As in water face reflects face, so the heart of man reflects the man (vs 15- 19)*

The crucible is for silver and the furnace for the gold, and a man is tested by the praise accorded him… Though you pound a fool in a mortar with a pestle, along with crushed grain, yet his folly will not depart from him (vs 21-22)*

Know well the condition of your flocks, and pay attention to your herds; For riches are not forever; Nor does a crown endure all generations. (vs 23-24)*

WISDOM FOR LIVING, DAY BY DAY
(Verses Written From Wisdom of Passages above from Proverbs 17)*

From the mouth and pen of an ancient King, a wise old man,
Come timeless words of wisdom, that will, the eternal test of time stand.
For He tells us in relevant and practical terms, the way that we should live,
To use daily, the mind, the heart, and the senses, that God did to each of us give.

He says, do not boast about what you will tomorrow, or next year do,
For we don't even know what the rest of the day holds, until it is through.
And do not praise ourselves, for the mighty things we think we have done,
But let any acclamations of your accomplishments, come from another one.

Wrath, anger and jealousy, he counsels, will overcome us like a flood,
For these emotions will bring us to evil, may even lead to shedding of blood.
And, it is better to display, by what we do, and to tell others of our love,
By withholding, our most precious gifts wasted, no matter how well thought of.

And even the gentle, truthful, yet painful words of a friend, are to be revered,
Much better than the pretentious kisses, of the pseudo friend, who is insincere.
For sweet as honey, is the wise and gentle counsel of a genuine friend,
A friend who is near, is better than a faraway brother, who may his good wishes send.

A contentious spouse, is like the steady dripping of raindrops on a rainy day,
Better is the spouse, who like apples of gold, speaks a chosen word, knowing what to say.
He who tends his fruit trees will enjoy the fruit, he who honors his boss will be rewarded,
But he who cheats and dishonors his master, will, in time, be entirely discarded.

Know the condition and extent of your colleagues, your flocks, and of your goods,
For any one or all may be lost, even before you know it, as you should.
For your wealth is not forever, fleeting as a wild bird, must be cared for like a friend,
It can be quickly lost, though slowly won, leaving you with nothing, in the end.

The crucible molds the silver, just as the furnace tests the gold,
Just as man's mettle is tested in times of success, will his principles fold?
And some who are foolish, you can pound to grain, as with a pestle in a mortar,
It doesn't change his chemical elements, his folly, which will give no quarter.

And, just as a pool of clear water, reflects the image of our body, our outer face,
So too, our inner heart reflects the depth of our love of our neighbor, the human race.
And, just as iron strengthens iron, and three strands of hemp, strengthens a rope,
So too, men bound together in a common purpose, strengthen their common hope.*

So much more wisdom, in the pages of Proverbs, from one, who had and lived it all, in ages past,**
So read it daily and carefully, learn from his experience, a knowledge that will last.
Yet even he, the sagest of us all, concluded, that all is vanity, when all is said and done,
That young and old alike, are dependent upon, and must, one day, for our life lived, stand before the Holy One.
*(**Ecclesiastes 11:9-14)*

WISDOM OF THE AGED ONE, FOR THE AGES (KING SOLOMON)

"Vanity of vanities," says the Preacher, "Vanity of vanities, all is vanity." … Indeed, if a man should live many years, let him rejoice in them all… Rejoice young man during your childhood, and let your heart be pleasant during the days of your young manhood. And follow the impulses of your heart and the desires of your eyes. Yet know that God will bring you to judgment for all of them. So, put away vexation from your heart, and pain from your body, because childhood and the prime of life are fleeting. Remember also your Creator in the days of your youth, before the evil days come and the years draw near when you will say "I have no delight in them."…The conclusion, when all has been said and done, is fear God and keep His commandments, for this applies to every person." *Solomon, (Ecclesiastes 1:2; Ch11-12) (selected verses)*

WISDOM OF THE AGED ONE FOR THE AGES

Our view of life, often, depends on the point from which we're looking, which portal,
When we are young, we have no fear of life or death, and feel we're immortal.
And for youth, with all their life ahead of them, life seems eternal,
We have oh so much time, but no time to keep a record, a life's journal.

But as we grow to middle age, one day, we realize our time is not forever,
So we rush to "have it all", while we can, hurry, no time for the future, whatsoever.
Without a single thought about how fast our time clock is fleeting,
Hurry up, make a bundle, have the latest toys, make that next meeting.

As we move down the road of time, to the next stage,
We ask, "Where have I been, Where am I going, now that I'm at mature age?"
As best we could, we've climbed society's and the business' lofty ladder,
With age, we see, as the ancient sage cried out "Vanity, all is vanity!" we ask "What does that all matter?"

Only as we grow to later years, do we appreciate our limited time, or so it seems,
Unless we have some life changing event or crisis, to get our attention, and intervene.
Now we're ready for retirement, but just how many rounds of golf can one man play?
In our childhood years, time dragged incessantly, now, would that we could only slow the passage of our days.

For now we've come to the recognition that our mortality is all too real,
Instead of steak and caviar, our diet is Ensure, bran, and oatmeal.
There is so much left undone, that now we can't, but wanted to do,
Many opportunities lost, as we look back, at our life's overview.

And as we review our life, from this aging perspective,
We see all the things we missed, often winsome, yet without invective.
Maybe, it was more time, we could have spent with each child,
Or helped another by sharing our experience, or showed compassion to the reviled.

Or maybe to have taken more time to stop and smell life's roses,
Taken time, to search out, where our family or friends deepest need reposes.
Taken the afternoon to go our little girl's dance of the fairies,
Instead of spending untold times, reading and text messaging on our I-Phone or Blackberry.*

We would have learned not to worry about the future, to the depth of our soul,
About things we could and should have done, or things, over which we had no control.
Fretting about what others thought, and had envy, about the things we couldn't do, or afford,
And, instead, spent more time seeking to follow, and listening to the whisper of our Lord.

Oh, if we'd only known those things years ago, from experience, what we know now,
We could have focused more on the few, really important things of life, our time to allow.
But, we cannot relive our life, not even one moment, for it's not within our choice,
Yet we can, share with the young ones, what we've learned, and give our hindsight's vision, voice.

The Wise Man of old, who had tried it all, and who was more worldly, much wiser, than I,
Shared what he perceived was truly important in life, as seen, looking back, through his aged eye.
King Solomon concluded, whether our years be many, or few, we should rejoice in them all,
Enjoy each day, cherish each friend and loved one, each moment, for itself, before the last night fall.

And whether you are in young, mid-life, or in declining years, to your loved ones, and God, always stay near,
For the One who has given us life, will guide our life's choices, we then make, with neither pride nor fear.
Ah yes, so simple, yet that is the final wisdom of history's wisest man, from the aged, for the ages,
Would that we could learn these lessons of wisdom, well and early, rather than in our latter stages.

A TIME FOR THE MANY SEASONS OF LIFE*
(Ecclesiastes 3:1-8, 11) (With author's additional life seasons)

There is, under heaven, a time and season, for everything,
There is a time to work diligently, and a time to do nothing.
There is a time to laugh, and a time to cry,
There is a time to be born, and a time to die.

There is a time to build up, and a time to tear down,
There is a time for a smile, and time for a frown.
There is a time to let life end, and a time to heal,
There is a time to wait, and a time to do what we feel.

There is a time to dance, and a time to mourn,
There is a time to encourage, and a time to scorn.
There is a time to search for, and a time to let go,
There is a time for unbearable heat, a time for chilling snow.

There is a time to eat, and a time to fast,
There is a time to give away, and a time to amass.
There is a time to be angry, and a time to forgive,
There is a time to exist, and a time to live.

There is a time to push away, and a time to embrace,
There is a time to strike out anew, and a time to retrace.
There is a time to throw away, and a time to keep,
There is a time for alertness, and a time for sleep.

There is a time to be silent, and a time to speak,
There is a time to be bold, and a time to be meek.
There is a time to knit together, and a time to tear apart,
There is a time stop, and a time to start.

There is a time to look upon, and a time to turn away,
There is a time to listen to God, and a time to pray.
There is a time to be certain, and a time to have doubt,
There is a time to speak softly, and a time to shout.

There is a time to climb mountains, and a time to descend,
There is a time to be independent, and a time to depend.
There is a time of plenty, and a time of need,
There is a time to root up, and a time to re-seed.

There is a time to contest, and a time to accept,
There is a time to let pass, and a time to intercept.
There is a time for precision, and a time to be loose,
There is a time for explanation, and a time for no excuse.

There is a time for love, and a time for hate,
There is a time to stand up, and a time to lie prostrate.
There is a time to hold on, and a time to release,
There is a time for war, and a time for peace.*

———————————————

And though most of life, is spent between these extremes,
The pendulum swings daily, in which we test what life means.
Because it is often in the times of trial, that we grow the most,
That we learn the important lessons of life that will be our guideposts.

The test, then of our learning and wisdom, is to know what time for us it is,
That we take and learn from each time of our life, and not be remiss.
Then, being aware of what time it is, that we act and appropriately respond,
Knowing that others before us, have been in that same time, since life first dawned.

And even though we don't in this lifetime, know all of God's ways to infinity,
Nor do we know His timing of whatever was, whatever is, or whatever shall be.
But He gives us this promise that He makes everything beautiful in itself, in its time,
In His time, He will wipe away all tears, pain, death, the sun will forever shine.**

*We designate 80 seasons above there are many more. All of the seasons named in Ecclesiastes 3:1-8, are among them. See if you can find them.

**This verse from Ecclesiastes 3:10-12.

DO NOT FEAR, I AM WITH YOU
(Isaiah 43:1-3, 5-7)

He, who formed us from the fruit of his gifts, His earth and His air,
Says, "Because I am with you, do not despair.
For I am with each and every day, the whole night thru,
Do not fear, for I have redeemed you."

"I will be with you when you pass through waters deep,
I am with you when you must climb mountains steep.
And, I am with you when you must walk through fire,
I am with you when you must face predicaments dire."

"I will be with you, and comfort you in your doubts and fright,
I am with you in the great unknowns, and in your darkest night.
And, I am with you because you are precious in my sight,
For I have loved you, know you by name, will teach you to follow right."

"And though you may be taken, or wander, to the ends of the earth,
I will bring you, my children, home, to My place of your birth.
Do not fear, then, for I am with you, beside you, each day,
Until that time, when I shall call you, to My Home to stay."

THEY SHALL WALK AND NOT GROW WEARY
(Isaiah 40: 9-12, 18, 27-31)

The messenger of God is sent to teach us of great tidings and good news,
Shout it from the mountain tops, and in the towns the message that renews.
God is coming, on a date only He knows, but He hears our daily cries,
So broadcast the message through the valleys, to the heavens, and the skies.

He is a sovereign God, who rules the worlds of the universe, in strength and power,
Yet, He is a God of compassion, knows us fully, from whom we need not cower.
For He shall come to us as a Shepherd, to feed and nurture his flock,
Will carry His lambs on His shoulders, lead His sheep through dangerous paths walk.

Who then can compare, who can stand up to, or with this Wondrous God,
He, who walks with each of us, whether we be noble and mighty, or the down trod.
He, who holds the oceans in His hands, and who can measure the Heavens with His hand,
It is only He, who was there, even before the universe was conceived and planned.

If then, our God knows all things, He hears and knows, our every call and trouble,
He looks down, and reaches with His gentle hand, lifts us from the depths of life's rubble.
Have you not heard, of His great love and wondrous deeds, do you not understand?
This God of the universe, who created every living being, and each grain of sand.

He never grows faint or weary, of listening to our prayers and plaintive cries,
For He will feed His sheep spiritually, physically, wipe each tear from our eyes.
None can comprehend the depth of compassion, He has for each and every one,
His love, far beyond our understanding, from life's first breath, until life is done.

In life's journey, then, even the young and the strong will stumble, grow weary and tired,
But for those who wait upon the Lord, they shall gain new strength, be awe inspired.
And they who wait, shall mount up with wings like eagles, given by our mighty God,
They shall walk and not grow weary, run, not grow tired, nor through life aimlessly plod.

STUDY WAR NO MORE

Man has lived with men in anger and conflict, for thousands of years,
Fought many wars, which have brought mass destruction, death, and tears.
For man continuously prepares for war, turning his pruning forks into spears,
And he beats his ploughshares into swords, to raise his enemies' fears.
Joel 3:10

But there shall come a time when God will come to judge the nations,
When there shall be peace, old enmities cast aside, for loving relations.
There shall come a time when man will neither study nor make war no more,
When neither race, nor creed nor nation shall hate, and men shall war abhor.
Micah 4:3

The time will come, when man shall turn spears into pruning forks, throughout the land,
And shall beat his sword into ploughshares, grow crops, no more shed blood in the sand.
And in that time no nation shall lift up its sword in anger against another,
A time when all the peoples of the world shall live together as brothers.
Isaiah 2:4

And in that time the leopard will be gentle, and the wolf will be docile and tame,
And the suckling lamb, will lay down with the lion, and play in the lion's mane.
It will be a time when the bear and the cattle will lay down together side by side,
For the Child of God shall lead them all, and there will be no need to hide.
*Isaiah 11:6-9**

And that day shall come when there will be peace in the valleys of the world,
When the King of Kings shall come in all His glory, with banners unfurled.
And on that day all of the earth and all of the people and creatures that live within,
Shall have the forbidden knowledge of the Lord, live in peace, no more war no more sin.*
*Isaiah 11:9**

Also see the spiritual "Peace in the Valley", by Thomas A. Dorsey

WHAT GOD ASKS OF US
(Micah 6:6-8)

What is it that my CREATOR wants of me,
I've often pondered, and thought on this mystery.
Will HE be satisfied, if I become King,
Or all through night and day His praises sing.

Will HE be pleased, if I conquer the world,
In all the Nations, with my banners unfurled.
If I gain great status, position or power,
Have the accolades of men on me showered.

Or would it be, for me, HIS desire,
That men call me rich, to that I should aspire?
For surely, if I have the praise of men,
HE would be honored, and pleased with me then.

Or, how much of my treasure will it take,
Does HE want all I have, make or break?
Would HE be content, with say ten per cent, or even half,
Or will a sacrifice be sufficient, a fatted calf?

And as I have searched, I have come to see,
It is not all of my treasure that HE demands of me.
For I cannot buy HIS Pleasure, at any price,
Not even with great inventions, or sage advice.

For HE has told us, clearly, what HE asks of us,
It seems so simple, with not much fuss.
HE asks that we do justice, with all whom we live,
To be loving, compassionate, understanding, and forgive.

Finally, HE asks that our Life's walk, be done, humbly with HIM,
To acknowledge our need of HIM, through thick and thin.
To give of our talents and treasure, in love, without cease,
His Promise of blessings, if we give my first fruits, my silos will increase.

And, I've found that all the treasures, power, and expensive toys,
Are not the things that bring us inner peace and joy,
For those things are but passing, and do not last,
Love is the answer to our present, our future, as well as our past.

THE OVERFLOWING BLESSINGS OF GOD
(1st Chronicles29:10-16; Malachi 3:6-10)

"I, the LORD OF HOSTS am Omnipotent, Eternal, and Unchanging,
MY Grace is sufficient for you, yet it is you MY people, who are estranging.
For many generations now, you have turned your hearts against ME."
Yet, you say "How have we turned from YOU, we do not see?"

"Surely, no man would rob God" you say. "But this is what you have done,
You have sought after your own desires, in every way under the sun."
"You have withheld from ME your gifts, your offerings and your tithes,
You have squandered what I have given you, and have not been wise."

"Yes, you claim ME as your GOD, but you have all, at times, from ME turned,
You have reverted to selfish lives, and GODLY ways, you have spurned."
"But I do not cast you out, and I ask that you to try ME, to see if it is not true,
Bring to ME your first fruits gifts, and tithes, and I will pour out blessings on you."

"Even go to your storehouse, that there may be food and shelter for the poor,
And see if not many blessings and good things will come to you, for sure."
"Test ME on this", says the LORD OF HOSTS, "that I may prove to you and show,
I will open the windows of Heaven, pour out blessings upon you beyond your wildest dreams until they overflow."

I AM WHO I AM
(Exodus 3:13-14; John 6:35;8:12;10:7;10:11; 11:25;14:6;15:1)

From across the millennia of years, and across the distant seas,
God, the Creator of all life, and His Son, Jesus Christ, speak to you and to me.
For, as God told Moses, it is "I AM that I AM", that sends you out,
I AM, is forever in the present, in all time past, and the future throughout.

And His Son, Jesus, tells us precisely who He is, loud and clear,
"I AM the Light of the world, I AM the Bread of Life," without peer."
"I AM the Door, I AM the Good Shepherd, I AM the True Vine,"
"And, "I AM the Way, the Truth, and the Life," for all time."

"I AM the "Resurrection and the Life," says He, who gives us eternal assurance,
To meet each days trials and triumphs, with courage and endurance.
He is the Rock, upon which our Faith is built, and upon which it will stand,
As we travel our pilgrim's path, across this earth, and its arid land.

Yes, He is the Door, our access, our shelter, and our passage, to the other side,
And, He is the Good Shepherd, who will always be with us, whatever betide.
He is the True Vine, who connects us to each other, and to eternal life,
He is The Way, the Truth, and the Life, the Advocate and the Gatekeeper, to the road to which we follow, to the
afterlife.

And, He is the Bread of Life, who feeds all of our physical and spiritual needs,
He is the beacon Light of the World, shedding Light, where darkness breeds.
He is the Resurrection and the Life, our assurance, in the times to come,
It is He who meets our every need, when all has been said and done.

So, whether we speak in the past, the present, or the future, yet to be,
God is "I AM", and CHRIST IS, the present and true answer, for you and for me.
HE is the Alpha and Omega, the First and the Last, the Beginning and the End,
And I thank the God of Love, "I AM", that He did His only Son, to us send.

WHO IS THIS MAN
(Matthew 16:13-16)

Who is this Man, who says, "You shall know the truth that sets us free"?
This Man, who lived and died, in tiny Judah and Galilee?
It was two thousand years ago, that He proclaimed a new Belief,
The impact of His Life, so simple yet profound, to bring joy, and relief.

There is no person who influenced the world's thinking more,
Than this Man of Sorrows, from Nazareth, on Galilee's shore.
Though He hung from a Cross, with criminals, centuries ago,
His Life and Words, are alive today, and still sets lives aglow.

He spoke of Love, Giving and Sharing, to all, who would hear,
Said the Great Creator, Loved all of his children, to Him so dear.
HE spoke of forgiveness, and that He would give up His Life,
Promised a New Life, a New World coming, without strife.

Yet, some said He was a fraud, a magician, the leader of a cult,
Others said He was a rebel, a man without a father, born in shame, words of insult.
Some said He was blasphemous, in the claims that He made,
Others said He was a satanic antichrist, who should make men afraid.

He asked his followers, what others were, about Him saying,
They answered, "Some say John the Baptist, some Jeremiah, or Elijah praying.
He asked all of them, then, "Who do you say that I Am?",
"Thou art the Christ, the Son of Living God", answered just one man.

But He died ignominiously on a Cross, on one dark day,
For the failures of many, then as now, our soul's price He would pay.
Those who knew Him, claimed in three days, He rose from the dead,
He said that He had died for others, now and forever, gave His Life instead.

But, who do people say that He is, in this troubled world today,
Some say a prophet, a great teacher, who had charisma, with people to sway.
With the things He said, the claims He made, He is either Savior, or master of deceit,
We must either call Him insane, or call Him Master, and fall at His Feet.

And, when He asks me the question of "Who do you say that I AM?
I'll call Him my Lord, Comforter, my Strength and my Redeemer, my Sacrificial Lamb.
I'll call Him Grace, Love, King of Kings, my Hope and my Shield.
I'll call Him my Shelter, my Friend and the Shepherd of my life, to Him shall I yield.

I ask you, then, if you know Him, He who healed minds and souls, this Man of Galilee,
This Man, lived long ago, In Spirit He who lives today, for those who seek him, even me.
And, if you don't know Him, He stands at the door, to meet you, this very day,
He gives new and eternal life freely, will love you unconditionally, never to stray.

HE IS THE GREATEST

For GOD So Loved the World, that He gave His only Begotten Son,
That whosever believes in HIM, shall not die but have everlasting life.
For GOD sent HIS SON into the World, not to Judge the World,
But that through HIM we might be acquitted of all of our human flaws and saved.
(John 3:16-17)

GOD	The Greatest of Everything Ever and Forever
So Loved	The Greatest Love to an Unfathomable Degree
The World	The Greatest Number and Expanse
That HE Gave HIS Only Begotten Son	The Greatest Gift Sacrifice Human/Eternal Miracle
That Whosoever Believes	The Greatest Invitation
In HIM	The Greatest And Only God/Man Creation
Shall not Perish	The Greatest Rescue
But	The Greatest Difference
Have	The Greatest Certainty
Eternal Life	The Greatest Future Destiny Imaginable!
Not to Judge Us	The Greatest Amazing Grace and Forgiveness
Through and In Jesus	Both God and Man

GOD AND HIS SON, JESUS THE CHRIST, GOD WHO BECAME HUMAN, MAN AND GOD- THE "I AM"- ALWAYS PRESENT, IN THE PAST, THE PRESENT AND THE FUTURE- THE GREATEST OF ALL LIVNG BEINGS IN ALL TIMES!

SERMON ON THE MOUNT

BLESSED AND AT PEACE
(Matthew 5:1-12)
THE BEATITUDES OF THE SERMON ON THE MOUNT
*Numbers on left margin represent the verses.

(1) Jesus spoke to throngs on that hillside, as He speaks to us today,
He gives us a way of living in all times, from which we should not stray.
Eternal road signs of values rather than the temporary values of society,
A real living Faith, that is not superficial, will meet God's propriety.

(2) Blessed and at peace will be those who humbly acknowledge their spiritual need,
For in seeking eternal spiritual goals, their life will be correctly keyed.
(4) Blessed and at peace will be those, even who grieve and mourn,
For through God's grace, they shall be comforted, though their lives have been torn.

(5)Blessed and at peace will be those who have Christ's qualities of gentleness and humility,
For in their humbleness, they shall be respected for their inner peace and outward civility.
(6)Blessed and at peace, will be those who seek justice, and to speak and do the right things,
For God shall give to them a peace that passes all understanding, that only He brings.

(7)Blessed and at peace are those who show mercy and compassion,
For into their lives, God will, for them, in the same measure, mercy fashion.
(8)Blessed and at peace will be those who are righteous in their thoughts and deeds,
For they shall see the Face of God, and He shall meet their every need.

(9) Blessed and at peace, will be those who seek peace among and between men,
For they shall be called the children of God, and shall be judged, free of sin.
(10)Blessed and at peace, will be those who have been ridiculed, persecuted, for doing good,
For by their actions and attitudes, in God's kingdom, they shall be a royal priesthood.

(11)Blessed and at peace, are they, who when faultfinders insult and persecute them, on His account,
(12)For their trials will be remembered, as were the persecutions the prophets did surmount.

TOUGH LOVE AND WISDOM FROM THE MOUNT
(Matthew Chapters 5: 13-48; Chapters 6, &7)

Wonderful Words of wisdom, freely from His mouth flow,
Wisdom that will pierce our hearts, as from a marksman's bow.
Words given to a crowd, who gathered long ago on that hill,
Words spoken two thousand years ago, that even today, ring true still.

Christians are as salt of the earth, giving flavor to walking in the Christian way,
They are the light of the world, as a city on a hill, with a dazzling light display.
Being light, do not hide your light under a basket, but give off light to all around,
So, we must let our light shine that our good works will glorify Him, through the world abound.
(Matthew 5:13-16)

For Jesus came to explain and live God's Word, as one of us, not to abolish the Law,
He Came to fulfill God's Law, steeped in God's Grace and Love, God's Love for all.
We know that to murder, steal, injure, hate and destroy we should not commit,
Nor should we harbor anger, but reconcile with others before we come before God, as fit.
(Matthew 5:17-24)

And a settlement of our disputes with others, rather than lashing out with hurt and angry retort,
Else the other may strike back in kind, or secure his judgment against us in court.
And though adultery, or considering it, will destroy the vow of trust, and is a sin,
For it will corrupt a marriage, and destroy a family from without and within.
(Matthew 5:25-32

For marriage is intended as a life commitment, not to be dissolved nor given up with every whim,
So seek to love, defer, and forgive, reconcile your differences, from the beginning to life's end.
And when you make a vow, honor it throughout day to day, from dusk 'til dawn,
Let your word be your sufficient promise, your word given as your life's bond.
(Matthew 5:32-37)

The tough love and wisdom He gives, telling us not to respond to evil, in kind,
"Do not retaliate", He says, kill them with kindness, seeking the ties that bind.
And even though the world's measure is "an eye for an eye, a tooth for a tooth"
"Rather", He says. "Whoever should slap you, turn the other cheek, without reproof."
(Matthew 5:38-39)

"And, if someone takes the shirt off your back, give him your coat too,
And if one forces you to go one mile, then go with him for two.
Give to him, who asks of you, and even though he wants to borrow,
Whether or not he pays you back, what he has promised for the morrow."
(Matthew 5:40-42)

"In our prayers, and in our giving, each should be without trumpet nor fanfare,
That others know when and, how we pray or what we give our own to care.
Nor should we stand on the corner, praying loudly and cloudly into the air,
That others may see and hear the meaningless and repetitious flair.
(Matthew :6:1-4;5-7)

THE LORD'S PRAYER

"Pray like this,Our Father in Heaven, to You we pray, You the Only One,
May your name be revered and praised, and Your Will be done.
The very essentials of life, will you on us bestow,
And may we forgive others' debts to us, as You forgive us the debts we owe."

"And may we not fall to the temptation of evil and sin,
Nor turn away from Your Plan from without or within.
And may we lift unto You, and give to You all the praise, power and glory,
And may this be forever our life's true story."
(Matthew 6:9-13)

―――――――――――――

"And, forgive all of your brothers for the evil things, they have done to you,
For if you do, your heavenly Father, will by that same measure forgive you, too.
But if you do not leave your anger at the altar, forgiving those who've done you wrong,
Then you too, will wait for God's forgiveness, through the night, and all the day long."
(Matthew 6: 14-15)

*"And, build not your treasures in tangible things, which are destroyed by moth or rust,
But build your treasure on spiritual things that last, as love, faith mercy, and being just.
For where your treasure and focus is, there also will be your heart and your priorities,
Leaving behind those passing things that will only temporarily gratify or please."
(Matthew 6:19-21)

"You cannot carry water on both shoulders, serve two masters, both mammon and God,
For you will hold on to the one, and hate the other, as nothing more than a dirt clod.
And "Do not judge, lest you be judged", the Master has warned us, and said,
"For in the measure and way we judge others, the same measure, shall be on our head."
(Matthew 6:24; 7:1-2)

"And, do not worry about what tomorrow, or the next day, may bring to your plate,
For the problems and trouble of today, are about all we can handle, or tolerate.
Your worry solves nothing, helps nothing, adds not a cubit, or a day, to your life's span,
For all things that happen in our life, are woven into the tapestry of God's master plan."
(Matthew 6: 25-34)

"And, do not be anxious about even our next meal, as God will provide for all our needs,
If He clothed in beauty the lilies of the field, and all the food upon which the robin feeds.
So, we of little faith, if He cares enough to provide even for each of these little ones,
Then, He will provide even more for us, valued highly, all of our needs under the sun."
(Matthew 6:25-34)

"And why do you look at the speck that is someone else's eye,
When you do not even notice the log in your own eye.
You are being hypocritical, first take out the log in your eye,
Then will you see and help another take the speck from his eye.
(Matthew 7: 3-5)

"Ask, and it shall be given unto you, seek and you shall find,
Knock and the door will be opened to you, and you will not be left behind.
For would a Father whose son asks him for bread, give him a stone?
So also, your heavenly Father, will give you what is good, not leave you alone."
(Matthew 7:7-11)

The Golden Rule is that you should treat others, as you would want them to treat you,
But, we are also to love our neighbors, even those who've been our enemy, too.
And we are to pray for others, yes, even those who have persecuted us,
For God causes the sun and the rain to fall, on both the evil and the righteous.
(Matthew 7:12, 5:43-45)

Beware of false prophets, who are as wolves, who wear sheep's clothing,
They are not what they appear, bear bad fruit, which is a fruit of loathing.
And, not everyone who proclaims he is of God, will enter the gates,
For it is what is in one's heart, not outward appearance that will, with God rate.
(Matthew 7: 13-14, 15-20, 21-23)

Real faith then needs to be built on a solid Rock, the Christ, God's Son,
For if it's built only on words, sand and fluff, it will not stand, when the storms come.
There shall surely come times, to all, when the storms of life, shall on us descend
Our life constructed with Christ as the Cornerstone, shall stand through all, 'til the end.
(Matthew 7:24-27; 21:42)

NOTE 1. In the above verses we have noted twice the verses 7:1-2, and 7:3-5, intentionally for emphasis.

NOTE 2. There is not one of us who will meet the standard of perfection He lived by, because we are each human and subject to human frailties and imperfection. He does ask of us that we strive for excellence, following each day, even if never achieving perfection, as best we can, the tenets of The Great Commandment (Mathew 22:34-40) and the direction of Micah 6:8.

There will be some days when we fail miserably, some days when we do well. There will be many days when we do better or worse than others. In the race of life we will fall, we will grow weary. If we begin again each day in repentance of the failures of yesterday or yesteryear, striving each day with what time, talents and gifts we may have, His Grace, His forgiveness will be sufficient for us- that is His Amazing Grace

**Amazing Grace, How sweet the sound, That saved a wretch like me,
I once was lost, but now am found, Was Blind but now I see.

**"Twas Grace that taught my heart to fear, And Grace my fears relieved.
How precious did that Grace appear, The Hour I first believed.

**Through many danger toils and snares, I have already come.
'Tis Grace hath brought me safe thus far, And Grace will lead me home.

**The Lord has promised good to me, His Word my hope secures.
He will my shield and portion be, As long as life endures.

**Yes, when this heart and flesh shall fail, And mortal life shall cease.
I shall possess within the veil, A life of joy and peace.

When we've been there ten thousand years, Bright shining as the sun.
We've no less days to sing God's praise, Than when we'd first begun.*

*Verse added by John Rees.

**Melody of song as sung today, not as John Newton wrote it. Melody was an early Virginia folk song melody sung by slaves.

LEAN ON ME
(Matthew 11: 28-30)

He speaks with words of compassion, from far across the sea,
"All of you who are weary, and heavy laden, come unto Me,
I say to each of you, lean on me, and I will give you rest,
I will give you comfort, as a father draws his child to his breast."

"The rest I give to you is healing, love and peace,
When the burdens of the world, weigh you down without cease.
So, I shall place my yoke upon you, help you carry your load,
All the stuff and baggage, life has put upon you, on our pilgrim's road."

"Turn them all over to Me, that I may show you, and you may see,
I will not condemn you, I have a gentle heart, will set your burdens free.
And though I have great power, I give to you freely, for I am humble,
I will lift you up, whenever your load makes you falter and stumble."

"And in Me, you shall find a peace that only I give, rest for your soul,
I will give you Living Water, and spiritual food for your life's bowl.
So, come to Me, all of you, for my yoke is easy, and my load is light,
And together we shall walk through your darkest valleys of the night."

RECOVERING THE LOST CHILD WITHIN US
(Isaiah 11:1-9; Matthew 18: 1-5; 19:13-14)

The Master has given us direction, that, to us, may seem strange,
That we must become, as like a child again, our self-serious selves, to exchange.
In our Faith, then we adults, must once again, become as a little child,
As the Prophet foretold, a Child will lead them, even the beasts of the wild.

Being transformed then, as a child, we must recover our innocence and humility,
Learn again to love, unconditionally, to the best of our ability.
And, we must learn to trust, in all things, our Heavenly Father,
Just as a little child trusts his parent, without a fear, worry, or bother.

And, as a child, sees not self or others outward beauty, status or color or skin,
Without learned prejudice or judgment, He sees through, to the person that lies within.
No shame to laugh or cry, no boundaries to a child's possibilities or expectations,
Anything is achievable to the child, impossible is not in his equation.

A child has an innocence, and inquisitiveness, and a joy for life, that does not exhaust,
Yet, when he grows older, his unfettered view of life and innocence, is lost.
For as we grow and "mature", we build protective, and self-limiting walls around us,
Built to hide our insecurity, our fear, prejudice, pride and self, to surround us.

Oh, that we might follow the Master's plan, become as a little child once more,
Trusting that God will provide for us, be with us, from this day and for evermore.
Oh, that we might rediscover that selfless, trusting abandon, and joy,
That we once had within us, as a little girl or little boy.

For that is what He has directed each of us, that we should do,
To live not, with the hardened edge of aged life, and our childhood trust renew.
For I perceive that one of the true measures of a real woman or a man,
Is how much of the little child, he or she has retained, in their life's span.

THE GREAT PRETENDERS
(Matthew 23:13-15, 23-27, 33)

Something that has plagued us all, at times, to some extent, from peasant to aristocracy,
Tis the wearing of masks, acting, pretending to be something we're not, that's hypocrisy.
And this is a fault, a shortcoming, that is most vigorously attacked and condemned,
By the Savior, which by His strong words, would seem to any other fault transcend.

For the hypocrite is truthful with neither himself, nor others, nor with God,
And when we evidence this deceitfulness, it demonstrates our character is flawed.
For He found fault with the legalists, who shut off the kingdom, kept others out,
He preached of seeking the outcast, all inclusive love is what His message was about.

And to those who took advantage of the poor, but gave lovely, high sounding prayers,
Who paraded around in their trappings and garments of wealth, with their pious airs,
He condemned them, those who went to great lengths to proselyte others to think as they,
Yet exclude those who didn't follow their rules, thought different, in seeking God's way.

He called hypocrites, those who parsed their words and Scripture to justify their position,
Then condemned loudly, all of those who interpreted differently, in opposition.
And those, as well, who tithed only their herbs, mint and dill, so that their sacrifice was small,
Rather than showing love and mercy, giving from all their treasure, for the needy all.

He chastised those who make an issue of detail, while overlooking the important things,
"You blind guides, who strain out a gnat, and swallow a camel" His condemnation rings.
Those who have the stench of impurity inside, but on the outside appear clean,
Like deadly vipers, or a whitewashed tombs, outwardly pure, inside poisoned and "unclean."

And He directed the Pharisees of old, as with cup and dish, clean the inside first,
For only cleaning the exterior may look good, yet leaves the interior still cursed.
So it's not just our outward appearances, our trappings, clothes, and words that count,
It's what we do, our attitudes and motives, our purity of heart that are paramount.

So, as we read the Master's condemnation, thinking how evil those hypocrites were,
Without ever considering that maybe He also speaks to us today, perchance to infer.
We need to search our hearts, our minds, our actions and our motives, for sure,
To guard that we not exclude, judge, and condemn those different, keep our hearts pure.

Could it be that when I, with all my faults, think less of others, who don't believe just as me,
That I am no different, and no better than the hypocrites that Jesus called out the Pharisees.
For though others may worship, speak, and understand God's Grace in a different way,
If they too, are seeking to live God's life of love, to denounce them, who am I to say.

UNTO THE LEAST OF THESE MY FRIENDS
(Matthew 25:31-40, 22: 34-40)

And JESUS said "When the SON OF MAN comes again in His Glory,
The people of the world will be gathered together", as HE continued the story.
"At that time, the SON OF MAN will separate the goats from the sheep,
Those ones, the sheep, who sought to follow the HIM, will HIS blessings reap."

Then HE said to them, "I was sick, weary and homeless, and you took ME in,
You bound up MY wounds, ministered to ME, and washed away MY sin.
I was down and out, a stranger to you, but you became MY friend,
I was naked and you clothed me, without and in my heart within."

"I lay in chains, in dank and darkened prisons, and you visited ME,"
"I thought no one cared, entombed in the fears of my Inner Self, for infinity."
"And you showed ME the Love of the FATHER OF LIGHTS, that I might see,"
"That a life can have meaning and purpose, yet, even in ME."

"MY Body was gaunt, frail, MY stomach empty, you gave ME food to eat,"
"You gave ME refreshing cold water, lifted ME up, and stood ME on my feet."
"You told ME of the Living Water, that "God so Loved the world", O so sweet."
"You gave ME the assurance of the Kingdom's victory, took away MY defeat."

And, his followers said to Him, "LORD, when were YOU thirsty that we gave YOU drink?
And, when were YOU hungry, fed YOU, naked and clothed YOU, served as YOUR life link?
And when were YOU sick, that we nursed YOU in prison that we came to visit YOU?
And, when did we lift YOU up, give to YOU, GOD'S love that YOU already knew?"

Then, HE said, "I have told you this parable, that you might come to know and see,
When you've done these things, even unto the least of these, you've done these things unto ME.
I commission each of you to bring this good news of the Gospel to all mankind,
That they may love neighbor as self, and love GOD, with all their heart, soul and mind."

A FAITH PARADOX
(Mark 8:34-37, 2nd Corinthians 12:8-10, James 1:2-4)

Oftentimes, in this life, things are not always as they seem,
We must look beneath the surface, for the true meaning to glean.
What seems to be the truth of the matter is sometimes not,
We must examine carefully to see what real truth has wrought.

So it is, sometimes, what appears to be clearly black, is white,
Is at other times a muddled gray, in finding what is right.
And so it seems, as we read about the life of our Lord and Savior,
To find what Truth Scripture tells us, as to what is to be our behavior.

For we are told that He is both the Lion of Judah and the Sacrificial Lamb,
He is both the First and the Last, the Alpha and Omega, Son of God, and Son of Man.
He is Master of all, and Servant of all, at the same time, both Human and Divine,
That He gave His life, to give us life, and save our life, and that of all mankind.

And many things that He told us are seeming paradoxes to confound,
That we must die to be born again, to lose our life to save our life, in a new one abound.
He is a King who came to bring new life, not to be served, but to others serve,
Lord of all, Servant of all, giving to each by His Grace, a gift not deserved.

He told us that the first shall be last, the last shall be first, our goal is not to control,
That it profit us nothing to gain the whole world, and yet forfeit our own soul.
He said, "Whoever wants eternal Life, must deny himself, take up his cross and follow Me,"
For He was telling us, that we should serve others even before ourselves, you see.

And, we are told by the Master, it is more blessed to give than to receive,
That our lives will be measured not by our works, but by the Faith we believe.
Yet, in our Faith lives, it will be evidenced by our works, and the way that we live,
Even good works fall short, if not done in love, and we're forgiven by the way we forgive.

Saint James tells us to have joy, when trials and troubles intrude into our life,
For it is in these trials, we learn patience, maturity, and endurance, to meet all our strife.
While Paul counsels that strength and power will be perfected out of our very weakness,
For through the Holy Spirit, we will find new strength, exchange our ego with meekness.

In all of these things what seems to be a paradox, really is not,
It is teaching us what an inward and selfish attitude, will and has begot.
That our life needs to be refocused, from inward to out,
That Love is the answer- that giving of ourselves is what life is about.

So, what does it all mean, how is it our life's challenges and trials we are to face,
To live and love by Faith, knowing when we will fall, He forgives us by gift and by Grace.
To give ourselves away in service, to love those around us, the very best that we are able,
That He will make our wrongs right, this wonderful King of Kings, born in a stable.

A PROPHET IS WITHOUT HONOR IN HIS OWN HOMETOWN
(Luke 4: 16-34)

That a cobbler's children has no shoes to wear,
That a barber's son lives with shaggy, unkempt hair.
That a lawyer who represents himself, has a client, who is a fool,
That a doctor whose child is always sickly, is the rule.

But ONE who was greater than all of these folks of renown,
Said, "A prophet is without honor in his own hometown."
What HE meant in part, was familiarity breeds contempt,
For those who know us best, our best efforts are often misspent.

There are many reasons why this might be so,
Maybe because with those closest to us, only our love we bestow.
Or maybe it's because to be objective, with these, is most difficult,
To give friends and loved ones, wise advice, and expect the desired result.

Or maybe, it's because, our human frailties, they've often seen,
So that our advice and "wisdom", are viewed within our homegrown backdrop, with less esteem.
Or maybe, it's because it's easier to speak with another not so well known,
Rather than with the one, with whom so much of our life has been thrown.

Or, maybe it's uncomfortable for them, to fully confide,
In one, from whom their failures, they'd rather hide.
Whatever it be, it seems to be a principle, if not a law,
It's tough to give advice, to those persons, to whom we're closest of all.

Even though we may find they don't hear the best advice we've ever given,
They discover the same truth, comes from a stranger, seems to them God-given.
Just be happy, if they finally get the solution to their problem right,
Even though the memory of your same counsel is far out of sight.

This is not to say we shouldn't share with loved ones our best advice,
Because the wisdom we share, may well change their life.
But whatever we say, must be with all gentleness and care,
Words carefully chosen, not just to correct, but to repair.

So don't feel discouraged, or like a failure you've been,
When you can help others to see the truth, yet not your own kin.
For if this be the case, join the club of the greatest One of All,
The Master, the Prophet, without honor, in His own town hall.

NOTE: Appearing in different form and verses elsewhere in Section IV book.

WITH A LITTLE HELP FOR OUR FRIENDS
Luke 10:29-37
The Parable of the Good Samaritan*

God's Law tells us to love the Lord with all our heart and our soul,
To love our neighbor as our self in order to find our inner compass, and life's role.
But, the question we must then ask is "How is 'my neighbor' to be defined?"
And do we have the concept of "our neighbor", too narrowly refined.

So, the Man from Nazareth, told a story about a man who went down to Jericho,
And, on the road, he was beset by robbers, beside the roadside, they did him throw.
He lay there, groaning, stripped of his clothes and goods, and profusely bleeding,
As many travelers passed, looked at him, and walked on by, without heeding.

A certain Jewish Priest went by, garbed in religious finery, reading his unctuous prayers,
Saw the man, but he was too busy, bound for an important meeting somewhere.
Then another man saw him, a wholly religious lawyer, who knew all the ecclesiastical law,
But, he was preoccupied, on an important mission, to argue a finer point of law, without flaw.

Then a common man, a Samaritan, one whose kind was looked down upon, by most,
Yet, he saw and heard, observed, stopped, helped, and felt compassion, to the utmost.
And, though he knew not this battered man, he knelt beside him, bound up his wounds,
He clothed him, gave him water, picked him up, did, with comforting words, commune.

The not well thought of Samaritan, placed him on his donkey, and walking, led him to an Inn,
Paid for his food, his care, said "Take care of him, and I will pay, when I return again."
And, all of these things, the lowly Samaritan did, for someone he did not know,
Jesus asks us today, "Which one of these three men, was a neighbor, and did mercy show?"

We must answer, "Surely not the priest, nor the lawyer, but the common Samaritan man,"
He says to us, "Go and do likewise! Let not your words, but your actions, be your plan." "Observe the pain and
needs of those around you, reach out and minister to them."
"For in this way, you love by your life lived, not by passing by, nor meeting religious rules and religious diadem."

*Another version of the story of The Samaritan appears earlier in this book. We thought the message of the story
was important enough for a re-run.

THE "I'S" HAVE IT, OR DO THEY?
Luke 12:13-21, A Parable; Psalm 39:5-6

Someone said to the Son of God, "Make my brother share his inheritance with me!"
And He answered him, "Who am I to stand as judge or mediator, for thee."
"Hear Me now, let Me tell you a parable of life about a rich young man,"
"Who gathered up great wealth, stored it away, only to have it slip from his hands."

"Be on guard," He said, "for your life is not to be measured by what you own,"
"One who hoards what he's given, will reap a bitter harvest of the seeds he has sewn."
"For there was once a rich self-centered young man, who thought only of himself,"
"He, already rich, made more each year from his harvest, stored it all on his shelf."

"Then he had so much money from his grain, he had no more space to store it,"
"He reasoned with himself, I will build a new vault, a secure place for it."
"And, I will continue to pile up my riches, that I may become even more wealthy,"
"I will hide my money in my massive vaults, safe from thieves and the stealthy."

And, over the years, he'd accumulated great wealth, possessions, a mountain of "stuff,"
He said to himself, "Now, I have plenty, to enjoy my passions, even if things get rough."
"So, I'll just eat, drink, and be merry, and shower myself with whatever I want,"
"For I am so accomplished, I am so rich, I will just tap into my never-ending fount"

But, God said, to this greedy and selfish man, whose favorite word was "I,"
"You foolish man, this very night, I may call upon your soul, and you will surely die."
"You have spent your life, rationalizing, and pursuing only your selfish desires,"
"Now, it will all depart from you, who will spend all your riches when you expire?"

The message of this parable, an eternal truth, two thousand years ago, as well as today,
For he who centers on himself, amasses fortunes, to please only himself, as his forte.
How foolish he is, thinking his treasure and his "stuff" will bring joy, life's true pleasure,
Better to share what God entrusts to you, with Him and others, there lay up your treasure.

THE TROUBLE WITH WORRY
(Luke 10:38-42; Matthew 6:25-34; Mark 4:14-19)

One day, Jesus and his followers were travelling in Bethany, near Martha's home,
Martha invited them in to rest and eat, and welcomed them with shalom.
Martha began feverishly and meticulously, planning and preparing their meal,
While Mary, her sister, sat at Jesus feet, to listen intently, to what His wisdom revealed.

Martha became perturbed, she doing all the work, said to Jesus, "Can't you see?"
"Lord, I am doing all of the work, don't you even care? Tell her to help me!"
Jesus replied, "Martha, Martha, you are worried and troubled about so many things."
"Mary has focused on spiritual matters, only one thing, is really important to cling."
(Luke 10:38-42)

Jesus said, "Do not be anxious and worried about your life, even your basic needs"
"For God will take care of you, as He has the birds of the air, even their water and seeds."
"For worry does not help provide your necessities, nor add one cubit to your life span."
"Don't worry about tomorrow, it will take care of itself, let today's problems be your plan."
(Matthew 6:25-34)

So it is worry does nothing to solve any of the things that trouble,
Worry often merely breaks us down, turns our life into rubble.
Worry is rooted in "Vergen," which means to strangle or choke,
And, to one who lives with worry daily, it is clearly no joke."
(Mark 4:1-20)

Worry begins, almost as a droplet of water, a passing thought,
Develops into a continuing stream, from that one thought wrought.
And, if we let it, it will become an obsessive, raging flood,
Will dominate our lives, 'lest we seize control, and nip it, in the bud.

To worry about what is past, it is folly, for it is over and done,
We can't relive re-live or change yesterday, there is no time rerun.
We can correct what is correctable, learn from our mistakes, do it different next time,
But, we can't take back the past actions, retrieve words spoken, never in a lifetime.

So too, worry about what might happen tomorrow, or the future, is futile,
For worry never solved a problem, and things may change meanwhile.
Many times we find in our worry about the future, the anticipation,
Is, more often than not, much worse that our worry's realization.

So deal with the problems on your plate that stand before you today,
Tomorrow's problem, will find tomorrow's solution, along the way.
And, if we confront squarely the issues of this day, at any rate,
Done correctly, and completely, will give us, for the present, a full plate.

It may help our angst, to understand, that we can completely control, only a few things,
And there are other matters, in which we may have some say, but not resolution, bring.
There are yet many more situations, over which we have zero dominion or deliverance,
May these truths ease our anxieties, and may we have the wisdom, to know the difference.

Worry never passed a test, paid a bill, solved a problem, nor cured a disease,
It never destroyed the wall of Jericho, slew Goliath, defeated the Persians or the Medes.
In our life, yes in all of history, worry never accomplished a single solitary goal,
But to make us less effective, cause us stress, and pain, deep within our soul.

So, when worry comes to knock at your mind and heart's door,
Simply say to it, no thanks, I have no need of you anymore.
Knowing that anxiety has nothing to offer or benefit you,
That things will go better, without adding worry, to your life's menu.

LOST AND FOUND
(Luke 15:11-32)
The Parable of the Prodigal Son

There once was a Father, who owned many lands, and who had two sons,
The elder son was loyal and responsible, but not the younger one.
For the younger came to his Father one day, and asked for his inheritance,
That he might travel, learn from and explore the world, and its great expanse.

So his Father honored his request, and gave to him generously, his share,
His son went to a distant country, and lived as one without a care.
He squandered all that had been given to him, and sowed his wild oats,
Expensive things, lived lavishly, with women, expensive garments and coats.

Then, after a time, he found that he had wasted all that he had been given,
For he had lived the wild life, spent his gifts and inheritance, in scandalous living.
He reached the point where he had no money, no job, and nothing to eat,
Said he'd even eat with, and after, the farmer's pigs, had come to total defeat.

He hit the bottom of an emotional, spiritual and physical pit, into which he had fallen,
Then came to his senses, knew he had failed his Father, and himself, was crestfallen.
He saw that with his wasted life, he was not worthy to be his Father's chosen son,
And wondered, if his Father might take him back, even as a servant, a hired one.

So he got up from the pit he was in, and began to travel home to his Father,
Thinking rightfully, his Father would cast him out, and say, "Don't even bother."
But as he approached his Father's House, his Father saw him from afar,
Ran out to meet him, embraced and kissed him, His love as an endless reservoir.

His Father said "Get him my best robes for his body, and sandals for his feet.
For my son was dead in spirit, is now alive, for he now has lost his old self conceit.
For My son was blind, lost in life, but now can see, and has been found.
And we shall celebrate his renewed life, with rejoicing, let the heavens resound."

The celebration began, with singing and dancing, with a feast fit for a king,
The Father, and his servants, rejoiced in His son's return, with joy the halls did ring.
The Father proclaimed, "My son was lost, but now is found, with Grace I welcome him home.
And may he begin to learn, the way that he should live, never to again roam."

As the feast of celebration went on, the older brother stood by, arms crossed, alone,
He asked, "Why this jubilation for him, who has wasted his life, while I tended to things at home?"
His Father embraced him too, and said "My son, you have always been with Me,
I treasure your service, which shall be rewarded, all that I have is for you, one day you will see."

"But, we need to rejoice, when your brother, who was spiritually lost and dead,
Has even belatedly found the Truth, returned to the fold and come to his senses in his head.
And, you will find, that if you too, will forgive him, your joy will be magnified,
As your Father has forgiven you, you should do likewise, that your Father be glorified."

"So, I say to you, dear son when any of your brothers, who were lost in mire, then found.
Even though you have labored in the fields without ceasing, let not your anger abound.
But rejoice in the new found life, the blindness that has been replaced by sight.
For, as I, your Father in Heaven, loves all of His children, rejoices when any of their lives are made right."

LOVE, THE ULTIMATE GIFT

"For God so loved the world that He gave his One and only son, that whosoever believes in Him, shall not perish, but have eternal life. For God did not send the Son into the world to condemn the world, but to save the world through Him. (*John 3:16-1-17*)

"Beloved, let us love one another for love is from God; and everyone who loves knows God. The one who does not love does not know God for GOD IS LOVE. (*1ˢᵗ John 4:7-8.*)

"He has told you o man, what is good and what does the Lord require of you? But to do justice, to love kindness, and to walk humbly with your God. (*Micah 6:8*)

"Teacher, what is the great commandment in the law? And HE said to them "You shall love the Lord with all your heart, and with all your soul, and all your mind. This the great and foremost commandment. The second is like it, 'You shall love your neighbor as yourself. On these two commandments depend the whole Law and the Prophets." (*Matthew 22:36-40*)

God cares more about you and I, than we could ever imagine or know,
He gave the ultimate gift to and for us,that carries us through life's ebb and flow.
For God loved each of us so much, He gave us in life and in death, His only Son,
Who, as one of us, lived among and died for us, the ultimate sacrifice, our victory's won.

The Word proclaims, "Whoever believes," heart and deed, no exclusions, no one left out,
Forgiving our flawed lives, "What a priceless gift!" to the heavens we'll shout.
That we shall not perish, death shall not conquer us, immortality, man's ultimate dream,
In accepting this gift, we are irrevocably chosen, to be one of God's heavenly team.

And all that God asks of us, in return, is that in Him, and His Son, we believe,
That if we will but have faith in Him, then through Him, eternal life we will achieve.
He specified no creeds, no catechisms, yet belief is more than just saying that we do,
But taking Him into our heart and soul, living a new life, a new me, and a new you.

For God gave His Son, Jesus, to and for us, not to judge or condemn mankind,
But to save the people of the world from themselves, in Him, Peace we would find.
No greater gift, as God reviews, than this singular promise to you and I, could human bestow,
This gift of eternal life, assurance, that our life is cleansed, white as the driven snow.

HE asks of us that we love God with all our heart, and others as our self,
To love by sharing generously all that we have and is in our life's shelf.
For what does a man profit who tends only to his own needs and desires,
He asks that we do justice, love kindness, walk humbly with God, we seek to aspire.

WHAT IS TRUTH?*
(John 3:16-17, 8:32, 14:6, 18:37-38; 1st John 3:7-12)

Two thousand years ago a Man from Nazareth said, "The reason I am here,
Is to bear witness to the Truth, that all men may come to know, see and hear."
Another man, Pilate, said to Him, "What is Truth?" this difficult question he posed,
"For I have been searching for years for the answer, to the question on you, I repose."

For The Nazarene had said "If you abide, live, in what I say, and you will listen to me,
You shall know the Truth, and that Truth, shall set you free.
For I am the Light of the World, the Good Shepherd (The Gatekeeper) I am the Truth, the Light and the Way,
The Word of God is the everlasting Truth, in which the root of all faith must lay."

The Truth is the reality written by God's inspiration, across Scripture's pages,
The Word which is unimpeachable, the Truth, yesterday, today, and for the ages.
The Truth that God created all, and cared enough to give up, by death of His Son,
For all people, for all time, the Son gave up His life, and has our victory won.

The Truth then that we can know, and sets us free, to live our life without fear,
That we need not prove, that we cannot earn, but live our life, with this message clear.
That God loves us, that God is Love, this Truth that came through Jesus,
That he or she, who truly lives in this Truth, lives in His love lived, God shall never flee us.

And if we have this ultimate Truth, in our minds and hearts permanently etched,
Then the Truth will envelope us daily, throughout our life's span stretched.
The Truth, that God is Love, and through Christ he has shown he loves us each,
Truth that Love is of God, we need to seek to love God, ourselves, and others, in our every thought, action and speech.

*In the above Scripture, Pilate asks the question of Jesus "What is truth?" Scripture does not report any answer by the Nazarene. We have transposed what he said elsewhere in the Gospel of John- to presuppose how He might have answered Pilate.

CASTING STONES
(John 8:1-11)
A Woman Caught in Adultery, The Men not caught

Jesus came to the temple one day, sat down and began to teach those gathered there,
As He began, the Pharisees brought in a woman, cast her down, in the morning's glare.
They said to test Him, "Teacher, we've caught her in the very act of adultery today."
Moses law says she should be stoned to death, what then, Teacher, do you say?"

For they knew if He decreed, "Stone her!" He would then violate the Roman Law,
Yet, if He said, "Release her!", then He'd go against the Torah's Law, which Moses oversaw.
But He did not answer them, instead He simply knelt, and began to write in the sand,
We do not know what He wrote, perhaps the sins of her accusers, who were there, on hand.

Then He spoke quietly, yet firmly, "Let he who has never sinned, cast the first stone."
And as He wrote in the sand, the Pharisees looked down at it, and uttered a collective groan.
With consternation, beginning with the eldest, the stones dropped with a thud, one by one,
Then all of her accusers left, leaving only the woman and Jesus, standing there alone.

He stood up, and said "Woman, where have they all gone, did no one condemn you?"
Relieved, she replied, "No Lord, not one, neither Pharisee, nor gentile, nor Jew."
He looked her square in the eyes, saying "Neither do I condemn you, go your way, and sin no more."
For through Jesus, God had forgiven her, and she as we, our sins washed away, forevermore.

This does not mean that we can do wrongful things, hurt others, without having consequence,
Even though held accountable, if truly repentant, God will forgive us every circumstance.
So it is, through the blood of Jesus, God forgave her, and forgives us daily, for our faults,
Imperfect as we are, who then are we to condemn others, casting stones of guilt, with our assault.

WHEN GOD'S PERFECT PLAN SEEMS TO GO AWRY
(John 9:1-7, Matthew 6:45b)

We don't understand the purpose, as we hear a mother's soulful cry,
When her child dies, is born imperfectly, is afflicted, we ask why?
It's so difficult to find a reason, as we survey all of life's horizons span,
To find a present purpose for this seeming unfairness, in God's Great Plan.

Sometimes we search for months or years, through life's events gleaning,
What it is, that will give our affliction, some purpose and meaning.
Yet if we search without cease, that we'll find an explanation, even in our pain,
For God has told us that none, good or bad, will be denied life's sun, nor spared its rain.

The damaged or lost life, for which there is no replacement or correction,
May yet give the afflicted or those who've loved, a new life's direction.
To the disabled, his disability, through striving may become a challenge to achieve,
That will inspire others like him, to try harder, and in themselves believe.

Or it may be, that in one less able, we see exposed the simple key to simple love,
That we may learn what unconditional love, given freely, is consistent of.
Or it may inspire us to find answers to our cause, that we may help others,
That they may not be plagued as we, our loved one, child, sister or brother.

For some, it may inspire them to a solution, as their new life's purpose,
How many wonderful healing programs, have begun from this inspired service.
For others it may be a ministry, hewn out of the rock where their life has gone wrong,
To bring hope to the lives of others, that their life be healed, might have a new song.

So, when we have things in our life or those we love, which seem so unfair,
And, even though we'd rather roll back time, and have things as they were.
We don't have that choice, we need to search for opportunity in things, as they are,
And seek to bring about good, from even our anguish, may that purpose be our lodestar.

For then, and only then, will our crisis, loss or pain have any real purpose,
It is portioned to us to find our cause, that will bring good to the surface.
And some day, we may be able to look back, and say "Now I understand!"
Even in our grief, God guided us through, to use even our trial, in His Great Plan.

NOT SEEING, YET BELIEVING
(John 14:1-6; 20 :24-29)

There was a man in Jesus time named Thomas, with whom I can identify,
He doubted some things had happened, 'lest he see it with his own eye.
The writing and the words of others, who have seen before are great,
But their just saying its so, doesn't always in our mind illuminate.

For I've never seen a burning bush, nor seen a parting sea,
And I've never seen a blind man healed, who was close to me.
And I've never seen someone raised from the dead,
Yet, I'm supposed to have it all straight in my head.

Not having seen then, there are times when I've had my doubts,
Is it all really true, what the preacher from the pulpit shouts.
That this man, Jesus, really is the Truth, the Life and the Way,
Since I haven't seen, how can I believe, and all my questions allay.

Then I hear the Master's words to Saint Thomas, "Before I leave,
Because you have seen, you Thomas, have now believed."
"Oh, how blessed are those who have believed, but have not yet seen."
It's a comfort to me, that even the saints had doubts, before they felt serene.

But as I reflect upon my life, though I know that I've been led,
Even if I've had no lightning revelation, striking 'round my head.
In the silence of my heart, I know HE walks with me each day,
That HE gives me answers, guides my direction, as I my life survey.

Though I've often slipped, made mistakes, not done the things I should,
And though I've been far from perfect, I've sought to do the best I could.
But that's the very reason that He hung upon that Cross,
That His life and His death for us, should not be for loss.

So, I am confident in the promises to us, that HE has made,
That I am HIS child, and HE will tend to me, in my evening shade.
I shall be duly blessed, though cosmic events did not my faith mold,
I'll be welcomed as those who've gone before, who now walk the streets of gold.

THE SEVEN MESSAGES FROM THE CROSS

1. THE PRAYER FOR FORGIVNESS OF TRESPASSES. "Father, forgive them for they know not what they are doing." *Luke 23:24*

2. THE PROMISE OF ETERNAL LIFE FOR EVEN THE BROKEN (THE CONFESSING CRIMINAL). "Truly I say unto to you, you shall be with me this day in Paradise." *Luke 23:43*

3. LEAVING, BUT STILL LOVING (GONE BUT NOT FORGOTTEN). When Jesus therefore saw His Mother, and the disciple whom He loved, He said to His Mother, "Behold thy Son." Then He said to the disciple "Behold your Mother." And from that day forward the disciple took her into his own household. *John 19:26-27*

4. THE ANGUISHED CRY OF LONLINESS. And at the ninth hour Jesus cried out with a loud voice, "Eloi, Eloi lama sabachthani," which is interpreted "My God! My God! Why hast thou forsaken me?" And when some of the bystanders heard it they began saying "Behold He is crying out for Elijah." *Mark 15:34-35; Matthew 27: 45-47*

5. CALL FOR HELP OF HIS HUMAN NEEDS. "After this Jesus knowing that all things had already been accomplished, in order that Scripture might be fulfilled, said "I am thirsty." *John 19:28*

6. THE SHOUT OF TRIUMPH "It is finished!" *John 19:30*

7. TRUSTING GOD (THE ULTIMATE HEALING PHYSICIAN) "Father, into Thy hands I commit My Spirit." *Luke 23:46*

WHEN OUR FAULTS ARE WIPED AWAY
(John 3:16-17; Romans 5:1; Galatians 2:16, 3:23-26)

For God So Loved the world, He gave up the life of His only Son,
That through Him, Jesus, eternal life, for you and I, would be won.
There is nothing we could do, on our own, to achieve life's perfection,
It is only in Christ's blood and Life, He takes us as imperfect, without rejection.

And He told us that whosoever believes in Him, would not perish,
But have eternal life, as a gift, too precious to buy, yet one to cherish.
So, this exquisite gift, can be neither bought nor earned, at any price,
All because one Man, Jesus Christ, was willing to die for us, the ultimate sacrifice.

So, we shall not earn our way, by works, or meeting some religious law,
For it is given freely, for our commitment to His life's message, The One without flaw.
Yet, even now, He knows our weaknesses, failures, does demand perfection,
But, that we seek excellence, our eyes focused on His Love teaching, and direction.

We are then justified, our failures wiped away, by our faith in Him,
He knows our humanity, that we're not flawless, as angels in a seraphim.
For through Christ, His life and death, we are no longer bound by Law's detail,
And all who earnestly seek His will, shall receive the eternal promise, without fail.

NO CONDEMNATION
(Romans 7:14-25, 8:1-3)

"For I joyfully concur with the law of God in the inner man, but I see a different law in the members of my body, waging war against the law of my mind, and making me a prisoner of the law of sin which is in my members. Wretched man that I am! Who will set me free from this body of death… So then, on the one hand I myself with my mind I am serving the law of God, but on the other, with my flesh the law of sin… There is therefore now no condemnation for those who are in Christ Jesus. For the law of the Spirit of life in Him has set us free from the law of sin and of death…"(Selected verses of the above)

Sometimes the things I do and say, I don't really comprehend,
I strike out at others, pursue my selfish aims, these things I need to mend.
The very things I don't know which direction I'm heading, my life askew,
At these times, I feel I am a walking civil war, each day to start anew.

And the things I want to do right, are those that are left undone,
Why in heaven, on earth, could God love me, I fear must be the worst under sun.
At these times, I don't understand myself, from the one hand to the other,
I am the walking antithesis, wanting to do right, while not loving my brother.

I know then, there are two forces working deep within me,
One who seeks self, yet one who seeks the good, could I but set him free?
I look at who I am, and cry out, "Oh, wretched man that I am!"
Who can free me from this inner turmoil, ah yes, none but the Sacrificial Lamb.

In all of this, I give thanks to God, for the gift of His son Jesus Christ,
Who lifts me up, forgives my failings, died for me, and paid for me the price.
When I don't understand myself, and am mired in my frustration,
I give thanks to God, that through Christ, there is now no condemnation.

For me, it is impossible to fully escape the curse of sin,
Because I am a part of humanity, human and imperfect both without and within.
For in Christ, from the convictions of my sin, He has forever set me free.
By taking Him into my life, He will make and mold me, though still human, a new me.

THE INSEPARABLE LOVE
(Romans 8:28:31-35, 37-39)

All things work for good, and for His purpose, for those who love the Lord,
Nothing can separate us from the Love of God, neither fire nor sword.
Yet, that does not mean that only good things occur, just as they should,
But, that even with the tribulations in all life, with God, can work for good.

So, what can we say to and about all of these things?
That God has a purpose, His love overflows, and makes our heart sing.
For, as we read His Word, and each word and phrase examine,
Nothing separates us from Him, not peril, trouble, distress, nor famine.

And I know, that if God be for us, none can be against us, no defeat.
In all things, we shall have victory, whatever foe we may meet.
And, who can separate us from the love of his Son Jesus Christ?
It is He, Christ, who upon the Cross, paid for us the full and eternal price.

And, since God freely gave His only Son, for us, surely He must truly love us all,
None then, can condemn us, for it is only He, who justifies, both noble and small.
It is Christ, His Son, who lived, who died, was raised, and sits at God's right hand!
It is Christ who intercedes for us, is our advocate, who will our failures, understand.

Knowing this, I am, then, convinced that neither death nor life,
Nor angels, nor principalities, neither past, nor present, nor future strife.
Nor shall height, nor depth, nor anything, anywhere, separate me,
From the love of God, through Christ, from here and now, to eternity.

DAILY TEMPTATION BATTLES IN OUR WAR OF LIFE
(1st John 4:4, Romans 7:14-15, 22-25,8:1; Ephesians 6:10-20)

Temptation comes to each of us in many disguises, from many angles and directions,
It confronts us in many shapes and sizes, has many seamy connections.
It is like the Siren's song that beckoned Ulysses, and his men,
Yet as soon as we navigate thru one seduction, lies another enticement just around the bend.

Like an irresistible attraction, the Prince of Darkness, summons us to his lair,
Whatever be our weakness, he knows, will lure us, to almost more than we can bear.
Like a magnet, we are drawn to the very things, that we want to avoid,
The gaping hole within us, our Achilles heel, for us as an inward carcinoid.

So, whatever are our weakest spots, and each has them, that we're subject to,
It is our personal stumbling block, our downfall, our nemesis, Achilles heel, and our Waterloo.
We can take consolation, in knowing that others have and now wrestle with their debility,
That they understand our inner battle, constantly waged, despite our outward civility.

For the war over temptation, is never done and over, by a single blow or fight,
But won, inch by inch, day by day, a daily struggle, to set our life's ship aright.
And, take courage in the One in Whom we can entrust our very lives,
Who will be with us each day, as our war's daily battles reprise.

By remaining constant, sober, ever vigilant, persevering, our personal battle will be won,
By the One, who has won our ultimate victory, for He is God's only Son.
So when the weakness that grips us, and the pull of the Father of Lies, around us swirls,
Put on the armor of God for Greater is He that is in you than he that is in the world.

SIGNPOSTS ALONG THE GOOD LIFE ROAD
(Romans 12:4-21)

His Word has given us signposts of direction, along the good life road,
As we travel through life, often struggling to carry our own life's load.
These signs are directions, as to how we should other travelers treat,
Yet knowing that we'll not always succeed, these high standards to meet.

Unto each of us are certain gifts given,
It is by these special talents, our life should be driven.
Whether our forte be leadership, service, or teaching,
It is in those areas we should be constantly reaching.

Serve then when called, teach the unteachable, give with liberality,
Lead with diligence, give mercy with cheerfulness, beyond all practicality.
And give love unconditionally, and without any hypocrisy,
Giving to the great and small, rich and poor, peasant or aristocracy.

Turn away from evil, and seek to only do the good,
Put others before you, turn the other cheek, as Jesus would.
Rejoice with those who rejoice, and weep with those who weep,
Practicing hospitality, helping others at times when havoc wreaks.

Bless those who persecute you, and curse not those who curse you,
Never pay back evil for evil, nor stoke the fires of resentment anew.
Show respect for the right, never praise, nor tacitly support, the wrong,
Be at peace with all, in so far as it depends on you, harboring no anger for long.

Persevere in times of tribulation, rejoice when times are good and times of hope,
Don't be haughty, feel superior, befriend the downtrodden, help them to cope.
Practice not vengeance for wrongs done you, rather let your forgiveness shine,
For we are told by the Giver and Sustainer of Life, that "Vengeance is mine!"

And if your enemy is hungry, then give him food to eat,
If naked cloth him, if thirsty, given him drink, and as a brother treat.
For to do so will be as coals on his head, drown his anger with your kindness,
In doing all these things, you will live out God's plan, in all its fineness.

DIFFERENT STROKES FOR DIFFERENT FOLKS, ONE GOD, A COMMON FAITH
(Matthew 15: 1-20; John 10: 14-19; Acts 10:9-22; Romans 14:1-5, 17-22)

Not all who profess their faith in God, agree on all Faith or Theology things,
What is important to one's faith, for another, it may be sent off on eagle's wings.
One may believe strongly that God should be honored only in a certain way,
While others may feel just as passionately, that the opposite should hold sway.

Some believe that we should not eat any meats, others only certain kinds,
Some believe we must be immersed to have salvation, others have a different mind.
And some believe that certain days are more important in faith than others,
While another believes that all days are alike to pray, worship, and to serve our brothers.

Whatever our beliefs, we need to determine if our differences are substance or form,
For who are we to judge another, to determine what for them should be their norm.
We should not condemn, those who believe and worship differently than we,
Not get sidetracked in details, nor flaunt our faith, but only the core of the Gospel we should see.

For those who differ, just as we, shall each stand before the Judgment seat of God,
Our task is not to criticize, judge, condemn, look down and conclude their way is flawed.
Our job is rather to put aside differences, pursue those things God would have us do
To be just, love mercy, help others, walk humbly with God, and others life renew.

And, if there is something we do that makes our neighbor stumble or fall,
Then we should not do it, even if we find in it no fault, if it trips him at all.
What we should be focusing upon, is growing goodness, peace and joy other's lives,
Rather than judging and condemning others faith, seek to make His Kingdom thrive.

LIFE'S FAITH RACE
(1st Corinthians 9:24-27; Philippians 3:13-14; Hebrews 12:1-2, 2nd Timothy 4: 6-8)

In so many ways life and faith are like a long distance marathon race,
We must discipline our minds and bodies, and confront our weaknesses, face to face.
The race we run for life is not a short sprint, where we run as fast as we can,
But a well thought out distance race, we seek to finish, then pass the baton, to do God's plan.

All are not relegated the same distance race they are to complete,
Some will run a lengthy race, others but a shorter journey, in which to compete.
So each must run his own race, not knowing when his race ends, making his own mark.
Each racer runs as in a relay, following others, setting excellence as his own benchmark.

In our race of life, there will be times we forge ahead, and times we fall behind,
During our life's run, though daily fortunes vary, we keep the final goal in mind.
Inspired by the endurance of earlier and other runners alongside us, and those who've passed,
While also encouraging others, who've grown weary, and feel they've been outclassed.

But there is lengthy training and preparations we must pursue, before we've begun,
We train, build our endurance, learn self-control, and test our strength, in life's hot sun.
So that in life's race, we may have had a purpose, that the valued future for to win,
The prize we seek is more than a medal or wreath, but an eternal prize that conquers sin.

So, we train, by the way we live our life, that we might finish well the course,
And having completed it to the best we are able, are empowered by a Greater Force.
There will be those times when we are out of breath, become weary and tired,
Having trained in the eternal plan, will struggle on, by the imprint of others, be inspired.

To those who run the race of faith and life, as with all, there will be joy and pain,
We have trained hard to run well, finish the course that we not run and toil, in vain.
So at race's end, we have kept the Faith, finished the course, and fought the good fight.
Then, we pass the baton, and Cross, to another runner, while keeping our Lord Jesus in our sight.

AN EXPLANATION OF LOVE GOD IS LOVE, LOVE IS OF GOD
(1st Corinthians 13; 1st John 4:7-16)

It is impossible to define completely, unconditional love in human terms,
To find the words that the full significance of God's Love would confirm.
For love is like God, you can neither see, nor touch, nor hear Him,
You can feel His presence, know God's Love is here and everywhere among men.

So it is with love, you can't see it, hear it, or touch it, but can observe its presence,
For the eternal truth of love is of God, God is Love, at its very essence.
And when one abides in God, he or she also abides in His love,
If God then loves us, we should love each other, as His Love comes from above.

Even if I could speak eloquently in all the languages of heaven and earth,
But have not Love, I'm just making noise like a clanging cymbal, of no worth.
And if I can prophesy and know the future, have all knowledge about all things,
But have not Love, it all amounts to zero, nothing, it has a hollow ring.

And, even if I have faith so strong, I can move mountains, but have no Love in me,
It is again worthless, my great acts of faith, are like, as if washed to the sea.
And even though I give all that I have to the poor, and my body burned for my faith,
But have no attitude of Love, do for my own praise, my good works would negate.

Love then is difficult to define, but can be seen as something like this,
Love is patient, is kind, forgiving, never jealous, always stable, never amiss.
And Love is never proud, nor arrogant, never keeps a record of wrongs,
So too, Love never rejoices in evil, rejoices in truth, is never headstrong.

Love will prevail, and bears all things, in the troubled times and the good,
Love believes and hopes for the good in all things, and endures, even if misunderstood.
So, even though prophesies, men's knowledge, and eloquence will all pass away,
Love will never fail, will conquer all, and is the path to Heaven's Gateway.

For while we often think we know it all, when in truth, we only know, in part,
When the perfect Love comes, we shall have all knowledge in our heart.
Again, it is like this, when I was a child, I spoke, thought, and reasoned like a child,
But when I grew up, I laid aside my childish things, my childish dreams were reconciled.

So, also, now I see myself and truth, only as in a poor reflection mirror, a fog in dim light,
But when Love and life is fulfilled, in that day, I shall see truth and myself, in full sight.
For now I only know, and see, only a part of the portrait of life, and all life, that is shown,
But then, I shall understand all things, just as I have been, by God's Love, always fully known.

And so it is that all temporal things, without Love, shall wither and disappear,
But those things that are immersed in Love, shall remain and prevail true and clear.
Of all things in life, there shall be but three things in our life which shall last for all of eternity,
Faith, Hope, and Love, yet the greatest of these is God's Love, as demonstrated by you and me.

THE TEMPLE TREASURE WITHIN THE JARS MADE OF CLAY
(Isaiah 64:8; 1st Corinthians 6:19-20; 2nd Corinthians 4:7-9)

Our lives and bodies, molded by the Master Potter's hand, likened unto jars made of clay,
Molded in the image of God, but with man's imperfections we have gone astray.
Formed, shaped by the hands of others, and baked in the world's grueling sun,
With the stresses and cracks of life, breaking down what the Potter had spun.

Through countless outward coats of paint, the jars made to look valuable from afar,
But a closer inspection would show the defects and frailties of these fragile jars.
Yet each of these vessels was designed by the Master Potter, to hold within,
As a temple for the Holy Spirit within, that others might see thru us, God's plan for men.

And within this jar, lies a beautiful, unseen, and heavenly treasure,
That has more value than all of the diamonds and gold, by any measure.
For through the power of God, in these jars, we may yet be made strong,
To withstand all of the blows that may strike us, that are done in wrong.

And though we be pressed and struck from every side, the Spirit within not be destroyed,
Worried and perplexed, but not despaired, persecuted, but not abandoned, in a void.
Though injured, beaten, knocked down, but not knocked out, and able to rise again,
For it is the Treasure within these jars that restores, and gives joy, even in pain.

The treasure within these cruses, is Jesus Spirit, His life death, for you and me,
Yet also His resurrected Life, now transparent in Spirit, jars of clay, for others to see.
It is through His death and new life, that these cracked, broken, even ugly earthen urns,
Are transformed into beautiful perfect vessels, emitting God's love, for all to discern.

SOWING, REAPING AND SHARING BOUNTIFULLY
(Luke 12:48b; 2nd Corinthians 9:6-7; Acts 20:35; Leviticus 19:9-10; Proverbs 11:24-25; Malachi 3:10)

What we sow today, thus shall we reap on a coming morn,
Sow a flower's seeds, reap beautiful flowers, sow seeds of thorns, will reap thorns.
And, if you sow what you plant sparingly, a sparing harvest will be your fate,
But sowing good seeds you may reap bountifully, and your harvest will be great.

So it is with our giving, the one who gives, for him, giving little, is not giving smart,
God asks only of us, that we each give as we prayerfully, purpose in our heart.
To the poor widow, the gift of her penny or her mite, is generous,
Yet, to the rich man, the gift of grand sums, may be for him penurious.

For the one who gives as bountifully as he can, will be truly blessed,
But giving should be done cheerfully, not grudgingly, under compulsion or stressed.
Sowing generously then, in our giving, we get back manifold blessings, even more,
While the one who gives none, small and miserly, may well end up, in spirit, poor.

Giving well, as we purpose, then, not to gain more, but for the joy of helping and giving,
The Master's words, "It is more blessed to give than receive," should govern our living.
And to each who has been given and entrusted much, much more may be required,
Help for the needy children, the helpless, the sick, the yearning to be free, and the tired.

For in sowing, reaping and giving bountifully, it will be returned to us, and even more.
As God has told us, if we give our best, He will pour out blessings, open Heaven's door.

A DECLARATION OF EQUALITY
(Galatians 3:25-26, 28; 4:7)

In the New Kingdom, God's World, there are neither higher stations nor castes,
What our status in this world may be, is all in the past.

There is neither Jew, nor Greek, neither free man, nor slave,
All our exclusive titles, stations, and societies, are as buried in the grave.

There is neither black, nor white, male nor female, royalty nor commoner,
Neither the amount of money we have, nor the title we claim, will be our worth barometer.

For while we are not all given the same strengths, opportunities and talents,
These are all, by God, who makes us one, put in their proper balance.

As we each stand before the Cross, regardless of earthly rank, we're all on equal ground,
And, for those of us who have been lost, we are no longer lost, but now are found.

We are no longer then either slave or master, but are each daughters or sons,
We are according to the promise, heirs to the Kingdom of the Holy One.

It gives us hope to know that in God's eyes, there are none better than we,
For it is what is in our hearts and lives, that only He sees.

THE HARVEST OF THE SOWER'S SEEDS
(Hosea 8:7; Galatians 6:7-9)

Don't deceive yourself, for God is neither fooled, nor mocked,
He knows your every thought and action, since your birth was clocked.

You cannot hide from him in darkness, or in the shadows of your mind,
For just as with Adam, He sees right through us, will seek us and will us find.

Whatever it is that you sow in this world, you will eventually reap,
Sow seeds of anger, reap bitterness, sow evil, reap evil, and tears of sorrow weep.

Sow bad seeds of selfishness and flesh, and you will reap corruption,
Like a man covered with boils, oozing with infectious eruptions.

Sow the wind, reap a harvest of the hurricane, or tornado whirlwind,
That destroys everything in its path, from the beginning to the end.

But sow ye good seeds of the Spirit of love, and you will find peace,
A peace that is beyond human understanding, gives you respite and release.

Sow seeds of justice and mercy, and you will be called blessed among men,
They will honor you, seek your wisdom, to come back again and again.

Yet even though it is seeds of good that you have nurtured and sown,
The harvest time of seeds, good and bad, is in God's hand, at a time His own.

So, do not lose patience, in the planting, and the flowering of your good seeds,
God will, in His time, bring forth in glory, the harvest of all your worthy deeds.

ENDURING ALL TIMES AND CIRCUMSTANCES
Finding the Peace That Passes Human Understanding
(Philippians 4:4-13)

Rejoice in the Lord always, and do not be dragged down by anxiety and worry,
Don't be in a rush, God is in control, so you need not be in a hurry.
Whatever anxiousness that is strangling your joy, pray about it, without ceasing,
Turn it over to God, you'll begin to feel a Peace within you that He is releasing.

And the Peace that comes from God, which is beyond all our human understanding,
For through Him, when you get up tight, He will give you a safe landing.
For the Peace He gives is of the mind, body and heart, not as the world gives,
Of money, of position, of tangible things, that slip through our fingers, like a sieve.

Our part in having God's Peace, is accentuating, in our lives, the positive things,
Make and do things that are honorable, true, right and pure in our minds and hearts spring.
Always look for the positive, for excellence and lovely, things of good repute,
Rather than looking for the negative, the ugly, and the things that bring dispute.

If something is worthy of praise, then give it your wholehearted acclaim,
Even if not perfect, find the positive that is in it, that you can proclaim.
So think and dwell on the worthy things that you see around you,
Rather than focusing on the imperfections, that will keep us in a stew.

For if we see the good, we will learn to live, and be content in all conditions,
Whether we are rich or poor, good times or bad, in pursuing our life's missions.
Then, with God's help, we will find the strength to meet whatever life decrees,
Wherever and whoever we are in life, we can make it through in life, in Him, into eternity.

BEARING ONE ANOTHER'S BURDENS
(Galatians 6:2-5)

Each of us has daily and life burdens to bear,
Many different kinds, but our own burdens to care.
Yet God calls us to service, to help carry the load of another,
Whether it be family, friend, even stranger, a sister or brother.

For the burden which we help, by our presence, to shoulder,
Is only half as heavy, gives the other courage to become bolder.
Do not deceive yourself that your job of help is too big, too small or beneath you,
And share the gift of mercy, God has given you, to share with others too.

And if your load is heavy, and you see the load of another, as light,
Do not compare yourself with them, for God judges you, in your own sight.
And do not judge others in the way that they carry their load,
Until you've walked in their shoes, and traveled down their road.

This then, is one thing we learn in life, for certain,
That each, must ultimately, bear and carry his own burden.
Yet, Jesus said, "Come to me, all who are heavy laden, with weight,"
So, we too, should help carry another's burden, if need be to Heaven's Gate.

THE PERIL AND PROMISE OF RICHES
(1st Timothy 6:6-12; 17-19; Luke 12:48)

We bring absolutely nothing tangible into this world, but the skin on our bones,
No Jaguars, no large bank accounts, no stock, no big houses or cellular phones.
Likewise, when we check out, we take nothing more than whence we came,
Regardless of our earthly successes, or the way we played the game.

So, if while we are here, if we have food, clothing, essentials, we should be content,
Knowing the temptation of riches, a trap for the unwary, can give us a selfish bent.
We are told, from those who are given much, much more of them, is expected,
That it's easy for those who are rich, to be drawn off course, of a life, God's Word directed.

Money itself is not our bane, but the love of its power, is the source of much evil,
It can ruin our lives, cause us much grief, bore through our hearts, like a weevil.
And, since our obsession with money may be addictive, and cause many a pain,
If our life is God centered, we will keep it in perspective, whatever we attain.

If then, you are one who has been tangibly blessed, and to whom much has been given,
That much more, will be expected of you, use it wisely, for good purposes be driven.
In all things pursue godliness, faith, gentleness, and with your wealth be sharing.
Fight off the curse of wealth, fight the good fight, that you may keep your bearing.

And do not be haughty about your successes, what you have amassed in your hands,
For it can be as quickly taken from you, your stocks, your money and your lands.
Fix your mental compass, to be humble, rich in good works, and be willing to share,
Laying up your treasure with compassion in helping others, in need of your care.

All of the status, power and money in the world, will not peace and contentment bring.
It is the love of family and friends, helping those in need that makes one's heart sing.
Consider yourself blessed, then in all that has, by your work and labors, entrusted to you,
Sharing bountifully, content with who you are, what you have, your whole life through.

REFINING THE PRECIOUS METAL AND METTLE OF OUR LIVES
(James 1:2-4; Malachi 3:1-3; Isaiah 43:1-3,5; 64:8; Proverbs 27:19)

PREFACE

One day not long ago, as I was reading the verses above from the prophet Malachi, when he was speaking for God. As I read the words again I was puzzled by the words which made the analogy of the coming Messiah being like "a refiner" who will refine us "like gold and silver", so that we may live and give an "acceptable" offering to God by our lives.

Knowing nothing about how gold and silver were refined either in Biblical times or today, how would this heating process make us better able to serve? What purpose does the refining serve? First, as we know from the time of early man, more than 4,000 years ago, gold and silver were discovered and considered valuable. They were valuable, for in their purest form, that man could create, they were considered rare, stronger, brighter and more malleable than iron or lead, and could be molded into useful objects. Even copper, though much less rare was valuable by itself, when mixed with other metals, it too was a malleable and useful metal.

So it was, man later found that iron could be made much stronger by adding copper to the iron, creating an alloy which we call steel, by heating and smelting, mixing the two together under great heat.

And as I read on, I found that even what was later to be called sterling silver, was not fully sterling or pure at all, but only 92.5% pure, containing 7.5% copper. Moreover, that even refined gold was not completely pure, that it was measured by its carat weight, and that what I thought were "pure gold coins were not were likewise not completely pure- and at the very best 99% pure.

As I began to study the early refining process, I found that before science had created the precision of the modern refining and smelting processes, that the silver refiner--- sat and personally watched the process, and knew when the heating was "just right" to melt out most of the impurities, and yet not "overcook" the silver.

At this point, when he could remove the liquid metal from the fire and see his image in the liquid, as it, the molten metal was a mirror image of the refiner. Only then was the process complete. Then I began to think about the Prophet Malachi giving the comparison of the metal refiner as being God and "we" being the metal. Also, what the prophet Isaiah had said about God being the Potter, and we were like the clay, and He would work and mold us into something beautiful and good (Isaiah 64:8). Further what Isaiah had said about the times we are in deep waters, that the rivers would not overflow us, and when we walk through fire we would not be burned, because in those times He would be with us (Isaiah 43:1-2,3a,5a Psalm 23:4.) So too then, is HE like the silver refiner, HE is there with us and watches over us, but he doesn't necessarily "save" us from all distress and discomfort. That is a part of life, a part of the strengthening process.

But then what of the fact that even gold and silver are never fully purified by human hand? Ah yes, we are still human, we are frail and live our lives in imperfection. We still are subject to jealousy, greed, self-centeredness, vanity and lust. It is only through the gift of the Messiah who Malachi said would come, and His blood, are we fully redeemed, and only made 100% wholly pure, when our time comes to meet our Maker. In this life we will not be fully purified.

What then of the molten gold and silver, the painful process of the deep waters and the burning fires of life, and what of the refining process of the metal refiner. Just as with the metal, while the Great Refiner, sees and knows these are often difficult times for us, He is with us in these times, and, as the sword is made stronger by the searing heat, so it is through these times that we grow wiser, stronger, and more complete- if we put our lives in His hands and trust Him.

So it was, a long way around, to understanding the refiner seated by and watching the fire, as it worked its purifying of the precious metals of gold and silver, just as God will purify His precious sons and daughters. But, from His Words in Malachi what I now see:

… That God is with us each day of our lives, watching, waiting and with arms outstretched, to help us on the way, and giving us encouragement in difficult times.

… That even though we may follow Him, we have no protective "life storms umbrella", as with all people, our lives will include times of storm, fire, and deep water, (see Matthew 5:45b) even though He walks with us, and His plan for us is always ultimately for our good (Jeremiah 29:11), many human and natural forces intervene.

… That even in the refining times of fire and deep waters, God is with us and walks with us, that though we may be wounded and die in this world, we shall not be destroyed and will have continuing life through and with Him.

… That not only our life's metal (and meddle) the fires of our stress are purified in the fires and deep waters of life— but our mettle, our character is strengthened. (James 1:2-4)

… That we may become more "pure", better, stronger, wiser and more useful to ourselves and others through Him even in and in spite of the deep waters and fires of life.

… That we all have value, though we may be of different metals, some considered more valuable than others by the world, some more pure than others by our life process, but that we all will stand on equal footing at the Cross of His Son, Jesus, and are all precious in His sight.

… That even as gold and silver are not fully purified, so too we shall in this life remain not fully purified, though some will be more purified (and less imperfect) than others; because we are humanly flawed, but we shall be cleansed through the Blood of His Son, and through His Grace, in His own time, we shall be made perfect (not just 92% as in sterling silver). We shall be as in the words of the Apostle Paul- "sewn (buried) perishable, in dishonor, weakness, imperfect, and natural, but raised (to a new life)- imperishable, in glory, power, perfection, and spiritual (1st Corinthians 15:41-44).

… That though we are not wholly purified, and imperfect in this life, by adding the life of Christ and His two great Commandments (Matthew 22:34-40), we will be as copper added to iron to create steel, stronger, more pure, and that our life and our values will neither mold nor rust, nor may they be stolen by thieves as may tangible things, that our light and life will shine (Matthew 5: 14-16) as does steel for others to see, and that our life lived may have meaning on earth from our legacy lived, long after our earthly body and life are gone from this earth.

REFINING THE PRECIOUS METAL OF OUR LIFE

Understanding that often our greatest growth and enlightenment may come in times of distress, difficulty or trial
(James 1:2-4; see also especially Malachi 3:1-3; Isaiah 43:1-5; 64:8)

The metallurgist has refined metal, in the same manner, as from the days of old,
Whether the precious part of the raw ore be comprised of platinum, silver, or gold.
When the priceless ingot hits the fire, he watches closely as it heats,
Holding and studying the process, as the impurities begin to secrete.

Yet the Smelter knew that if the silver is heated a moment too long,
The precious substance will be damaged, rather than being hearty and strong.
He knows instinctively, when the process of heating, is finally done,
For in it he sees his own image reflected clearly, the value process begun.

So it is with us, in life's storms, deep waters, or burning fires, though pain and stress we feel,
As with iron, when copper "mettle" of God thru the Holy Spirit is added with searing heat, comes the unbreakable strength of steel.
May we too, as we add HIM and trust in HIM in our lives, HE stands with us each day, holding tightly, giving our life more meaning,
Watching until HE purifies, strengthens and may see HIS image in us, becoming a precious metal gleaming.

Yet, even the refined metals, as we in human form, contain impurity traces of ore metals,
Through life's fires and storms, events have brought us, the REFINER has strengthened our mettle.
Even if we become 24 carat gold or sterling silver, we are never fully free of all the old imperfect mud,
We have greater value, strength and purpose, yet only perfectly purified, when washed by the Grace and gift of HIS cleansing BLOOD.

LIKE A TWO EDGED SWORD
(Psalms 57:4; Proverbs 5:1-4, 12:25, 16:24, 25:11; Hebrews 4:12, James 3:4-11)

The most powerful organ within each of us, ounce for ounce,
The ne that gives our personality a hefty bounce.
Is that two ounce wagging monster lying in wait, within our mouth,
The tongue, like a ship's rudder, sends us on a course, either north or south.

God planted the tongue behind the cage of our teeth,
To keep it in check, to only carefully, take out this sword, from its sheath.
For the tongue, though small, has awesome destructive power,
With one blow, it can bring down the mighty, turn a whole life sour.

Or it can just rattle on, just to be talking like so much palaver,
'Tis wasted energy, misuses God's gift, just to use it for jabber.
Sometimes the talk is empty, just so much hot wind,
With no real purpose, no message to send.

The tongue, like so many things, was not created to do bad,
Even though we use it to hurt, all too often, when we get mad.
Yet it can be used not only to destroy, but to do great good,
If only its great power were completely understood.

For the words we speak, are as arrows from a cross and bow,
Sometimes thoughtless shots can injure or destroy, more than we know.
And yet the same tongue, can with words, that are like a skillful surgeon's knife,
Heal a wound, excise an emotional cancer, or even save a desperate life.

There are then, things about the tongue, and its sounds, we need to comprehend,
That the words we speak, may, know it or not, create an enemy, or win a friend.
Yet the tongue should not be condemned, for it is simply the messenger,
Of an angry, hurt or malicious heart, that is striking out, or create a stir.

The very same mouth may with words, give compassion, build up, encourage or heal,
Can change or set new direction for a young life, or renew an older one to feel.
That their very existence is important, a life to be treasured and prized,
With words that calm fears, create new horizons, in ways, that leave, even the speaker, surprised.

Our words are like a two edged sword, one edge pierces deeply, the other restores,
One edge affirms, the other batters, one edge brings joy, the other remorse.
Carefully choose then, and carefully speak, the right words for the occasion,
That your words might lift another up, or bring about, friendly persuasion.

Sometimes our most effective words may be no words at all,
Just our very presence may speak volumes, and tragedy forestall.
Using words then as our tools, as our refined instruments of healing,
Choose your words selectively, just the right implement, for the circumstance we're dealing.

Because our spoken words have the power to create or destroy,
We need to carefully consider, when and how our words to deploy.
Our words need to be thoughtfully molded and carefully conceived,
For their impact on others, may go far beyond, what we could have ever believed.

WHAT FAITH IS!
(Hebrews 11:1-3)

PREFACE

What is Faith? Young's Analytical Concordance to the Bible contains some 243 entries where the word faith is used, but in only a few places is it defined. Probably the best known definition of Faith, in Scripture, is the one above, found in the Book of Hebrews.

In the Apostle Paul's "Love Chapter" (1st Corinthians 13), he concludes that all knowledge will pass away, but three things, those being Faith, Hope and Love, shall never pass away. In this chapter, he gives us a beautiful exposition of what love is. If only Paul in some of his writings had given us in the same manner, in one place, so clearly defined love, pinpointing also faith and hope, we would have been blessed in "triplicate."

Webster's New World College Dictionary (fourth Edition) gives as its first definition of faith: "Unquestioning belief that does not require proof or evidence." That seems all inclusive, but many of us claim to have faith- but we still have questions. There are still things we just aren't sure about! Yes, and there are times, when life seems unfair and our concept of justice fails, if we are honest with ourselves, deep in our hearts, we as the Apostle Thomas, can have questions about the great scheme of things.

So what is faith? Men and women much wiser than I have attempted to define it, books have been written on the word "Faith", but even with that, it does become confusing. So, I went back to Scripture searching for how the men who wrote God's Word, endeavored in human terms, to define faith. "What Faith Is," that follows takes some of those inspired words, and seeks to piece them together in verse, adding in, of course some thoughts of our own.

My hope is that it might make you begin to think, and to clearly define in your own life and mind, what Faith means to you. If it does that, then it has been well worth the effort.

WHAT FAITH IS.

Now Faith is the assurance of things hoped for, the conviction of things not seen. For by it men of old and even men and women today gain God's "approval."
By Faith we understand that the worlds were prepared by the spoken Word of God, so that what is seen was not made by The One, or out of things which are visible.
Hebrews 11:1-3

Faith is received more readily, by those who have with their senses, seen, felt, and heard,
Faith is even more blessed for those who have not seen, yet still, abide in His Word.
John 20:29

Faith is an unfaltering trust in God's plan, that all things, will work out,
That all things work for good, for those who love the Lord, and cast aside their doubt.
Romans 8:28

Faith is the promise, that there is, for us, no condemnation, through God's only Son,
For those who are humble, repentant, and trust in Him, their eternal victory is already won!
Romans 8:1

Faith is the knowledge that all that we are and possess, are but gifts from our God,
Given to us for a time, to be wise stewards, and not by our own successes, be awed.
1st Chronicles 29: 14-16

Faith is the confidence that God hears, listens to, and will answer our prayers,
Even when His answers seem to us delayed, and our plans may impair.
Matthew 7:7-8

Faith is expecting a field of flowers, from our life's barren lands,
Claiming His strength, as our courage and shield, our life, in His hands
Philippians 4:13

Faith is the certainty that God has an eternal plan for me, though I cannot see,
Even when I feel helpless and useless, thrashing about in life's turbulent seas.
John 20: 26-29

Faith is realizing that God is the Lord of time, will act in His own time,
Especially as I wait impatiently, when His timing isn't mine.
Isaiah 4:28-31; Psalm 40:1-4; Psalms 37:2-9

Faith is believing that God will use me, even with only my own mere five loaves and two fish,
That through Him, even small and great miracles will come, as He may wish.
Mark 6: 32-44

Faith is the boldness to know that we will not sink, in life's waters deep,
If we trust in Him, and on Him our focus keep. Isaiah 43:1-3 *Matthew 14: 25-33*

Faith is our walk in His path, even when the sight we have, is as in a mirror dim,
Knowing that the goal we strive for, is to live our life, that we might please HIM!
1st Corinthians 13:12-13; 2nd Corinthians 5:7-9

Faith is the conviction, that even when my life's circumstances, are spinning out of control,
That God, has not left me, stands alongside me, will one day make my body, mind and soul whole.
Psalm 23:4; Isaiah 43:1-2

Faith is evidenced, not in just what we profess, but in the way we live out our lives,
So others may see our faith, for it is our faith through our actions that survives.
James 2:14-18

Faith is saying and doing the right thing, when the wrong thing is the world's way,
Knowing that God will right the wrongs, in His time and way, as we earnestly pray.
Psalm 73: 1-14

Faith is refusing to think that God loves only the beautiful, the powerful, those with success,
And knowing God loves each of us, even as we are, when our life is a mess.
John 3:16-17; Romans 7:18-25, 8:1-2

Faith is trusting that there will be justice, even when the unjust seem to prevail,
That God will work it all into His plan, judge the wrongdoers, and His plan unveil.
Psalm 73: 16-28

Faith is remembering that even in times when I feel my life is useless,
In God's eyes, I am the one lost sheep to be found, the treasured pearl that is priceless.
Matthew 13:45; 18:10-14

Faith is as the child who squeals with delight, when cast in the air, knowing His father will not let him fall,
Just as we, if we follow His way, He will make our steps firm, will catch us and hold us in His hand, through it all.
Psalm 37:23-24

Faith is stronger, gains endurance, even in times of hardship, trial and loss,
Rather than through celebrant robes and rituals, stained glass, and cathedrals that embellish and emboss.
James 1:2-4

Faith is letting go, past hurts, anxiety for the future, and living each day in the present,
Knowing that worry never wins, only tears down, and is wasted time spent.
Matthew 6:25-34

Faith is never giving up on ourselves, and God, through all of our years,
Knowing that His promises are true, He will come again, He will wipe away all death, pain and tears.
Revelation 21: 1-5; 22:12-13

SHOW ME YOUR FAITH
(James 2: 14-26)

A man may proclaim that he has faith, but the living of his life denies it,
He may see another, hungry, naked, or thirsty, say "God bless you, Oh how I despise it."
Yet the blessing is hollow, unless he acts upon that need which he sees,
Gives water to the thirsty, food to the hungry, clothing to the naked, medicine to one with disease.

For if he simply says, "Go in peace, my brother" what good has he done,
He shows his faith by his words only, but from doing the mercy he has shunned.
So it is with real Faith, if it is not followed by action, to help another in need,
Then the faith one claims is just words, dead, a lifeless thing, of no real use, indeed.

Then some will say, "Hear my words, watch my praise, see the faith that I have."
I say to them, "For a serious wound, all you provide are unctuous words, a useless salve."
And I will say to them "You show me your faith, I'll show you in my works, by how to live."
"And how you should honor your God, by helping others, and in the way that you give."

"For our labors for God, our works are but the visible evidence of a faith that is real.
How you have reached out to others each day, with words and hands that heal.
So, more important than all your memorized prayers, scriptures recited, and read,
Is a living, working, active faith, for faith, standing alone, without works is dead."

MY ADVOCATE*

(1st John 2:1-2, 1st Corinthians 13:12; Micah 6:6-8; Matthew 18:10-14; Revelation 20:10-15)

In GOD'S Own Time, there shall come a day,
When I shall have finally passed this way.
And I shall stand at the Bar, of HIS Great Throne,
Before I go, to my Eternal Home.

On that Great Day, HE shall judge my life,
Which has seen both beauty, failure and strife.
And, then, I shall see my life past, so clearly,
What I had seen before, only in a mirror dimly.

And while I know I should stand in trembling and fear,
With the Mighty Power of My GOD so near.
But I shall fear no more, with Jesus thru GOD'S GRACE,
When I shall meet my MASTER, FACE to face.

For JESUS gave HIS Life, HIS very Blood,
That I might stand amidst Life's raging flood.
And on that Day, all my sins are laid to rest,
By HIS Blood and Life, I have passed the test.

Oh, what a comfort it is to me,
To know when I pass o'er the Crystal Sea,
That standing by me in that Judgment Time,
Is JESUS, my ADVOCATE, I, the lost one, of the ninety an nine.

For HE is greater than all the Prophets of old,
Greater than all the Angels, playing their harps of gold,
Greater than a thousand Jennings Bryans and Clarence Darrows,
JESUS, my ADVOCATE, my DEFENDER, my BOW and my ARROW.

For when the BOOK is opened and I am asked, Why?
It shall be JESUS, the RIGHTEOUS, Who speaks for me, not I.
And HE shall say, "Though he often failed, he earnestly tried,
It was for his failures that I willingly died."

"And though he stumbled day by day,
He tried as YOU asked, to show kindness and justice, along the way.
And even as he faltered he sought to do the right,
Knowing that every step he took was always in YOUR sight."

And, so it is armed with this Blessed Assurance,
That I need not fear, when I give up my last, and all my endurance.
For JESUS, my ROCK, my ADVOCATE, my DEFENDER,
Shall take me HOME, to that ETERNAL PLACE OF SPLENDOR.

*Written to and for the concerns of a dear friend in his last illness.

235

A NEW DAY COMING
(Psalm 40: 1-3; Isaiah 11:6-9, 65:17-19; Revelation 21:1-5,22:1-5, 12,13)

In God's own time, there shall come a New Day,
When He shall come down, with His Son, a new earth for to stay.
For They, in this New World, shall come to abide with us,
To mark a new Beginning of true righteousness and justice.

In that New Day, He shall, with all of His people, find joy,
For all the things of evil in the past, He shall destroy.
He shall create a New Jerusalem, where all shall live in peace,
Where man shall no hate his brother, and wars shall forever cease.

The wolf shall live with the lamb, the leopard with the lion, all animals be tamed,
And the beasts of the wild shall be led by a child, the creature of Man, be changed.
And all the nations of men, shall walk by His Light,
And kings shall praise His glory, give justice, and do right.

There shall be no more weeping, for He shall wipe away all tears,
No more death, neither sadness, nor pain, through all eternity's years.
Man shall no longer dwell in the darkness of the night,
Neither there be Sun, nor lamp, for God's New World shall illuminate in light.

For the first things, when man moved east of Eden, shall have all passed away,
No longer will there be evil or greed, when God comes down to stay.
And, in this New World, shall be Rivers of Living Water, from his Throne,
Beside the Rivers, a Tree of Life, bearing life giving fruit, from Heavenly seeds sewn.

Though we know that God is The Alpha and Omega, the Beginning and the End,
We know not when the present earth shall pass away, and the New Jerusalem descend.
And though we know not the day nor the time this New Heaven will come down,
He says, "Be ready, I am coming soon, to make all things new," in His time, a new song, throughout the universe
will resound.

A SOMEWHAT QUICK JOURNEY THROUGH THE BIBLE IN VERSE

NOTE: Some time ago I saw a ten line rhyming poem of the Bible, in a periodical that was called a "Bible Summary." I was intrigued with the idea of telling the Bible Story in a nutshell fashion, in verse. So, I began my own adventure, even as flawed and incomplete as it is.

Beginning in Genesis and tracking through the Bible to Revelation, we sought to touch on some of the best known stories and messages of the Bible, with which many would be familiar. Needless to say, what came out is not even cooked "once over lightly" of just a few of the stories, and touching on the relationship of God with His people, and with us today.

In the terminology of poetry, certainly it is not an epic, maybe an "Ode" to God's love and care for mankind. Whatever, the result are thirty seven multi-lined rhyming couplets, which together we call "A Somewhat Quick Journey Through the Bible in Verse," together with book, chapter and verse references to the Bible. I hope that it will either bring to you memories of Biblical stories of old, you heard as a child, or even if not, that it might encourage you to search further for how "The Bible Speaks To You."

A SOMEWHAT QUICK JOURNEY THROUGH THE BIBLE IN VERSE

In the beginning, God created, and all things in the heavens and earth made,
But, while and by eating the forbidden fruit of all knowledge, Adam and Eve played.
So out of the Garden, And east of Eden, they were sent,
This, only the beginning of man's imperfections and descent.
Genesis 1-3

At God's call, Noah began to build an ark, on the flooded waters to float,
While his neighbors, scoffed, said "You fool," made fun of him, and did gloat.
Then, as he finished, the rains and floods, for forty days came,
It was man's sin and wretchedness that were to blame.
Genesis 6-8

Abram offered his son, Isaac, as a sacrifice to God, in an act of Faith,
Yet God, after testing Abram's faith, spared his son, by His Grace.
God's Covenant with Abram, because of his faith, his heirs, twelve tribes, would be the chosen ones. Chosen as God's people, to follow Him, but with responsibility, from birth 'til life is done.
Genesis 21

To Isaac and Rebekah, two sons, named Esau and Jacob, were born,
But through Jacob's guile, his brother Esau's inheritance was shorn.
Genesis 25

Because of his brother's jealousies, Joseph was sold into bondage,
Joseph remained steadfast, forgave his brothers, became a ruler in Egypt at a young age.
Genesis 37-49

Then Moses, a Jew, but future Egyptian leader, fled to the desert, where to him, the Burning Bush talked,
But Moses, at eighty, doubted his calling, and to God's call, he balked.
Exodus 2-4

Hesitantly, Moses signed on, and through God's Hand, the Pharaoh's land was plagued,
Finally, after many plagues, Pharaoh saw the light, and God's power, and a release deal was made.
Moses and Israel left Pharaoh's Egypt with great haste, and a shout,
Released by God's power, as freed men and women, they walked out.
Exodus 14

Then God, through Moses' rod, for Israel's children, the Red Sea was divided,
Through the wilderness, by the Ten Commandments, Israel, God's people, He guided.
Exodus 26-40

And, after forty years of travelling over and around the Desert's sand,
'Tis Joshua who led Israel, into Canaan, and divided among 11 of the 12 tribes, the Promised Land.
Joshua 1-19

After the Judges, at Israel's demand, God appointed a handsome, reluctant Saul, as Israel's first king,
But power, anger and jealousy, and deceit, did later, down the King Saul, bring.
1st Samuel 12-15

David, the shepherd boy, with stone and sling, slays the Philistine giant, Goliath, at the start,
Plays his harp, writes many Psalms, and though imperfect, is a man, after God's own heart.
1st Samuel 17, 1st Samuel 16

King Solomon's kingdom, his wisdom and proverbs, are known the world wide,
But, Solomon, lost his way, found all is vanity, but re-found his Father's God, before he died. *1st Kings 1-4,
Proverbs, Ecclesiastes*

Elijah, Elisha, Isaiah, and all the major and minor Prophets of old, foretold and saw,
That a new day was coming, a new King, a New Gospel, to fulfill the Old Law.
1st Kings

Elijah and Elisha performed miracles, and taught, that to God, we must aspire,
Then God, to show Elijah was His prophet, took him to Heaven, on Chariots of Fire.
1st Kings 17-22, 2nd Kings 1-2

Satan told God that Job's righteous faith was rooted in his wealth, health, family, and his vanity,
So Satan tested Job's faith, stripping his life away, with physical, emotional and spiritual calamity.
Yet even though he lost all that he had, and his friends claimed his travail was punishment for his sin,
Job, though he cried out with questions, proclaimed "I know that my Redeemer lives, and will take me in."
The Book of Job

Isaiah prophesied precisely, the coming of the Messiah, a Nazarine Child, the Holy One,
Who would be both God and Man, give up His life for ours, He, Emanuel, God's only Son.
Isaiah 2-12

The prophet Micah asked, "Does God require of us rivers of oil and thousands of sheep?"
Nay, God thru Micah said only that we should do justice, love mercy, walk humbly with our God, these three laws
to keep.
Micah 6:6-8

And God so loved us all, with a New Covenant, He sent into the world His beloved and only Son,
Not to judge us, but whosoever believed in Him, Love's victory would be won.
John 3:16-17

Jesus, born in a manger, of Mary, as shepherds and wise men came from afar to see,
He grew up as a carpenter's son, in the despised town of Nazareth, near the Sea of Galilee.
Matthew; Luke 1, 2

Jesus preached love, and forgiveness, healed body, mind and soul, both inside and out,
Many marveled at his Word and miracles, yet others, would plot His death, scheme and doubt.
Through God's Grace, Man's Old ritual Laws and additions, while still man's tutor, are forever repealed,
And, God's New Covenant of Grace, Love and Forgiveness through his Son Jesus, is sealed.
Mark (The shortest of the 4 Gospels), Galatians 3:23-29

When the Pharisee Lawyer sought to trick Him, asking "Which if the greatest of Ten Commandments of The Law,
He answered clearly, "You shall Love the Lord you your God with all of your heart, mind and soul, and love your
neighbor as your neighbor as well as yourself, is The Great Commandment of All."
Matthew 22:34-40

After three years of ministry in Judea and Galilee, He was whipped, gave up his life, and was crucified,
The hope of despondent followers, and disciples would fall, His authority, even by Peter, denied.
Mark 14-15

Taken down from His Cross, placed in Joseph of Arimathea's tomb, which was sealed and closed,
But after three days, an Angel appeared, to announce that Jesus, the Christ, had Arose.
John 19-20

As tongues of fire, rained down upon the disciples, to them, the Holy Spirit came,
Gave to them new power, ushered in a New Life, where the Risen Christ would reign.
Acts 2

Christ's Good News, as to why He came, He lived, and died, is the Gospel,
For through Him, our failures are washed clean, Death and Sin, will be felled.
The Four Gospels; John 3:16-17

Paul traveled and preached, often rejected, beaten, as he taught and wrote,
Yet through him, a very human, imperfect Paul, The Word of Faith and Grace, God spoke.
2nd Corinthians 11; Romans 7, 8:3

The Disciples, Peter, Matthew, and John, and Mark, Luke, James, though persecuted, they too, preached,
And through their spoken words and writings, all of the then known world was reached.
Mark 16:19-20

And, though since then, Faith has spread throughout the world, and made many gains,
Fleshly sin, greed, selfishness, jealousy, and anger, within us, as within Adam, still remains.
Yet, God does not give up on us, and Jesus loves us, this we know,
For the Bible, and the Holy Spirit working within us, tells us so.
John 3

And there is nothing that shall separate us from God's unfailing, everlasting Love,
Neither height, nor depth, nor death, nor life, things past nor present, nor things below or above.
Romans 8: 31-39

And, in and through Christ, our failures are forgiven, and there is no condemnation,
Of our repentant failures, this message, we are commissioned, to bring to every nation.
Romans 7, 8; Luke 24

God through Christ continues to seek after us, knows us from our conception, and forgives,
His Spirit, within us, though we, like jars of clay, forever lives.
Psalm 139; 2nd Corinthians 4: 6-7

The Great Commandment, that we Love God, love self, and love our neighbor,
These three things, He asks, to meet God's command, and His favor.
Matthew 22:24-36

For Love is of God, and God is Love, and to the extent we live love, God is within us
Three things endure, Faith, Hope and Love, but the greatest of these is Love, we trust.
1st John 4:7-16; 1st Corinthians 13

So, rejoice in the Lord always, in all times, He tells us this message through Paul, loud and clear,
For in Christ Jesus, in good times and in bad, we can do and endure all things, without fear.
Galatians 4:4- 13

For Jesus said, He will come again, at a time only God the Father knows, to set things right,
He will cleanse the world, defeat evil, bring justice, and peace, with all of His might.
Matthew 24:27-31; Revelation

In that time, we shall live by the River of Living Waters, there shall be no more sorrow, pain nor tears,
And Peace shall reign forever, there shall be no night, only God's light through eternity's years.
Revelation 21

May we all come to know by God's Word and Christ's life, the Truth of Life that sets us free.

John 8:32b

That this free gift of Love and Eternal Life, we cannot earn, but 'tis simply a gift, to you and to me.
So, through God's Grace, Christ's life, and death, may we become humbly, the best that we can be,
For by Christ's sacrifice, you are His child, He is our Advocate, and you will live with Him for eternity.

Galatians 3; 1st John 2:1

I AM WHO I AM, BUT WHO AM I

GOD: "I AM WHO I AM"

"And Moses said to God, "Who am I that I should go to Pharaoh and that I should bring the sons of Israel out of Egypt?" And God said "Certainly I will be with you, and this shall be the sign that it is I who sent you: when you have brought the people out of Egypt, you shall worship God at this mountain." Then Moses said to God, "Behold, I am going to the sons of Israel, and I shall say to them, "The God of your fathers has sent me to you". Now they may say to me, "What is His Name? What shall I say to them?"

And God said to Moses," I AM WHO I AM", and He said "Thus you shall say to the sons of Israel, I AM has sent me to you." And God furthermore said to Moses "This you shall say to the sons of Israel, 'The Lord, the God of your fathers, the God of Abraham, the God of Isaac, and the God of Jacob has sent me to you.' This is My Name forever, and this is my memorial to all generations." *(Exodus 3:11-15)*

My life was in a state of turmoil. Storms were swirling all around me. I felt as if I were in a small boat, being hopelessly cast about in a tumultuous sea. So many things I did not understand- So many unanswered questions, so much injustice I saw in the world. I looked up to the Heavens and cried out "Lord where are You? Lord, who are You?" And then, the storms and seas seemed to subside, and a quiet came over me. Then I heard the Whisper of the Wind, and I heard His answer:

"I AM! I AM HE who created you, and all that exists in the universe. I AM omnipresent, ever present. I AM was there before the beginning, I AM continued to be in everything that has been created in the heaven and the earth. I Am in the present moment, and in every moment and thing that shall come in the future of eternity. My Name I AM describes me because I AM in all things and create all things –I AM at the same time IN the past from before the beginning of time, the present moment, and all of the future that shall ever be. It was I, I AM, who spoke and the worlds came into being, and it is I, I AM who breathes life into every living being. I AM THE WORD, AND I AM THE WORD WHO BECAME FLESH IN JESUS CHRIST. And, I AM was both in My Son called JESUS, and I AM the COMFORTER, (The Holy Spirit) whom my SON sent to follow ME, IAM. Let ME explain more in MY WORDS (written by Inspired men, as they understood Me) from THE WORD, so you may better understand, even better who I AM:

❖ I AM the God of your refuge, and your strength, a present help in all your troubles (Psalm 46:10)
❖ I AM the Rock, and the Stronghold of your salvation (Psalm 61:1-2)
❖ I AM your HOPE, and your glory rest, so wait patiently for ME (Psalm 62:5-8)
❖ I AM your refuge that you may tell of MY works (Psalm 73:28)
❖ I AM your Dwelling Place for all generations, from everlasting to everlasting (Psalm 90:1-2)
❖ I AM the Chief Cornerstone that the builder rejected (Psalm 118:22-24)
❖ I AM a Light unto your path, a Lamp unto your feet (Psalm 119:105)
❖ I AM The Lord your God, who created you, I call you by name you are mine, (Isaiah 43:1)
❖ I AM the One who will be with you when you pass through deep waters and fire (Isaiah 43:2-3)
❖ I AM HE who will be the refiner and purifier of silver and gold, I will refine and purify you like silver and gold, and you will bring in offerings in righteousness (Malachi 3:3)
❖ I AM He who will overcome all things the Morning Star (Revelation 2:28)
❖ I AM the Alpha and Omega, the Beginning and the End of all (Revelation 22:13)

THE APOSTLE JOHN'S JESUS AS "I AM"
The Seven I AM's of Gospel of JOHN
(MY Son JESUS who came As and for ME, in MAN)

- ❖ "I AM , and he who believes in ME shall never thirst- I AM the Living Bread of Life, that came down out of Heaven, if anyone eats this Bread, he shall live forever, and the Bread which I shall give for the Life of the world is MY Flesh" (John 6:35, 48,51)

- ❖ "I AM the Light of the World, he who walks with ME shall not walk in darkness, but shall have the Light of Life, while I AM in the world, I AM the Light of the World" (John 8:12; 9:5)

- ❖ I AM the Gate (Door) of the sheep… I AM the Gate (Door), if anyone enters through ME, he shall be saved, and shall go in and out, and find pasture" (John 10:7-10)

- ❖ "I AM the Good Shepherd, the Good Shepherd lays down His life for His sheep… I AM the Good Shepherd and I know My own and My own know Me… And, I have other sheep which are not of this fold; I must bring them also, and they shall know My Voice, and they shall become one flock of the One Shepherd. For this reason the Father loves Me, because I lay down My life that I may take it again." (John 10:11-18)

- ❖ "I AM the Resurrection and the Life; he who believes in Me shall live, even if he die" (John 11:21-28)

- ❖ "I AM the Way, the Truth and the Life, no one comes to the Father but through Me." (John 14:1-11)

- ❖ "I AM the True Vine… I AM the Vine, you are the branches, he who abides in Me, and I in him, he bears much fruit, for apart from Me you can do nothing." (John 15:1-5)

BUT WHO AM I?

Then I said in prayer to God:

"Father, I understand better who You are, that You are truly "I AM", always present with me, in the present tense, that you have been I AM since the beginning of time, and extending to all eternity, though, I must be honest, it is still hazy, I'm not sure I will ever fully understand it. AND I UNDERSTAND THAT BECAUSE HUMAN MAN DID NOT FULLY UNDERSTAND YOUR PLAN FOR HIM, THAT YOU SENT YOUR SON JESUS, THE ONLY MAN WHO WAS ALSO GOD "I AM', THAT YOU MIGHT UNDERSTAND WHO IS I M, AND MY PURPOSE FOR YOU.

But I still don't understand how I, as insignificant as I am, fit into Your plan, how I am a part of all that has been is now and will be, The Master Plan, which You have designed? Who then am I?"

Again, there was a quiet, a Peace that I felt, and there followed a gentle breeze. Then I heard the Voice of God of the Universe, and Worlds of Eternity, the "I AM", SAY TO ME:

"Ah yes, who are you? Let me tell you exactly who you are, how cherished and important you are to ME. It is I AM who created you, as well as every other thing in the universe, from the beginning of time and for time to eternity. It was I who breathed life into all living things and into you.

I created you and all men and women as living beings, just below the Angels, and I created you specifically in and after MY own image. I gave you a mind and a soul, a mind to make choices in your life, choices that affect you and others and things around you, for good or for bad, the choices are yours. And after I created you, I saw what I had created and made in you, and it is good. (Genesis 1:26, 27; 3:10)

❖ And, having created you, I shall be with you every moment of your life, to the ends of the earth, for I AM the Good Shepherd, you are as the sheep of My pastures. I will lead you to still water, and give you Peace, as only I can give. And, I shall walk with you in the valleys of shadows of life and of death, and when your life is finished, you shall dwell in My Heavenly Home forever for there are many rooms in My home. (Psalm 23.)

❖ Others may forsake and disown you, even if your Mother and Father reject you, you are mine and I will take you in. (Psalm 27:10)

❖ And while I have created you in your present state as mortal, and your life span shall be three or four score years plus ten, maybe more, maybe less, your human life is but an instant compared to your life in eternity, and your life on earth is in preparation for your life in eternity. Your life on earth is like a blade of grass which sprouts anew in the morning, flourishes during the day time, and at evening fades and withers away. (Psalm 90:5-6)

❖ I tell you now that all human life is like the loveliness of the flowers of the field that fades, that I have also given life, and will also give you eternal life in eternity. (Isaiah 40:6-7)

❖ You are so important to Me, that you are my sons and my daughters, you Are my people, and the sheep of my pastures. (Psalm 100:1-3)

❖ I knew you personally, even before you were born, for I formed you in your Mother's womb, that you might know how deeply I care about you and know you. (Psalm 139:13)

- ❖ So special to me I call you the apple of My eye. (Psalm 17:6-8)

- ❖ I am with you and come along side you, wherever you go, even to the remotest parts of the earth, whether you take the wings of dawn, go to the depths of the sea, there shall I be also. (Psalm 139:7-9)

- ❖ I have you in my thoughts day and night. My thoughts of you are more numerous than the grains of sand upon the seashore. (Psalm 139:17-18)

- ❖ I shall call you by your name, You are mine. You belong to me. (Isaiah 43:1-2)

- ❖ And I have plans for you in your life, and they are for your good, and not to harm you. (Jeremiah 29:11)

- ❖ You are so important to Me, and I love you so much, that I gave up the living human life of My Son, called Jesus of Nazareth, that you may have eternal life. I sent my Son, from My side in the Heavens, into the world to live a human life, to experience the joys and pains of life, yet He without imperfection. I sent Him that He might teach you the depth of My Love Even though He was sinless, He would suffer and die for the sin of the world. And, I sent my son Jesus into the world not to judge the world , nor to judge you, , but that through Him, you and all who seek to follow Him and what He taught, might be saved and inherit eternal life in another and beautiful existence far beyond your wildest imagination. (John 3:16-17)

- ❖ While there are many varieties of special gifts, I have given to you gifts which are unique to you in your time, for you are like no other whoever has been or shall be. Each of these gifts I give to you to share with others for their good, and for the common good of what My Son has taught you, all of which come from the same Spirit, I AM. (1st Corinthians 12:4-7-12)

- ❖ It matters not to Me to whom or where or when you were born, whether you be Jew or Gentile, male or female, entrepreneur or worker, slave or freeman, black or white, all are made as One through My Son, whom I sent to bring you peace and equality. (Galatians 3:28-29)

- ❖ So, now, while you are here on earth, be of good courage, Walk by Faith, and not by Sight, for one day you shall be together with loved ones passed, and the Lord your God. (2nd Corinthians 5:6-8)

- ❖ And, I say to you all earthly things concepts and actions shall in time pass away. Only three shall remain, they are Faith, Hope and Love, but the greatest of these is Love. For even though now you may only see as in a dim or broken mirror, but in that eternal life to come, you shall see and understand all things, you shall see things clearly, and you shall see and know Me then Face to face, and know me just as I fully know and behold you today. (1st Corinthians, Chapter 13)

- ❖ And there shall come a time when your life on this earth shall die, but only in the body which you now live, which is the Temple of the Holy Spirit which I have sent to you, and is likewise I AM. At that time you shall be raised from the dead just as was My Son, more than 2,000 years ago,, and at that time you shall receive a new and different body, from the perishable body in which you now live, to a new and imperishable Spiritual Body, and their you shall live with Me forever, and with your loved ones and the Saints of the past, while you too await the resurrection of those who follow you. (1st Corinthians 15:35- 58)

❖ And now My beloved Child, I trust that you might better understand how very special and unique you are, like no other who has or will live on earth. And, that you may know how important you and your life are to Me, for I AM the One, the True and only God of the Universe, I Am the God of Love, I AM Love, and that by this Love of Mine, I am manifested and reflected in you here and now, and if you abide in My Love, you abide in Me, and I in you. (1st John 4:7-21)

SO I, "I AM" ASK YOU NOW "DO YOU BELIEVE?"

❖ "Even though you have not seen me with your eyes, and Face to face as you shall one day,
even though you may not have fully understood all that has or may happen in your life and in your world, I shall show you these things in that time, that you may know that while I may not direct every daily and momentary event, I AM in ultimate control of all things and that all times and things I shall work into my Ultimate Plan for you and for all mankind.

❖ Even though it may not seem that man or nature, or even Satan is in control at times, do not forget that I Am created you and humans, just below the Angels, and give to you free will to make decisions for right or for wrong, but I AM and Will see that Justice according to My Will shall prevail in eternity, even if not always from day to day; that I do have a Master Plan and My Plan shall be in My own time be fulfilled.

I ask you then do you believe? Do you believe that I AM who I say I AM, I AM the One who sent my Son to live and die for you and for all the world, that you might have eternal life, and that I AM Love?"

––––––––––––––––––

I had listened intently to what my God had said, but so in awe was I from all that He had said to and about me, I replied barely in a whisper "Yes Lord, I believe. Take my life and let it be, consecrated Lord to Thee."

––––––––––––––––––

I heard His Voice, once again, as in a breath of wind saying:

"Blessed art they who have not yet seen, and yet believed, have persevered in their Faith, held fast to their Hope, and have Loved as they were endowed, and as I have taught them." (John 20: 26-29)

MAKING A SYNOPTIC GOSPEL DIFFERENCE

		MATTHEW (Synoptic)	MARK (Synoptic)	LUKE (Synoptic)	JOHN (Not Synoptic)
1	Genealogy From	Abraham	None	Adam	"In the Beginning was the Word"
2	Written To	Jews	Romans	Theopolis and the Greeks	Greek Speaking Gentiles
3	Time	2nd - Before 70AD	1st - Before 70AD	3rd - Before 70AD	4th - After 70AD
*4	Parables	20	9	17 (Unique)	None
*5	Miracles	21 (no I AM)	19	22	7 Events, 7 Signs, 7 I AMs
6	Prophesied	New King	Jesus the Servant	Jesus, Great Physician	Jesus, Divine Man and God
7	Apostle	Jon	Mark-Peter	Dr. Luke and Paul	James Sons of Thunder
8	Other Writings	None	None Known	Acts Vol II	The Revelation, 3 John's Letters
9	Begins	Jesus' Birth	John the Baptist	Jesus' Birth	"In the Beginning was the Word"
10	Jesus Baptized	Yes	Yes	Yes	No
11	Disciples Called	Yes	Yes	Yes	No
12	Similar Healings	Yes	Yes	Yes	No
13	Calming the Sea	Yes	Yes	Yes	No
14	Gerasene Demoniac	Yes	Yes	Yes	No
**15	Feeding 5,000	Yes	Yes	Yes	Yes
16	Beatitudes	Yes	No	Yes	No
17	Sermon on the Mount	Yes	No	Yes (Short)	No
18	Lord's Prayer	Yes	No	Yes	No
19	Jesus' Temptations	Yes	Yes	Yes	No
20	Galilee or Jerusalem	Both	Both	Both	Mostly Jerusalem
21	Transfiguration	Yes	Yes	Yes	No
**22	Palm Sunday	Yes	Yes	Yes	Yes
**23	Cross - Words	(1) – Ch. 27	(1) – Ch. 15	(3) – Ch. 23	(3) – Ch. 19
24	Great Commandment	Yes	Yes	No	No
**25	Holy Week	Yes	Yes	Yes	Yes
**26	Resurrection	Yes	Yes	Yes	Yes
**27	Reappears	Chapter 28	Chapter 16	Chapter 24	Chapter 20, 21 (4 times)

*As noted in New American Standard Version
**Appears in all four Gospels
***There are other common events in the three synoptic Gospels, and yet others that appear in two of the three Gospels.

Made in the USA
Middletown, DE
02 October 2016